4th Edition

Harnessing the Power of the Charitable Remainder Trust

Compliments of

GOLDENSELECT™

ISSUED BY GOLDEN AMERICAN
LIFE INSURANCE COMPANY

SPECIALIZING IN VARIABLE ANNUITIES AND VARIABLE LIFE

The contents and opinions in this publication are entirely those of the authors who are responsible for their accuracy as well as any required regulatory approvals.

Variable products are sold by prospectus only. This is not an offering of any security.

FOR BROKER/DEALER USE ONLY

Acknowledgments

The authors express their gratitude to Douglas K. Freeman, J.D., LL.M. and Fred J. Marcus, J.D., LL.M. of Freeman, Freeman & Smiley, Los Angeles for the many hours spent in refining and perfecting this treatise.

This edition is dedicated to the memory of our dear friend and colleague Ernest J. Schag, Jr., J.D., LL.M.

ISBN 0-9654692-0-4

Distributed by
PhilanthroTec, Inc.
10800 Independence Pointe Parkway, Suite F
Matthews, NC 28105
Voice 704.845.5527
Fax 704.845.5528
E-mail: pgdc1@ibm.net

Fourth Printing

About the Authors

MARC D. HOFFMAN

Marc Hoffman is the Editor in Chief of the Planned Giving Design Center, L.L.C., an Internet publishing company dedicated to assisting charitable organizations to provide comprehensive gift planning education and resources to members of the professional advisory community.

Mr. Hoffman is the former Executive Vice President of San Antonio Hospital Foundation, located in Upland, California, where he was responsible for all fundraising programs, and assisted individual donors and professional advisors in matters of charitable tax and estate planning.

Prior to joining the foundation, Mr. Hoffman was a Senior Vice President with Lexington Capital Management, Inc., a Registered Investment Advisory firm, where he assisted in the development of the firm's charitable trust and foundation investment management and administration division. He is a co-founder of PhilanthroTec, the country's first charitable tax planning software publisher and has also served as Director of Planned Giving at Hoag Memorial Hospital in Newport Beach, California.

Mr. Hoffman regularly conducts continuing professional education seminars throughout the country on matters of charitable financial and estate planning and has been a platform speaker at the National Conference on Planned Giving and National Society of Fund Raising Executives National Conferences. He is a founding board member and past president of the Orange County Planned Giving Roundtable and is a founding faculty member of the American Institute for Philanthropic Studies at California State University Long Beach.

LELAND E. HOFFMAN, JR.

Lee Hoffman is the President of the Planned Giving Design Center, L.L.C., Going Virtual, L.L.C., and PhilanthroTec, Inc., all located in Matthews, North Carolina. Going Virtual is a World Wide Web technology and service company that, among other things, specializes in the development and delivery of World Wide Web sites for not-for-profit organizations and professional advisors who work in the area of planned giving. PhilanthroTec specializes in the creation and distribution of planned giving and charitable estate planning software.

Since founding PhilanthroTec in 1983, Mr. Hoffman has taught thousands of planned giving professionals in the use of PhilanthroTec's software and the intricacies of planned giving. He has lectured at national conferences, not-for-profit seminars, and insurance company meetings.

Mr. Hoffman is recognized as an innovator in the planned giving industry. He was responsible for the first letter ruling regarding the use of a commercial annuity as a net income unitrust investment vehicle. He is also the principal author of PhilanthroTec's software, the country's first planned giving software program.

He is a member of the North Carolina chapter of the National Committee on Planned Giving and the National Society of Fund Raising Executives.

Foreword

Since *Harnessing the Power of the Charitable Remainder Trust* was first published in 1992, much has occurred in the charitable gift planning field. The application of charitable giving in estate, tax, and business planning has become widely accepted among professionals in the fields of law, accounting, finance, and insurance. Professional fundraisers too have become more experienced and creative, combining the philanthropic interests of their institution's donors with more sophisticated planning techniques. Institutional fiduciaries have developed specialized teams to manage these programs, and the public media seem more receptive and supportive of the ideas and concepts.

The charitable remainder trust is not a new tool. It has been in the law since 1969 and, unlike many more recent planning techniques, it is reasonably well understood and accepted by the Internal Revenue Service. Nonetheless, the concept has evolved in practice and is far more complicated than many practitioners and donors realize. And as practitioners apply this technique to a variety of new facts and circumstances, the rules continue to evolve.

Our charge, as participants in the gift planning process, is to understand these rules–both the spirit and the letter–and to facilitate their prudent application by our clientele and donors. This expanded and thoughtful book, perhaps the most comprehensive yet written, will enable another generation of professionals to serve their constituents better and, in doing so, serve our community as well.

> Douglas K. Freeman, J.D., LL.M.
> Senior Partner
> Freeman, Freeman & Smiley, LLP

Introduction

The Revenue Act of 1917 introduced the first income tax deduction for gifts to corporations or associations organized exclusively for religious, charitable, scientific, or educational purposes; and to societies for the prevention of cruelty to children or animals. For better or for worse, the federal income tax system and charitable giving had become intertwined—better because donors were provided a financial incentive to give—worse because donors now needed to consider the tax consequences of their altruism.

As charitable gift planning continued to evolve, so did the need to define the giving arrangements that had come into use. The Tax Reform Act of 1969 contained provisions intended to better define and regulate private foundations. The Act also gave formal recognition and structure to a device that had come to known as the *life income contract*. The new name for this device? The *charitable remainder trust*.

In the early years after their arrival, charitable remainder trusts remained fairly obscure. Charitable organizations and the donors who supported them quietly executed trust agreements, refining them and gaining experience with their use. Tax legislation was again to be the change agent for the charitable remainder trust—because of its impact not on the trust itself, but on the body of tax law surrounding it. Among its more salient provisions, the Tax Reform Act of 1986 defined the *tax shelter* as abusive. Overnight, a component of the financial planning industry was driven, not to extinction, but to seek alternative planning tools. For the first time, the charitable remainder trust, itself a creature of tax law, found itself in the spotlight of the financial services industry. To the chagrin of the not-for-profit sector, the charitable remainder trust was not always portrayed as a charitable giving vehicle that also provided personal tax and financial benefits to the donor. Rather, it was sometimes seen as a personal tax and financial planning tool that also provided benefits to charity. The way one perceived the trust was now based on one's vantage point. A clash of corporate cultures had begun.

A great deal has happened since 1986. The use of the charitable remainder trust has increased at an astonishing rate, and with it the refinement of its illustration, implementation, investment management, and administration. The IRS reported that as of March 1, 1996 there were over 61,000 charitable remainder trusts on file. A 1993 study commissioned by the National Committee on Planned Giving reported the percentage of trust companies offering planned giving services increased from 55.7 percent in 1991 to 86.9 percent in 1993. In the same survey, the percentage of life insurance companies promoting charitable remainder trusts increased from 44.6 percent to 90.2 percent over the same two-year period.

As the charitable remainder trust has become more widely understood and utilized, so has the temptation to stretch and test the envelope of prudent application. The charitable remainder trust has become a higher profile planning tool. And with increased visibility comes increased oversight. That oversight has now been manifest with recently enacted legislation and proposed regulations that will help ensure that charitable remainder trusts operate in the manner for which they were intended.

Although this book shows the professional adviser and prospective donor how to maximize the tax and financial benefits obtained through using the charitable remainder trust, its intent is to teach *efficient philanthropy* and to help those people whose primary intent it is to leave this world better than they found it.

Table of Contents

Operational Considerations   145

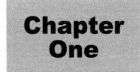

Overview

Who are the Candidates for a Charitable Remainder Trust?

Charitable remainder trusts were once considered the sole province of the wealthy. Before the mid-1980s an institutionally managed and administered trust often required a minimum account size ranging from $250,000 to $500,000. Times have changed. The early 1980s witnessed the arrival of the personal computer, and with it an explosion of highly specialized software. Today, the charitable remainder trust can be designed, the benefits illustrated, documents drafted, and administration performed at a cost that makes an initial transfer of as little as $2,000 economically feasible. Who then are the candidates?

A. Philanthropic Motivations

An individual's ability to benefit society through outright financial gifts to charity is limited only by their financial capacity. At one end of the continuum of donative intent are those individuals who make outright gifts, and do so anonymously. At the other end are those who give nothing at all.

Charitable remainder trusts are legally described as *split-interest* trusts. The term is appropriate because their use is predicated on a blend of philanthropic motivations and personal financial needs. *Financial wealth* can be defined as the ability to generate income. Charitable remainder trusts can increase a donor's income and, by this definition, increase their financial wealth. This result is opposite to that of an outright gift. Where charitable remainder trusts fall on the continuum of donative intent is, therefore, subject to debate and is probably different for every individual.

At one end of the spectrum, the most likely candidates for a charitable remainder trust include those individuals who have maximized their financial capacity to make outright contributions, yet desire to do more. At the other end are those individuals who are motivated solely by personal financial benefits. This latter group may paradoxically be willing to give *only if it doesn't cost them anything.*

The planner must be careful not to confuse donative *intent* with donative *capacity.* A person's donative capacity to make outright gifts is almost certainly less than their capacity to make split-interest gifts. Their intent to make larger gifts may be based on the paradigm that charitable gifts can be made only at the sacrifice of financial wealth (i.e., the ability to generate income). It stands to reason that donative intent may differ based on the type of giving technique one is considering. More than one donor has modified their definition of donative intent *after* they became aware of the personal benefits that accompany the use of a charitable remainder trust. This does not suggest they were not philanthropically predisposed. It does suggest they experienced a paradigm shift.

B. Personal Financial Motivations

There are many financial benefits to using the charitable remainder trust:

1.   Tax Free Asset Conversion

The charitable remainder trust is unique in its ability to sell appreciated assets free from the erosion of capital gains or ordinary income tax, and then provide the trustor or others with an income stream.[1] *Asset conversion* is the most visible financial advantage of using a charitable remainder trust.

2.   Current Income Tax Deduction

Like other charitable contributions, a gift to a charitable remainder trust can provide the trustor with a current income tax deduction. The deduction can be used to offset all forms of income.[2]

3.   Increased Cash Flow

An individual may own a highly appreciated asset that generates little or no income. The owner has thought of selling it, but is reluctant to do so because capital gains tax would consume one-third of its value *and* one-third of the resulting income.

Having the ability to sell low-income producing appreciated assets free from the erosion of income taxes enables the charitable remainder trust to generate more income for recipients.

4.   Asset Diversification and Risk Reduction

Studies in the securities markets demonstrate that a lack of adequate diversification serves only to increase risk with no incremental increase in return. Having all of one's eggs in one basket often means those eggs are highly appreciated. Therefore, repositioning an asset may be available only at a substantial tax cost. The tax cost of selling assets with a zero cost basis is analogous to a 2,240-point drop in the Dow Jones Industrial Average.[3] Who would voluntarily elect their own personal stock market crash? The charitable remainder trust can recover the benefits of cost effective asset diversification.

---

[1]   This is distinguishable from a tax-deferred exchange that merely allows for the replacement of one asset by another within the same class.

[2]   Deductions are subject to percentage limitations and AMT discussed in Chapter 4.

[3]   Calculation assumes a Dow Jones Industrial Average of 8,000 and a marginal capital gains rate of 28 percent.

5. Lifetime Cash Flow Planning

With careful design and investment management, the charitable remainder trust can defer income for later distribution. This feature enables rapid accumulation of income for retirement planning or for intermittent financial needs that may occur along the way. Income deferral can also enhance the value of the ultimate charitable gift.

6. Retirement Planning and Asset Management

Among other things, retirement denotes reduction of management responsibilities. This may be true not only in the work place, but also with personal assets. A 10-unit apartment complex carries greater personal management responsibilities than does *clipping* coupons. Asset conversion for relief of management responsibilities can be a strong lifestyle motivator. The charitable remainder trust not only provides the means to dispose of *management intensive* assets, it also supplies a mechanism to provide professional asset management during a person's later years when it may be most needed or desired.

7. Gift and Estate Tax Planning

The charitable remainder trust offers the individual an effective alternative to the payment of gift and estate taxes. Amounts transferred to a charitable remainder trust are not generally subject to gift or estate taxes.[4] The combination of capital gains, gift tax and estate tax avoidance can be very compelling for those who wish to benefit the charity.

In addition to the gift and estate tax savings generated by the trust itself, the cash flow created by the charitable remainder trust can be coordinated with other estate planning techniques. The most common combination involves gifts of cash from a trustor to an irrevocable trust or directly to family members who then used them to purchase insurance on the life of the trustor. Commonly referred to as *wealth replacement*, the concept often enables trustors to provide a significant legacy to charity without disinheriting their heirs.

---

[4]   This assumes one trustor or two married trustors are the sole noncharitable income recipients. See Chapter 5.

Involuntary Philanthropy

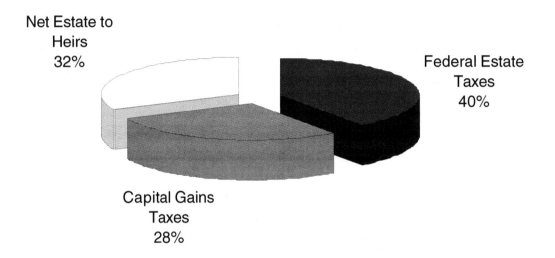

Net Estate to
Heirs
32%

Federal Estate
Taxes
40%

Capital Gains
Taxes
28%

Figure 1   This chart illustrates the erosion of assets caused by the combination of capital gains tax (at a federal and state rate of 28 percent) and federal estate tax (at a rate of 55 percent). The combination of the two taxes can reduce the value of the estate by, in this example, 68 percent. "The United States, states and governmental units" are included in the Internal Revenue Code as qualified charitable organizations. By this definition, the federal government is the largest charitable organization. Charitable giving allows the entire value of an asset to be directed to the charitable organization(s) of the trustor's choice rather than 68 percent being directed by the federal government.

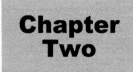

Asset Conversion Planning

Choices

Regarding the disposition of an asset, an individual has four basic choices:

- Keep it
- Exchange it
- Sell it, or
- Give it away

Because charitable giving and wealth accumulation have traditionally been considered mutually exclusive concepts, the thought of giving an asset away to maximize personal financial benefit can be a difficult concept to convey.

Case Study - Asset Conversion

The following case study illustrates the benefits of asset conversion planning using a charitable remainder unitrust. To illustrate how the trust can be incorporated into the trustor's overall estate transfer planning, the case includes the use of life insurance to replace for family members the assets passing to charity.

Converting Assets to Income

The Facts

Meet Mr. and Mrs. Smith. They both are sixty years old and have accumulated a $5,000,000 estate. Like many people their age, they are now thinking about retirement and shifting their investment posture from asset accumulation to one of conservation and maximizing income. On the personal side, they would like to give something back to their community in the form of time as well as financial resources.

The Smiths received founder's stock many years ago in a high-tech company that has since gone public. The shares are now worth $1,000,000. They have several concerns regarding their stock. First, the stock pays no dividend. This conflicts with their goal of maximizing income. Their second concern is volatility. With the market at an all-time high, the Smiths think the time is right to take some profits. Their third concern is diversification. Now that retirement is upon them, the Smiths feel having the majority of their investment eggs in one basket carries too much risk.

The Problem

The Smiths want to sell their stock. With a zero cost basis, however, they will recognize a $1,000,000 taxable gain. In a 28 percent combined federal and state capital gains bracket, they will pay $280,000 in tax, leaving them with only $720,000 to reinvest. [5]

Further, when the Smiths are both gone, the remaining value from the stock sale will be subject to federal estate tax at a rate of 55 percent, thereby reducing their children's inheritance from this asset from the original $1,000,000 to only $324,000. That represents a combined tax erosion exceeding 67 percent!

Planning Goals

The Smiths have identified the following goals:

- Convert their stock into an income stream without paying capital gains tax

- Create an investment vehicle to maximize their retirement income and relieve them of the burden of investment management should one of them die or become disabled

- Reduce their estate taxes beyond the amount provided for by their current Credit Shelter Trust planning while maximizing the amount passing to their children and grandchildren, and

---

[5]   Tax bracket reflects top 1998 federal marginal capital gains rate of 20 percent and 8 percent hypothetical state rate.

- Make a substantial financial contribution to the charitable organizations of their choice

The Solution

The Smiths will create a charitable remainder trust!

The Smiths transfer their stock to a charitable remainder unitrust

1. The Smiths **transfer their stock,** valued at $1,000,000, to the trust.

Benefits

No Recognition of Gain upon Transfer

Transfers of appreciated property to a charitable remainder trust are not considered a sale or an exchange.[6] Thus, the trustors avoid recognition of gain upon transfer. This provision is critical to those who desire to use the trust to sell appreciated assets free of capital gains tax exposure. In

---

[6] Reg. §§1.1011-2; 1.170A-6(b)(2). The transfer of debt encumbered property will be considered a bargain sale resulting in possible recognition of gain.

addition, the trustors will not recognize any depreciation recapture when property is transferred to a charitable remainder trust.[7]

The Trustee sells the stock and pays the Smiths a life income

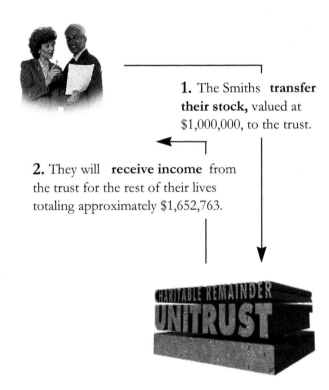

1. The Smiths **transfer their stock,** valued at $1,000,000, to the trust.

2. They will **receive income** from the trust for the rest of their lives totaling approximately $1,652,763.

During the Smiths' lifetimes, they will receive income from the trust based on a fixed percentage (the payout rate) of the trust's *annual* value.

Benefits

Capital Gains Tax Avoidance

If the Smiths sell the asset on a taxable basis, they will be left with $720,000 to reinvest. They will have to earn a 39 percent return on their money, on an after-tax basis, to recover the amount that was paid in taxes.

As an alternative, a charitable remainder trust takes on both the holding period and adjusted cost basis of assets transferred to it. When the trust sells a contributed asset, it will realize the same

---

[7]   Accelerated depreciation over straight-line will cause a reduction in the amount of the charitable contribution deduction.

amount of gain as would have the trustor. However, because the trust is tax-exempt, it will not generally be taxed on the gain.[8] Therefore, 100 percent of the asset's value remains intact.

Increased Cash Flow

More principal means more cash flow and asset growth when compared to a taxable sale and reinvestment strategy. In fact, in the first year the Smiths must generate an 11.11 percent rate of return on the net proceeds of a taxable sale to produce the same cash flow as the charitable remainder trust at an 8 percent payout rate.

Unitrust Income	Sales Proceeds	
$1,000,000	$1,000,000	
x 8.00%	($280,000)	
= $80,000 /	$720,000	= 11.11%

Figure 2   This table illustrates the calculation of the rate of return the outright sale of the asset must generate to equal the charitable trust income.

Reduced Investment Risk

Return on investment is commensurate with risk. Therefore, achieving the same cash flow outside the unitrust will force the Smiths to subject their assets to higher risk, or settle for less income.

Inflation Hedge

If the trust earns amounts in excess of what it is required to distribute, those amounts are added to trust principal free of tax. As the trust grows, so will the Smiths' income.

---

[8]   IRC §§1015; 664(c); 512. The trust will be subject to tax if it has any *unrelated business taxable income.*

The Smiths will leave a lasting legacy to charity

1. The Smiths **transfer their stock,** valued at $1,000,000, to the trust.

2. They will **receive income** from the trust for the rest of their lives totaling approximately $1,652.763.

3. When the Smiths both die, the trust assets of approximately $1,640,606 **will pass to the charitable organization(s) of their choice.**

When the trust terminates (in this case, when Mr. and Mrs. Smith die), the trust assets will pass to the charitable organizations of the Smiths' choice.

Benefits

A Philanthropic Legacy

The Smiths can select as many organizations as they desire to receive the charitable remainder. These organizations can be public charities, a supporting organization, or the trustors' own private foundation. Amounts can be given outright, designated for a specific purpose, or held in a perpetual endowment.

Asset Maximization

The Smiths have also maximized the financial, social, and spiritual value of their asset: financially, by reducing taxes and increasing their cash flow; socially, by earmarking the principal to fulfill a social need; and spiritually by knowing they have done something with their assets that reflects their own individuality, humanity, and personal values.[9]

---

[9] Asset Maximization™, Renaissance, Inc., Carmel, IN.

The Smiths will receive a charitable income tax deduction

1. The Smiths **transfer their stock,** valued at $1,000,000, to the trust.

2. They will **receive income** from the trust for the rest of their lives totaling approximately $1,652,763.

4. Because of their generous gift, the Smiths will receive an **income tax deduction** of $167,540.

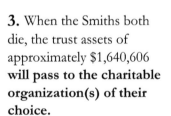

3. When the Smiths both die, the trust assets of approximately $1,640,606 **will pass to the charitable organization(s) of their choice.**

In addition to avoiding $280,000 in capital gains tax, the Smiths will receive an income tax charitable contribution deduction in the year the trust is created. Why? Upon termination of the trust, the trust assets will be distributed to the charitable organizations named in the trust instrument. The deduction is determined from Treasury tables that calculate the actuarial present value of the remainder interest passing to charity.

In the Smiths' case, the deduction will amount to $167,540 and will generate tax savings of $67,016.

Benefits

Deduction Offsets All Forms of Income

The charitable deduction can be used against passive, portfolio, and active income. When long-term capital gain property is transferred, the charitable deduction can be used against 30 percent of the trustor's contribution base (usually the same as adjusted gross income) with a five-year carryover of any excess deduction.

Deduction Creates Additional Cash Flow

The combined income tax savings from the charitable deduction and capital gains tax that was avoided total $347,016, or 35 percent of the value of the asset.

The Economics

The lifetime benefits of a charitable remainder unitrust can best be appreciated by comparing the pro forma cash flows of the trust to those produced by an outright sale and reinvestment of the after-tax proceeds.

Continuing with the example, additional assumptions are as follows:

Tax Assumptions	
Trustors' Contribution Base (AGI):	$0
Regular Income Tax Marginal Bracket:	40%
Long-term Capital Gains Marginal Bracket:	28%
Federal Estate Tax Bracket:	55%
Investment Assumptions	
Annual Total Return on Reinvestment:	10%
Tax Character of Income:	5% ordinary, 5% capital gain
Life Expectancies of Income Beneficiaries:	25 years

The following illustrations show the economics of the charitable remainder trust based on the above assumptions. The first illustration shows a comparison between selling the asset and reinvesting the proceeds versus contributing the asset to the unitrust. The second is an illustration of the cash flow of the unitrust.

Comparison of Benefits
Without Life Insurance Replacement
Prepared for Mr. & Mrs. Smith

A. Input Assumptions	Sell asset and reinvest	Standard Unitrust
Type of Technique		
Time Period Projected	25 Years	25 Years
Income Payout Rate	All Income	8% StdCRUT
Income is Paid	Annually	Annually
Investment Period Measured by	2 Lives	2 Lives
B. Contributions	**Sell Asset**	**Std. Unitrust**
Fair Market Value of Property	$1,000,000	$1,000,000
Income Tax Deduction	$0	$167,540
Capital Gains Tax on Sale	$280,000	$0
C. Cash Flow		
Net After Tax Income During Life	$1,188,000	$1,719,779
(=) Net Spendable Income	$1,188,000	$1,719,779
D. Estate for Heirs		
Gross Value of Estate	$720,000	$0
(-) Estate Taxes	$396,000	$0
(=) Net Estate for Heirs	$324,000	$0
E. Benefit Summary		
Net Income + Net Estate	**$1,512,000**	**$1,719,779**
(+) Endowment to Charity	**$0**	**$1,640,606**
(=) Total Benefit	**$1,512,000**	**$3,360,385**

Comparison of Benefits

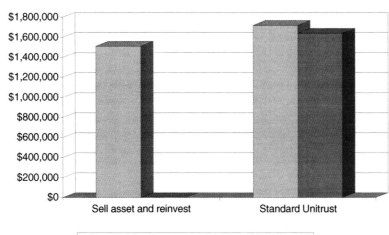

Net Income + Net Estate ■ Endowment to Charity

But what about the family?

Even though the charitable remainder trust can provide substantial lifetime income and tax benefits for the Smiths, there is an estate planning tradeoff to be considered. Specifically, the principal from the charitable remainder trust will ultimately pass to charity rather than to the Smiths' heirs.

It is important to note the opportunity cost to the heirs is not the $1,000,000 transferred to charity. It is the amount that would have remained after the payment of capital gains and estate taxes. It is assumed that all income is consumed.

The following chart illustrates the calculation of the net estate passing to the heirs:

Beginning Principal		**$1,000,000**
Minus	Capital Gains Tax	$280,000
Equals	Amount Available for Reinvestment	$720,000
Minus	Estate Taxes @ 55%	$396,000
Equals	Net to Heirs	$324,000
Tax Erosion		**67.60%**

The Smiths will create a wealth replacement trust

1. The Smiths **transfer their stock,** valued at $1,000,000, to the trust.

5. The Smiths will give $281,160 of their **increased income** and **tax savings** to a trust for the purchase of life insurance.

2. They will **receive income** from the trust for the rest of their lives totaling approximately $1,652,753

4. Because of their generous gift, the Smiths will receive an **income tax deduction** of $167,540.

3. When the Smiths both die, the trust assets of approximately $1,640,606 **will pass to the charitable organization(s) of their choice.**

The Smiths will create a second trust called a *Wealth Replacement Trust.*[10] Its purpose will be to replace, for the family, the value of the assets passing to charity via the charitable remainder trust.

Using this device, the Smiths will make annual gifts of $23,430 for twelve years to an irrevocable trust that will purchase and own an insurance policy on both their lives. The trust will be structured so the annual gifts will qualify for the $10,000 annual gift tax exclusion.

After the Smiths have both died, $1,355,521 will be distributed to the children (and grandchildren if desired) free of income, gift, and estate taxes. This represents an increase of $1,031,321 or 318 percent over their current plan.

What is the source of the insurance premiums? The premiums are more than adequately covered by the tax savings and increased cash flow generated by the charitable remainder trust.

Benefits

1. Planning Flexibility
The *Wealth Replacement Trust* can be designed to replace any portion of the trustors' gifts to charity. In this case, the Smiths chose to replace the entire $1,000,000 value of the asset transferred to the trust. The insurance policy grows to $1,355,521 by the time both of them die.

2. Estate Tax Avoidance
The Smiths will retain no *incidents of ownership* in the insurance policy within the *Wealth Replacement Trust.* The death benefit will, therefore, not be taxable in either of their estates. Further, the trust can be designed to avoid *Generation Skipping Transfer Taxes* if the Smiths wish to benefit their grandchildren.

3. Estate Liquidity
Wealth Replacement Trust proceeds are paid in cash, free of probate administration, and can be used by the heirs to purchase assets out of the estate. Cash can be a precious commodity in settling an estate.

4. Distribution Planning
The *Wealth Replacement Trust* can provide additional planning flexibility with respect to when and how assets will be distributed to the heirs through the terms of the trust instrument.

5. Estate Leverage
Life insurance can be the most economical method of creating estate dollars when they are needed. In this case, the total cost of replacing $1,000,000 was $281,160, or 20.74 percent, when divided by the eventual death benefit of $1,355,521. The combination of using the *Wealth Replacement Trust* and the discounted dollars of life insurance provides the greatest leverage in estate transfer planning.

---

[10]   The term, "Wealth Replacement Trust" is used to describe an irrevocable life insurance trust.

Payment of Premiums

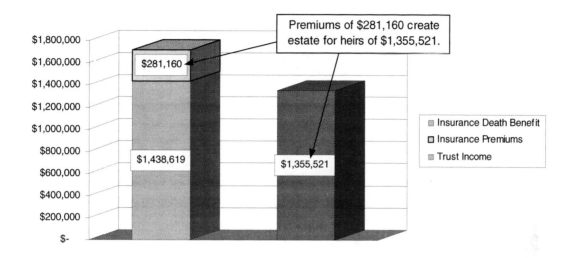

The Completed Plan

1. The Smiths **transfer their stock** valued at $1,000,000 to the trust.

5. The Smiths will give $281,160 of their **increased income** and **tax savings** to a trust for the purchase life insurance.

2. They will **receive income** from the trust for the rest of their lives totaling approximately $1,617,523

4. Because of their generous gift, they will receive an **income tax deduction** of $167,540.

6. The children will receive the life insurance proceeds of $1,355,521, **free of estate taxes**, upon the death of Mr. and Mrs Smith.

3. When the Smiths both die, the trust assets of approximately $1,640,606 **will pass to the charitable organization(s) of their choice.**

The following illustration projects the benefits of using the *Wealth Replacement Trust*. It compares the net after-tax cash flow and net estate to the heirs applicable to an outright sale with the net after-tax cash flow and net estate to heirs applicable to the combination of a charitable remainder trust and wealth replacement trust.

Comparison of Benefits
With Life Insurance Replacement
Prepared for Mr. & Mrs. Smith

A. Input Assumptions

	Sell asset and reinvest	Standard Unitrust
Type of Technique		
Time Period Projected	25 Years	25 Years
Income Payout Rate	All Income	8% StdCRUT
Income is Paid	Annually	Annually
Investment Period Measured by	2 Lives	2 Lives

B. Contributions

	Sell Asset	Std. Unitrust
Fair Market Value of Property	$1,000,000	$1,000,000
Income Tax Deduction	$0	$167,540
Capital Gains Tax on Sale	$280,000	$0

C. Cash Flow

Net After Tax Income During Life	$1,188,000	$1,719,779
(1) Premiums Paid for Insurance	$0	$281,160
(=) Net Spendable Income	$1,188,000	$1,438,619

D. Estate for Heirs

Gross Value of Estate	$720,000	$0
(+) Life Insurance Death Benefit		$1,355,521
(-) Estate Taxes	$396,000	$0
(=) Net Estate for Heirs	$324,000	$1,355,521

E. Benefit Summary

Net Income + Net Estate equals Total Family Benefit	**$1,512,000**	**$2,794,140**
(+) Endowment to Charity	**$0**	**$1,640,606**
(=) Total Benefit	**$1,512,000**	**$4,434,746**

Comparison of Benefits

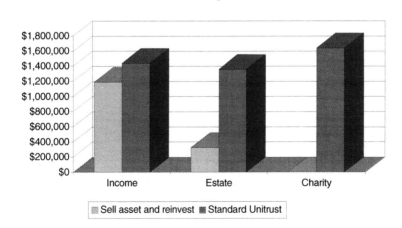

Sell asset and reinvest ■ Standard Unitrust

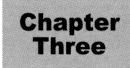

Technical Overview

Qualification as a Charitable Remainder Trust

In order to qualify as a charitable remainder trust, the trust must meet all of the requirements set forth in IRC §664, the regulations promulgated thereunder, Revenue Rulings, and Procedures.[11]

> In Rev. Proc. 91-3[12] the IRS announced that it will no longer issue advance rulings regarding whether a transfer to a charitable remainder trust described in section 664 of the Code that provides for annuity or unitrust payments for one or two measuring lives qualifies for a charitable income, gift or estate tax deductions under sections 170(f)(2)(A), 2522(c)(2)(A) or 2055(e)(2)(A). The Service will, however, continue to rule regarding provisions that deviate from those found in the sample documents published in the Revenue Procedures.
>
> **Caution:** A trust that does not contain a required governing provision or otherwise fails to qualify as a charitable remainder trust will cause the loss of the trustor's income tax deduction, will cause all transactions within the trust to be taxable, and may also subject the transfer to gift tax even though made to charity. Further, it may be impossible to amend or reform a defective trust.[13]

A. Tax-Exempt Status of Trust

A charitable remainder trust is exempt from all taxes unless it has unrelated business taxable income within the meaning of IRC §512. In any year in which a charitable remainder trust has one penny of UBTI, the trust is subject to tax as if it was a complex trust.

A charitable remainder trust that sells appreciated property within two years of the date the property is contributed to the trust is exempt from the requirement of IRC §644 that it compute the gain on the sale at the transferor's tax rate. Further, the grantor trust rules of IRC §§671 - 678 and the throwback rules of IRC §§665 - 668 are not applicable to a *qualified* charitable remainder trust.[14]

---

[11]   See Rev. Rul. 72-395, 1972-2 C.B. 340 as modified by Rev. Rul. 80-123, 1980-1 C.B. 205, and Rev. Rul. 82-128, 1982-2 C.B. 71; Rev. Proc. 89-19, 1989-1 C.B.841; Rev. Proc. 89-20, 1989-1 C.B. 841; Rev. Proc. 89-21, 1989-1 C.B. 842; Rev. Proc. 90-30, 1990-1 C.B. 534; Rev. Proc. 90-31, 1990-1 C.B. 539; Rev. Proc. 90-32, 1990-1 C.B. 546

[12]   Rev. Proc. 91-3, 1991-1 C.B. 364

[13]   IRC §2055(e)(2)

[14]   Reg. §1.664-1(c)

The trust assumes the trustor's adjusted cost basis and holding period in the transferred property based on the carryover basis provisions of the Code. If the trust sells the property, it will realize the same amount of gain as the trustor would have realized if he or she had sold the property. The trust is tax-exempt and, therefore, will not pay any tax.[15]

In practice, this feature makes charitable remainder trusts ideal for use by individuals who desire to dispose of highly appreciated, low yielding property free of capital gains tax exposure in favor of assets that will produce higher amounts of cash flow and appreciation. It is important to note the double tax leverage that can be accomplished by avoiding recognition of capital gain and creating an immediate income tax deduction.

B. Requirement of Annuity Trust or Unitrust

Anyone who wishes to create a charitable remainder trust must choose between the annuity trust and unitrust formats. A trust is a charitable remainder trust only if it is either a charitable remainder annuity trust or a charitable remainder unitrust in every respect.[16] No blending is allowed. The principle difference between the two is the way in which income distributions are determined.

C. Charitable Remainder Annuity Trust Defined

A charitable remainder annuity trust is a trust from which a sum certain (which is not less than 5 percent of the initial fair market value of all property placed in trust) is to be paid, not less often than annually, to one or more persons[17] (at least one of which is not an organization described in IRC §170(c) and, in the case of individuals, only to an individual who is living at the time of the creation of the trust) for a term of years (not in excess of twenty years) or for the life or lives of such individual or individuals.[18]

The annuity amount may be stated as a fixed percentage of the initial net fair market value, or it may be stated as a fixed sum. The annuity percentage or amount that is fixed cannot be changed regardless of fluctuations in portfolio value. For this reason, additional contributions to annuity trust are prohibited.[19]

---

[15]   IRC §§1015; 664(c)

[16]   Reg. §1.664-2

[17]   See the definition of "persons" on page 53.

[18]   IRC §664(d)(1)

[19]   Reg. §1.664-2(b)

Annuity Income Example

Payout rate   7%

Yr.	Earnings Rate	Trust Value	Annuity Amount
1	8%	$1,000,000	$ 70,000
2	6%	$1,010,000	$ 70,000
3	10%	$1,000,600	$ 70,000
4	8%	$1,030,660	$ 70,000
5	4%	$1,043,113	$ 70,000
6	12%	$1,014,837	$ 70,000
7	6%	$1,066,618	$ 70,000
8	7%	$1,060,615	$ 70,000
9	3%	$1,064,858	$ 70,000
10		$1,026,804	$ 70,000

Annuity Income Vs Trust Value

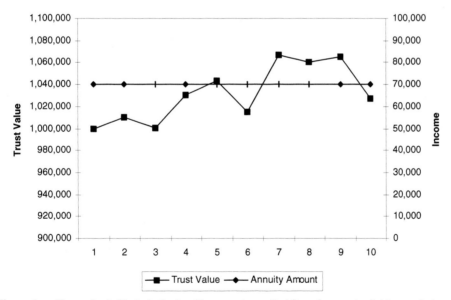

Figure 4   These charts illustrate the level income stream that flows from a charitable remainder annuity trust. Annuity payments are level regardless of the trust's fair market value. Annuity payments are NOT guaranteed, however. If the trust's asset value falls to zero, the annuity payments cease.

D. Charitable Remainder Unitrust Defined

A charitable remainder unitrust is a trust from which a *fixed percentage* (which is not less than 5 percent) of the net fair market value of its assets, *valued annually*, is to be paid, not less often than annually, to one or more persons (at least one of which is not an organization described in IRC §170(c) and, in the case of individuals, only to an individual who is living at the time of the creation of the trust) for a term of years (not in excess of twenty years) or for the life or lives of such individual or individuals.

Unlike the charitable remainder annuity trust, additional contributions to unitrusts are permitted.

Standard Unitrust Income Example

Payout rate 7%

Yr.	Earnings Rate	Trust Value	Unitrust Amount
1	8%	$1,000,000	$ 70,000
2	6%	$1,010,000	$ 70,700
3	10%	$ 999,900	$ 69,993
4	8%	$1,029,897	$ 72,093
5	4%	$1,040,196	$ 72,814
6	12%	$1,008,990	$ 70,629
7	6%	$1,059,440	$ 74,161
8	7%	$1,048,845	$ 73,419
9	3%	$1,048,845	$ 73,419
10		$1,006,891	$ 70,482

Unitrust Income Vs Trust Value

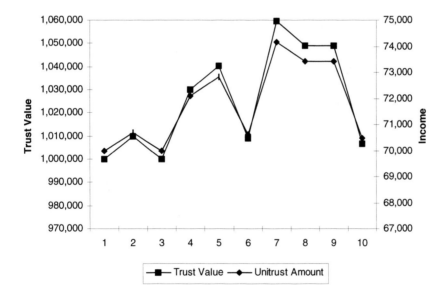

Figure 5   This table and chart illustrate the direct relationship between the value of a charitable remainder unitrust's assets and the unitrust amount it distributes.

1.   Annual Valuation

The net fair market value of the trust assets may be determined on any one date during the taxable year of the trust. It also may be determined by taking the average of valuations made on more than one date during the taxable year of the trust, so long as the same valuation date or dates and valuation methods are used each year.[20]

Multiple valuation dates, while helping to balance payout fluctuations, are usually impractical from an administrative standpoint. Therefore, the majority of unitrust instruments provide for one valuation date. However, if an additional contribution is made on a non-valuation date, the property is valued on the date of contribution and the unitrust amount is adjusted to reflect the unitrust amount attributable to the additional contribution for the balance of the trust's taxable (calendar) year.[21]

To enable the trustee to plan for required distributions and to easily determine the value of publicly traded securities held by the trust, most trust instruments designate the first business day of each calendar year as the annual valuation date. Designating an annual valuation date after a required payment date requires the trustee to estimate the future value of trust assets in order to determine the unitrust amount and, therefore, is not generally recommended.

E. Unitrust Format Options

1.   Standard Payout Option

A unitrust is required to distribute, at least annually, an amount equal to at least 5 percent of the annual value of trust assets. This is referred to as the *unitrust amount*. In the event income and gain are not sufficient to make the required distribution, the trustee is required to distribute corpus. This type of format is commonly referred to as a *standard* or *Type I* payout option.

The previous illustration and chart demonstrate a standard unitrust bearing a 7 percent payout rate. There is no statutory maximum payout rate.

2.   Net Income Option

Notwithstanding the 5 percent minimum distribution rule applicable to a standard unitrust, a unitrust instrument may include an optional provision that requires the trustee to pay, for any year, the lesser of the full unitrust amount and trust income (as defined in section 643(b) and the regulations thereunder). This provision is commonly referred to as a *net income, income only*, or *Type II* option.[22]

---

[20]   Reg. §1.664-3(a)(1)(iv)

[21]   Reg. §1.664-3(b)

[22]   Reg. §1.664-3(a)(1)(i)(b)

As originally envisioned by Congress, the net income option was intended to relieve trustees from having to distribute trust corpus in years in which trust income was insufficient to satisfy the unitrust amount.

According to IRC §643(b), the term *income*, when not preceded by the words *taxable*, *distributable*, *undistributed net*, or *gross*, means the amount of income of the estate or trust for the taxable year determined under the terms of the governing instrument and applicable local (state) law. For purposes of determining the unitrust amount for a net income unitrust, many states provide that expenses incurred in the administration, management or preservation of trust property, and all expenses reasonably incurred by the trustee are charges against trust income. Regular trustee's compensation is generally charged in equal portions against income and principal.

The *Revised Uniform Income and Principal Act* adopted by most states defines *income* to include interest, dividends, rents, royalties, and the discount element of original issue discount obligations.[23] Unless otherwise defined, and subject to state law, income does not include capital gains. Furthermore, a net income unitrust is never permitted to distribute corpus.

Reg. §1.643(b)-1 adds: Any trust provisions which depart fundamentally from concepts of local law in the determination of what constitutes *income* are not recognized for these (federal tax) purposes. The draftsman should always, therefore, conform to local law.

Net Income Unitrust Distributions

Payout rate   7%

Yr.	Income Rate	Trust Value	Unitrust Amount	Trust Income	Actual Payment
1	8%	1,000,000	70,000	80,000	70,000
2	6%	1,010,000	70,700	60,600	60,600
3	10%	1,010,000	70,700	101,000	70,700
4	8%	1,040,300	72,821	83,224	72,821
5	4%	1,050,703	73,549	42,028	42,028
6	12%	1,050,703	73,549	126,084	73,549
7	6%	1,103,238	77,227	66,194	66,194
8	7%	1,103,238	77,227	77,227	77,227
9	3%	1,103,238	77,227	33,097	33,097
10	10%	1,103,238	77,227	110,324	77,227

Figure 6   This illustration compares the unitrust amount that should be paid to the amount that can be paid based on the distributable net income of the trust. The shaded areas illustrate years in which the trust income is insufficient to satisfy the unitrust amount. Because this trust does not contain a make-up option, there is no opportunity for any income deficiencies to be recovered by the income recipient(s) in future years.

---

[23]   See discussion of zero coupon bonds on page 206.

3. Make-Up Option

If a *net income* option is adopted, the trust will pay income in excess of the full unitrust amount to the extent the aggregate of amounts paid in prior years were (by reason of the income only exception) less than the aggregate of the fixed percentage amounts for such prior years. The trust can, in other words, *make-up* past deficiencies from prior years by paying out excess income earned in the current year.[24] The concept is somewhat analogous to a cumulative dividend feature on preferred stock and is referred to as a *net income with make-up* or *Type III* unitrust.

Net income and make-up options are available only to charitable remainder unitrusts. They are not available to charitable remainder annuity trusts or to charitable income (lead) unitrusts. Furthermore, excess income from a prior year cannot be used to satisfy a deficiency amount arising in a later year.

Planning Note: The net income and net income with make-up unitrusts can solve the problem of funding a trust with a non-income producing asset by limiting the requirement for income distributions to times when the trustee has the capacity to make them. Further, as will be discussed, net income unitrusts provide planning opportunities for those income recipients who wish to defer income distributions.

Net Income Unitrust with Makeup

Payout rate 7%

Yr.	Income Rate	Trust Value	Unitrust Amount	Trust Income	Actual Payment	Annual Deficit	Amount of Make-up Payment
1	8%	1,000,000	70,000	80,000	70,000	0	0
2	6%	1,010,000	70,700	60,600	60,600	10,100	0
3	10%	1,010,000	70,700	101,000	80,800	0	10,100
4	8%	1,030,200	72,114	82,416	72,114	0	0
5	4%	1,040,502	72,835	41,620	41,620	31,215	0
6	12%	1,040,502	72,835	124,860	104,050	0	31,215
7	6%	1,061,312	74,292	63,679	63,679	10,613	0
8	7%	1,061,312	74,292	74,292	74,292	0	0
9	3%	1,061,312	74,292	31,839	31,839	42,452	0
10	10%	1,061,312	74,292	106,131	106,131	0	31,839
						94,381	73,154
Remaining Makeup							21,226

Figure 7 This illustration shows the amount of the annual deficit and the make-up payment occurring in those years in which trust income exceeds the required unitrust amount. Shaded areas show those years in which a make-up occurs, the deficit from previous years, and the remaining make-up at the end of the ten year period.

---

[24]   Reg. §1.664-3(a)(1)(i)(b)(2)

4. Flip Unitrusts

Can a unitrust instrument be drafted to permit the trust to switch or *flip* from having a net income option to a standard income provision? Under proposed regulations it can. The legislative history explains the rationale and applications of the flip unitrust.

In a 1987 letter ruling, the Service approved an arrangement whereby a unitrust was funded with restricted securities that could not be traded until the applicable holding period expired. The trust provided that if the shares were ineligible for sale to the public, the trustee would pay only trust income (as defined under IRC §643(b)) for such period during which the restriction or inability to sell the shares existed; provided that such income would not exceed the 10 percent unitrust amount. The trust also contained a make-up option.[25]

In 1995, the Service reversed itself.[26] In an independent case, two individuals had transferred real property to an 8 percent net income unitrust with make-up option. The taxpayers later realized that they had intended to include language that converted the trust to a standard payout format upon sale of the property. The taxpayers petitioned the Circuit Court to reform the trust agreement to include such language.

The Service ruled that pursuant to section 664(d) of the Code, the amount payable to noncharitable recipients from a qualified charitable remainder unitrust must be computed using one of three methods as selected by the terms of the trust's governing instrument, and that such method must be used during the entire term of the trust. In addition, the method of computing the unitrust amount may not be reformed to provide for a change in the method of computation of the unitrust amount without adversely affecting the qualification of the trust under section 664.

On April 18, 1997, Treasury issued proposed amendments to the regulations that would permit the use of a flip provision under certain circumstances.[27]

A. General Explanation.

The governing instrument of a CRUT must specify the method of computing the unitrust payments. Section 664(d)(3) provides that the income exception methods (either the net income method or the NIMCRUT method) may be used to pay the unitrust amount "for any year." The legislative history, however, provides that the method used to determine the unitrust amount may not be discretionary with the trustee. H.R. Conf. Rep. No. 782, 91st Cong., 1st Sess. 296 (1969), 1969-3 C.B. 644, 655.

Some donors may fund a CRUT with unmarketable assets that produce little or no income. These donors often want the income beneficiary or beneficiaries of the CRUT to receive a steady stream of payments based on the total return available from the value of the assets. The donors recognize, however, that the CRUT cannot make these payments until it can convert the unmarketable assets into liquid assets that can be used to pay the fixed percentage amount. These donors establish CRUTs that use one of the income exception methods to calculate the unitrust amount until the unmarketable assets are sold. Following the sale, the donors may prefer that the CRUT use the fixed percentage method to calculate the unitrust amount. A trust using such a combination of methods would be a "flip unitrust."

---

[25]   Ltr. Rul. 8732026

[26]   Ltr. Rul. 9506015

[27]   Reg-209823-96

The proposed regulations provide that a donor may establish a flip unitrust that qualifies as a CRUT if the following conditions are satisfied. First, to ensure that the CRUT has substantially all unmarketable assets prior to the switch in methods, at least 90 percent of the fair market value of the assets held in the trust immediately after the initial contribution or any subsequent contribution (prior to the switch in methods) must consist of unmarketable assets. Unmarketable assets are assets that are not cash, cash equivalents, or marketable securities (within the meaning of section 731(c)).

Second, because the legislative history indicates that a trustee should not have discretion to change the method used to calculate the unitrust amount, the governing instrument must provide that the CRUT will use an income exception method until the earlier of (a) the sale of a specified unmarketable asset or group of unmarketable assets contributed at the time the trust was created or (b) the sale of unmarketable assets such that immediately following the sale, any remaining unmarketable assets total 50 percent or less of the fair market value of the trust's assets. For making this determination, the remaining unmarketable assets are valued as of the most recent valuation date.

Third, to ensure that the CRUT will use the fixed percentage method after the unmarketable assets are sold, the CRUT must switch exclusively to the fixed percentage method for calculating all remaining unitrust amounts payable to any income beneficiary at the beginning of the first taxable year following the year in which the earlier of the above events occurs.

Finally, because the fixed percentage method does not provide for a makeup amount, any makeup amount described in section 664(d)(3)(B) is forfeited when the trust switches to the fixed percentage method.

The IRS and Treasury request comments on whether there are additional circumstances under which a combination of methods should be addressed in regulations.

B. Proposed Effective Date and Transitional Rules

The amendments allowing a flip unitrust are proposed to be effective for CRUTs created on or after the date the final regulations are published in the Federal Register.

If a trust was created before the effective date of this amendment and its governing instrument contains a flip provision other than the one permitted by the regulations, the trust may be amended or reformed to comply with the final regulations. If a trust is created after the effective date of this amendment and has a flip provision not expressly permitted by the regulations, the trust will qualify as a CRUT if it is amended or reformed to use the initial method for computing the unitrust amount throughout the term of the trust. If a qualified CRUT is created before or after the effective date of this amendment and its governing instrument does not contain a flip provision, the trust will not continue to qualify as a CRUT if it is amended or reformed to add a flip provision.

The IRS and Treasury invite comments on the least burdensome methods of changing the terms of a trust's governing instrument.

Although the flip provision offers planners a new and valuable tool for solving the problems of illiquid and non-income-producing gift assets, the proposed regulations, as drafted do not permit the use of a flip provision when securities that are restricted under Rule 144 are transferred.

The proposed regulations define the term "unmarketable assets" as assets that are not cash, cash equivalents, or marketable securities (within the meaning of section 731(c) and the applicable regulations).

Section 731 defines "marketable securities" as financial instruments and foreign currencies which are, as of the date of the distribution, actively traded (within the meaning of section 1092(d)(1)).[28] The regulations further define securities as actively

---

[28]   IRC §731(c)(2)(A)

traded (and thus, marketable) if "it is of a type that is, as of the date of distribution, actively traded within the meaning of section 1092(d)(1). For example, if XYZ common stock is listed on a national securities exchange, particular shares of XYZ common stock that are distributed by a partnership are marketable securities even if those particular shares cannot be resold by the distributee partner for a designated period of time."[29]

Hopefully, this omission is an oversight that will be rectified in response to the public commentary phase of the regulatory process.

5. Determination of Unitrust Amount in Net Income Unitrusts with Make-Up Options that Allocate Gains to Income

The concept of the make-up option is simple unless the definition of income within the trust instrument is modified. For example, in Letter Ruling 9511007, a taxpayer proposes to create a 10 percent net income unitrust with make-up option. The trust instrument directs the trustee to allocate to trust income all gains that are realized on trust assets after contribution to the trust (whether attributable to appreciation occurring *before* or *after* contribution). The trust further states, the liability to the income recipient resulting from any income shortfall (i.e., the deficiency account balance) shall be taken into account in determining the annual unitrust amount. The trust provides specifically that the net fair market value of trust assets as of the valuation date is to be determined by first subtracting the amount of the shortfall as of that date, provided the reduction is no more than the amount of the unrealized gain then inherent in trust assets.

In its analysis the Service stated,

> The income exception provision of section 664(d)(3) was enacted by Congress to permit greater flexibility for certain charitable remainder gifts, but it was crafted in such a manner as to prevent the manipulation of the trust assets to the detriment of the charitable remainder interest. If the income exception provision is included in the trust's governing instrument, this provision prevents the trust from having to invade corpus when income for the year is below what was originally contemplated. For purposes of this provision, the determination of what constitutes trust income is to be made under the applicable local law and, thus, is not to include items such as capital gains which must be allocated to the trust principal.

> As envisioned by Congress, the trust income used to pay the unitrust amount would never include amounts that in prior years had been included in the fair market value of the trust assets on which the fixed amount had been based. The allocation of capital gains to trust income creates the potential to manipulate the trust assets to the detriment of the charitable remainder interest. Year after year, the trustee naturally includes any unrealized appreciation in determining the fair market value of the trust's assets on which the unitrust amount is based. Then when the trustee chooses to realize the appreciation by selling the assets, the realized appreciation is taken out of the base. The realized appreciation becomes trust income that will be paid to the noncharitable recipient to the extent of the current year's unitrust amount and any deficiency in the unitrust amounts from prior years. The trustee has, thus, inflated the unitrust amount each year by amounts that will be payable to the noncharitable recipient upon the sale of the assets. Under these circumstances, the amount that will

---

[29]   Reg. §1.731-2(c)

be paid to the charitable organization at the termination of the trust may well be less than the amount that would be paid to the charitable organization if the fixed unitrust amount had been paid each year pursuant to section 664(d)(2)(A) of the Code (i.e., a standard trust).

The Service ruled,

> In determining the fair market value of the assets on the annual valuation date, the governing instrument must require the trustee to treat as a liability the amount of any deficiency for prior years computed under section 664(d)(3)(B). The amount treated as a liability need not exceed the trust's unrealized appreciation that would be trust income under the terms of the governing instrument and applicable local law if the trustee sold all the assets in the trust on the valuation date. This trust provision will ensure that the timing of the realization of the gain by the trustee cannot be manipulated to the detriment of the charitable remainder interest.

The key to this ruling rests in the fact that the trust instrument defines *distributable net income* to include all gains realized on trust assets after contribution to the trust (whether attributable to appreciation occurring before or after contribution). In theory, if the contributed assets have a zero dollar adjusted cost basis, the entire amount of the trust can be used to satisfy a deficiency payment, thereby exhausting the trust! If, however, the trust instrument limits the definition of income to gains that occur only *after* the contribution of assets to the trust (i.e., the contribution value is the basis for purposes of determining subsequent gain or loss), it becomes mathematically impossible, given identical investment assumptions, for such a net income unitrust to produce a lesser remainder interest than a standard unitrust bearing the same payout rate. In fact, there is a possibility the trust will terminate prior to gains being realized and distributed. In such case, the remainder interest will be greater than from a standard unitrust. Thus, the formula called for in the ruling should not, in the opinion of some practitioners, logically apply.

In a subsequent letter ruling, a similar fact pattern was presented. In this case the trustee was instructed to allocate gains to income only upon receipt of cash or other property, by reason of sale or distribution.[30] In addition, a portion of the net proceeds of dispositions of underproductive property was to be allocated to income. In both cases, however, how capital gains were to be determined (i.e., whether based on the donor's basis or the contribution value as basis) or what portion of the proceeds from underproductive property was to be considered income was not addressed. In the absence of a clear definition, and relying on the logic presented in the first ruling, the Service required the same formula to be used in determining the annual unitrust amount.

The latest ruling on this topic deals with a net income with make-up option unitrust in which any gain realized upon disposition of the specific assets contributed to the trust is treated for all purposes as principal. For purposes of section 643(b) and applicable state law, all other realized capital gains are to be treated as income and, therefore, distributable as part or all of the unitrust amounts. In addition, the trust instrument provides that, for purposes of determining the annual unitrust amount, the fair market value of the trust assets is reduced by the amount of any deficiency in unitrust payments in prior years, but that such reduction shall not exceed the amount of unrealized gain in the trust assets as of the valuation date.

---

[30]   Ltr. Rul. 9511029

The Service approved the arrangement citing the compatibility of the trust's allocation of specified gains to principal and income with local law and the requirement to take into consideration the deficiency account in computing the annual unitrust amount.[31]

How does the reduction requirement affect the unitrust amount? The illustration on the following page shows the calculation of the formula used in Letter Ruling 9511007 and its effect on the amount of the makeup account in a net income unitrust where pre-gift and post-gift capital gain is defined as income. In both cases, the payout rate of the trust is 9 percent and the earnings rate of the assets within each trust is 6 percent. In the tenth year of the trust, the trustee withdraws the maximum allowable amount under each trust's makeup formula. As can be seen, the trust on the right (Trust 2 - without the formula) allows the trustee to distribute a substantial amount of the original contribution. Trust 1 does not allow the trustee to withdraw income below the original contributed amount. The asset value of Trust 2 drops below the original contribution because gain attributable to pre-gift appreciation is defined as income and the post-gift earnings rate of the trust is less than the trust's payout rate.

---

[31] Ltr. Rul. 9609009, *See also* Ltr. Ruls. 9643014; 9643014; and 9711013

Ltr. Rul. 9511007 Deficit Example

Payout rate at 9%
Earnings Rate of Assets at 6%

	With Ruling Formula - Trust 1			Without Ruling Formula - Trust 2		
Yr.	Unitrust Value (at end of year)	Gross Income from Unitrust	Maximum Payment in Current Year	Unitrust Value (at end of year)	Gross Income from Unitrust	Maximum Payment in Current Year
1	1,060,000	-	90,000	1,060,000	-	90,000
2	1,123,600	-	177,300	1,123,600	-	185,400
3	1,191,016	-	262,467	1,191,016	-	286,524
4	1,262,477	-	346,036	1,262,477	-	393,715
5	1,338,226	-	428,516	1,338,226	-	507,338
6	1,418,519	-	510,390	1,418,519	-	627,779
7	1,503,630	-	592,122	1,503,630	-	755,445
8	1,593,848	-	674,157	1,593,848	-	890,772
9	1,689,479	-	756,930	1,689,479	-	1,034,218
10	1,000,000	840,859	840,859	655,261	1,186,272	1,186,272
11	1,000,000	90,061	90,061	655,261	58,973	58,973
12	1,000,000	90,061	90,061	655,261	58,973	58,973
13	1,000,000	90,061	90,061	655,261	58,973	58,973
14	1,000,000	90,061	90,061	655,261	58,973	58,973
15	1,000,000	90,061	90,061	655,261	58,973	58,973
16	1,000,000	90,061	90,061	655,261	58,973	58,973
17	1,000,000	90,061	90,061	655,261	58,973	58,973
18	1,000,000	90,061	90,061	655,261	58,973	58,973
19	1,000,000	90,061	90,061	655,261	58,973	58,973
20	1,000,000	90,061	90,061	655,261	58,973	58,973
		1,741,469			1,776,002	

As a result of these rulings, some practitioners have called into question the efficacy of using zero coupon bonds, common trust funds, and tax deferred annuities to defer income distributions from net income unitrusts. Because the Service has based its argument on the preservation of the charitable remainder interest, the deferral of income distributions by virtue of investment asset selection is not at issue. What is at issue is the language in the trust instrument, or lack thereof, that permits the trustee to convert trust corpus into distributable income. Limiting the allocation of gains to income to *post-contribution gains* prevents the invasion of principal and, therefore, makes it mathematically impossible for the net income trust to produce a smaller remainder interest than a standard unitrust.[32]

On April 18, 1997, Treasury issued proposed amendments to the regulations that would prohibit the allocation of pre-gift gain to trust income.[33] The National Committee on Planned Giving supports this proposal and has further requested that Treasury and IRS revoke the positions held in Ltr. Ruls. 9511007 and 9511029 (and other subsequent PLRs) that require charitable remainder unitrust governing instruments to treat the deficiency account as a liability in calculating the fair market value for purposes of determining the annual unitrust amount.

F. New Trust Qualification Requirements

In response to congressional concern that some charitable remainder trusts have been established with combined measuring terms and payout/annuity rates that will result in only a *de minimis* remainder interest passing to charity, the Taxpayer Relief Act of 1997 imposes two new requirements for all charitable remainder trusts:

1. 50 Percent Maximum Payout or Annuity Rate

Since their inception, charitable remainder trusts have been subject to a minimum payout, or annuity rate, of 5 percent; however, there has been no maximum rate. The new law imposes a maximum annuity, or payout rate, of 50 percent.

In application, this new rule will have little effect on most charitable remainder trust planning because it was intended to curtail the use of *accelerated* charitable remainder unitrusts as described in Notice 94-78. The trust cited in the notice carried a payout rate of 80 percent and a measuring term of two years. Conversely, the majority of traditionally designed charitable remainder trusts carry single digit payout or annuity rates and terms measured by the life of each income recipient.

With respect to charitable remainder annuity trusts, when such trusts are measured by the life of an individual, they are subject to the 5 percent probability test.[34] This test effectively limits the maximum annuity rate for a qualifying trust to between approximately 7 and 15 percent.

2. 10 Percent Minimum Present Value of Remainder Interest

In addition to establishing a 50 percent maximum annuity, or payout rate, the law also requires the present value of the charitable remainder interest to be at least 10 percent of the net fair market value of such property transferred in trust on the date of

---

[32]   As of the publication date, the Government Relations Committee of the National Committee on Planned Giving was in dialogue with the Service on this issue. The authors and NCPG are opposed to the Service's current position. At least five requests for ruling on this issue are pending.

[33]   Reg-209823-96

[34]   The five percent probability test is discussed on page ___.

transfer. A charitable remainder trust that satisfies the 10 percent test on the date of transfer will not fail to qualify if the present value of the remainder interest subsequently falls below the minimum original qualifying amount. Similarly, where a charitable remainder trust is created for the joint lives of two individuals, the trust will not cease to qualify because the value of the charitable remainder is less than 10 percent of the trust's assets at the first death of those two individuals.

The conference agreement provides several additional rules in order to provide relief for trusts that do not meet the 10 percent rule:

First, when a transfer is made after July 28, 1997 to a charitable remainder trust that fails the 10 percent test, the trust is treated as meeting the 10 percent requirement if the governing instrument is changed by reformation, amendment, construction, or otherwise to meet such requirement. This is accomplished by reducing the payout rate or measuring term (individually or in combination) of any noncharitable income recipient's interest to the extent necessary to satisfy such requirement. The reformation must be commenced within the period permitted for reformations of charitable remainder trusts under section 2055(e)(3). The statute of limitations applicable to a deficiency of any tax resulting from reformation of the trust shall not expire before the date one year after the Treasury Department is notified that the trust has been reformed. In substance, this rule relaxes the requirements of section 2055(e)(3)(B) to the extent necessary for the reformation of the trust to meet the 10 percent requirement.

Second, a transfer to a trust will be treated as if it had never been made where a court having jurisdiction over the trust subsequently declares the trust void (because, for example, the application of the 10 percent rule frustrates the purposes for which the trust was created) and judicial proceedings to revoke the trust are commenced within the period permitted for reformations of charitable remainder trusts under section 2055(e)(3). Under this provision, the effect of "unwinding" the trust is that any transactions made by the trust with respect to the property transferred (e.g., income earned on the assets transferred to the trust and capital gains generated by the sales of the property transferred) would be income and capital gain of the donor (or the donor's estate if the trust was testamentary), and the donor (or the donor's estate if the trust was testamentary) would not be permitted a charitable deduction with respect to the transfer. The statute of limitations applicable to a deficiency of any tax resulting from "unwinding" the trust shall not expire before the date one year after the Treasury Department is notified that the trust has been revoked.

Third, where an additional contribution is made after July 28, 1997 to a charitable remainder unitrust created before July 29, 1997, and that unitrust would not meet the 10 percent requirement with respect to the additional contribution, the conference agreement provides that the additional contribution will be treated, under regulations to be issued by the Secretary of the Treasury, as if it had been made to a new trust that does not meet the 10 percent requirement. The failure of the new trust to qualify will not adversely affect the status of the original unitrust as a charitable remainder trust.

The requirement that the present value of the charitable remainder, with respect to any transfer to a qualified remainder trust, be at least 10 percent of the fair market value of the assets transferred in trust applies to transfers to a trust made after July 28, 1997. However, the 10 percent requirement does not apply to charitable remainder trusts created by a testamentary instrument executed before July 29, 1997, if the instrument is not modified after that date and the settlor dies before January 1, 1999, or could not be modified after July 28, 1997 because the settlor was under a mental disability on that date (i.e., July 28, 1997) and at all times thereafter.

The effect of the new 10 percent qualification floor is more far reaching than the 50 percent annuity/payout rate maximum and has been the topic of intense public debate. Proponents of the new rule argue that in order for donors to enjoy the tax benefits that accompany the use of a charitable remainder trust, such as complete avoidance of capital gains tax on the transfer and sale of contributed assets, there should be a minimum charitable component. Those who oppose the new rule have suggested the new rule discriminates against younger donors by preventing them from creating charitable remainder trusts with measuring terms based on their lives. Others argue the new floor prevents the use of more creative trust designs that are based on the unique circumstances of each donor.

Although the 10 percent qualification floor will discourage the creation of some charitable remainder trusts, it will also serve to remind planners that the primary purpose of the charitable remainder trust is to be charitable. As an alternative, younger donors may consider a contribution to a pooled income fund or to the charitable gift annuity, which are not subject to the 10 percent minimum present value floor.

G. Payment Frequency

A unitrust can make distributions annually, semi-annually, quarterly, or monthly, at the beginning or end of the payment period prescribed in the trust instrument. In addition, an annuity trust can make distributions on a weekly basis if desired.

The majority of charitable remainder trusts make distributions at the end of each calendar quarter. This format offers a practical balance between the income recipient's desire to receive regular payments and the trustee's desire to manage the administrative burden of such distributions.

Although all charitable remainder trusts are required to make distributions at least annually, the regulations have permitted the trustee to make actual payment of the annuity or unitrust amount within a reasonable time after the close of the trust's taxable year. A reasonable time would not ordinarily extend beyond the date by which the trustee would be required to file Form 1041-A (including extensions) for such year.[35] Since 1987, all charitable remainder trusts have been required to operate on a calendar tax year.

On April 18, 1997, the Treasury issued proposed amendments to the regulations to require that all annuity trusts and standard payout format unitrusts distribute the full annuity or unitrust amount by the close of the taxable year in which it is due.[36] Unitrusts that use a net income format will be permitted to continue to make payment within a reasonable amount of time after the close of the trust's taxable year.

These changes were initiated solely by the Treasury's desire to curtail the use of *accelerated* charitable remainder trusts as described in Notice 94-78. Accelerated CRTs exploit legal fictions involving trust accounting income for the purpose of enabling trustees to convert trust distributions from taxable capital gains into a tax-free return of principal.[37]

In response to numerous objections that such a requirement would place undue hardship on trustees of conforming trusts, the IRS issued Notice 97-68 that exempts some charitable remainder trusts from the year-end payment requirement. Specifically, trusts created before January 1, 1998 may pay the annuity or unitrust amount for the 1997 tax year within a reasonable period following the close of the tax year, provided (1) the payout rate or annuity rate of the trust does not exceed 15 percent, and (2) that all distributions received by the income recipient for 1997 are characterized for income tax purposes as described in IRC 664(b)(1), (2), and (3), and not as trust corpus.

In the case of a testamentary charitable remainder trust, the obligation to pay the unitrust or annuity amount commences with the date of the testator's death. Actual payment can, however, be deferred (with accrued interest) until a reasonable time after the taxable year in which complete funding of the trust occurs.[38] These rules are unaffected by the proposed regulations.

H. Choosing a Payment Format

One the first decisions that must be made in the design of a charitable remainder trust is the trust's payout format. Will the trust be an annuity trust or unitrust? If it is a unitrust, will it be standard, or include a net income or net income with makeup provision? If it is a net income unitrust, how will income be defined? These choices of annuity or unitrust depend on a thorough analysis of a number of factors, including:

- the marketability, liquidity and cash flow producing capability of the funding asset

- the income goals and risk tolerance of the income recipients

- the trustor's goals regarding the size of the ultimate charitable gift

---

35 Reg. §§1.664-2(a)(1); 1.664-3(a)(1)(i)(a). Form 1041-B was discontinued for 1981 and tax years thereafter.

36 Reg-209823-96. The proposed regulations will amend sections 1.664-2(a)(1)(i) and 1.664- 3(a)(1)(i).

37 Notice 94-78, 1994-2 C.B. 555. Accelerated CRTs are discussed in detail on page 181

38 Rev. Rul. 92-57, 1992-2 C.B. 123

1. Marketability, Liquidity, and Cash Flow Producing Capability of Funding Assets

One of the first steps a planner can take in choosing a payment format is to examine the compatibility of contributed assets with various format options. The marketability, liquidity, and cash flow producing capability of contributed assets are an excellent starting point.

Suppose a trustor funds a charitable remainder annuity trust with an apartment complex and with the intent of an immediate sale. Suppose also that the current net rents are sufficient to make the annuity payments. However, what if unforeseen additional cash requirements arise prior to the sale? What if the owner is required to make unanticipated capital improvements prior to the sale? What if one or more major tenants move out, severely reducing net operating income below that of the trust's payout requirement? Can the trustor of an annuity trust make additional contributions to the trust? No. Additional contributions to annuity trusts are prohibited. Further, a net income provision is unavailable to an annuity trust. [39]

Can a trustee borrow money? Yes. However, the trust might have acquisition indebtedness / unrelated debt-financed income and lose its tax-exempt status for that year. Accordingly, all income (including capital gain upon the sale of trust assets) could be taxable. [40]

The consequences of not making a distribution may, however, be more severe. The regulations provide that the unitrust or annuity amount is includible in the gross income to the recipient in the year it is required to be distributed even though no distribution is made until after the close of the tax year of the trust. [41] Such a deemed distribution results in phantom income to the income recipient. As mentioned earlier, the trust is required to make the distribution no later than when the tax return is filed for the year in which the distribution is due. A failure to make such a distribution may result in the disqualification of the trust.

Illiquid, non-income-producing, or potentially non-income-producing property is most suitably transferred to a charitable remainder unitrust for two reasons. First, the unitrust can receive additional contributions if necessary. Second, the unitrust can include a net income provision that can relieve the trustee of the obligation to make distributions during periods when net cash flow does not satisfy the unitrust amount.

Should a trustor automatically select a net income unitrust over a standard unitrust when illiquid or low-income-producing contribution assets are contemplated? No, not without (a) considering the effect that selecting the net income format will have on the investment

---

[39] Reg. §1.664-2(b)

[40] IRC §§514(c)(1)(A); 664(c)

[41] Reg. §1.664-1(d)(4)(i)

management of the trust's ability to produce adequate net income to satisfy the unitrust amount, and (b) understanding the alternatives.[42]

2. Income Goals and Risk Tolerance

Because high returns and low risk are mutually exclusive, the choice of payment format is most greatly influenced by the income recipient's investment horizon, risk tolerance, and prevailing investment market conditions. The investment horizon of a charitable remainder trust is its measuring life, usually represented by the actuarial life expectancies of income recipients. Risk tolerance can be defined as the amount of fluctuation in asset value an investor is willing to accept.

Charitable remainder trusts have risk tolerances as well. A charitable remainder annuity trust, with its fixed distribution requirement, may have difficulty in recovering from a loss of capital because, when principal value is reduced, the relative annuity amount is increased. On the other hand, a unitrust is more risk tolerant because, in the event of a loss of capital, the payout is adjusted downward.

The annuity format is usually selected by individuals who are averse to risk or have short investment horizons. Upside potential is deliberately sacrificed in exchange for the assurance of a fixed income stream regardless of investment performance or fluctuations in trust value. For example, a seventy-five year old income recipient may prefer an annuity trust invested in U.S. Treasury bonds, purchased at par or a discount, thereby locking in and guaranteeing the rate of return.

On the other hand, the unitrust is most often selected by those with higher risk tolerances or who otherwise desire to protect the purchasing power of their income distributions over longer investment horizons. In times of inflation or economic prosperity, a unitrust format may be preferable because the income recipient's return varies with in direct proportion to the annual fair market value of trust assets.

I. Selecting the Annuity Rate or Payout Rate

The most significant design consideration regarding a charitable remainder trust is the choice of the annuity or payout rate. Not only will this choice affect the amount of income distributions, it will also affect the amount of the charitable remainder interest and the trustor's charitable contribution deduction. Further, the rate will influence the selection of investment strategies for the trust.

With respect to charitable remainder annuity trusts, the annuity amount will remain static for the life of the trust. This, however, assumes the trust does not deplete its assets in the meantime. Therefore, the choice of annuity rate must take into account the income recipient's income needs, prevailing investment markets, and the amount of risk the trustee is willing to bear in meeting the annuity amount. An annuity trust bearing a high rate (relative to prevailing market returns) not only runs the risk of depleting principal (which can be exacerbated if

---

[42]   For complete discussions of these issues, refer to "Effect of Net Income Provision Upon Investment Policy" on page 196 and "Taxation of In-Kind Distributions" on page 204.

principal falls below the initial funding amount), but the contribution may not qualify for a charitable contribution deduction. The 5 percent probability test is discussed on page 66.

The unitrust, with its variable payout format and more-flexible drafting options provides an opportunity for more-creative cash flow planning. A unitrust bearing a payout rate that is less than its return on investment will grow from year to year and, with it, the amounts distributed to income recipients. The concept of tax-free compounding and its effect on future income distributions adds another element to the payout rate design equation.

The following illustration shows the annual net cash flow and tax savings produced by two standard unitrusts bearing payout rates of 5 percent and 10 percent. The assumed rate of return on investment within the trusts is 10 percent. The term of the analysis is forty years.

Comparison of Income
5 and 10% Standard Unitrusts

Yr.	5%Std. CRUT	10% Std. CRUT
1	50,000	100,000
5	63,814	100,000
10	81,445	100,000
15	103,946	100,000
20	132,665	100,000
25	169,318	100,000
30	216,097	100,000
35	275,801	100,000
40	351,999	100,000
Totals	6,391,988	4,100,000

Comparison of Income

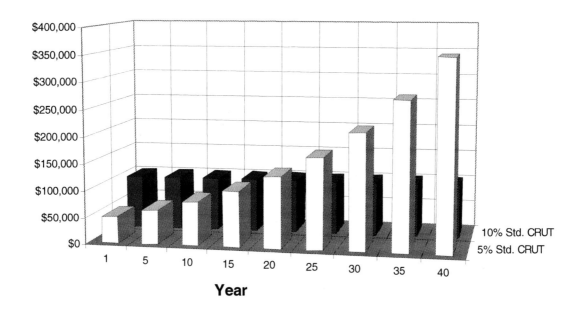

Figure 8   Although the unitrust bearing the 5 percent payout rate pays less initially than the unitrust bearing the 10 percent rate, the income from the 5 percent unitrust passes the income from the 10 percent unitrust in year fifteen.

As demonstrated, crossover points occur as the unitrust amounts of the trusts reach equilibrium with one another. Which trust produces the greatest aggregate cash flow over the period? The trust with the 5 percent payout rate. However, should a 5 percent payout be selected?

1. Using Discounted Cash Flow Analysis in Selecting Payout Rates

Variable cash flows are most accurately compared by discounted cash flow analysis. The following analysis illustrates the cumulative net present value of cash flows and tax savings, along with the net present value of the future charitable gifts. Trust assets are to be invested at an assumed rate of 10 percent. The discount rate is 6 percent. In this case, a 6 percent discount rate is used to simulate the after-tax opportunity cost of reinvestment (i.e., 10 percent taxable rate of return less 40 percent income tax).

This analysis presents a completely different result. As can be seen, the present values of cash flows are similar. What payout rate should be selected? The rate the trustor selects after seeing this type of analysis and making an informed decision.

Cumulative Income at 6% NPV
5 and 10% Standard Unitrusts

Yr.	5%Std. CRUT	10% Std. CRUT
1	46,296	92,593
5	259,187	462,288
10	444,108	713,896
15	604,733	885,137
20	744,254	1,001,680
25	865,444	1,080,998
30	970,712	1,134,980
35	1,062,150	1,171,719
40	1,141,574	1,196,723

Cumulative Income at 6% NPV

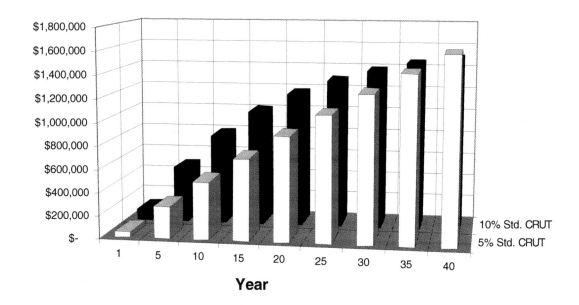

Figure 9 Based on a discount rate of 6 percent (the projected after-tax investment opportunity cost), the cumulative net present value income from 5 percent unitrust does not catch the cumulative net present value of income from the 10 percent unitrust until year forty. While the 5 percent unitrust produces less cumulative benefit in most years, the decision regarding payout rate selection is not as simple or obvious as this NPV analysis suggests. The donor also must examine the impact of payout rate selection higher upon the projected charitable remainder interest.

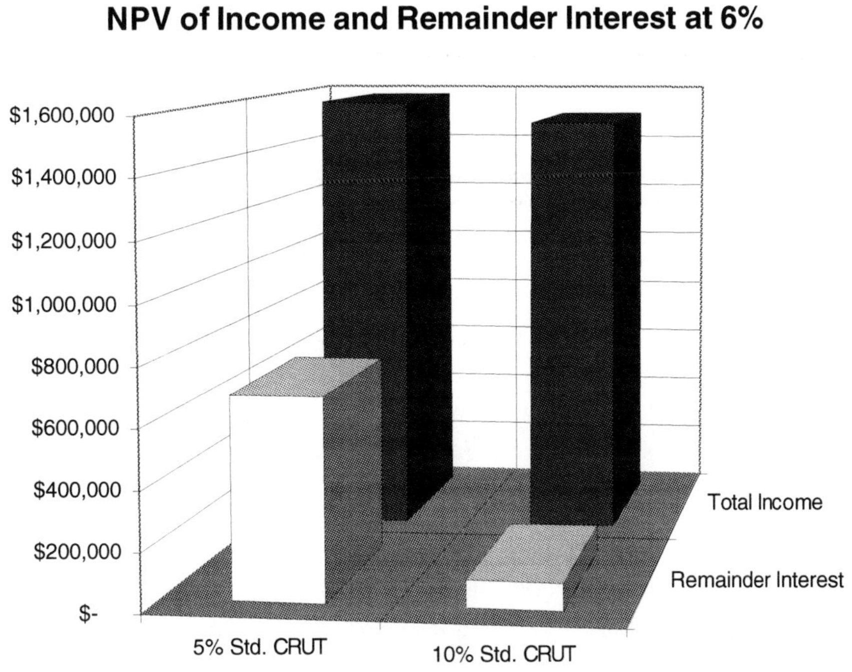

NPV of Income and Remainder Interest at 6%

Figure 10   This chart shows the cumulative net present value of income provided by the 5 percent and 10 percent payout rate unitrusts in the fortieth year and the net present value of each trust's charitable remainder interest.

Even though the difference in the cumulative net present value of the two income streams is negligible, the difference in the value of the gift to charity is significant. The analysis demonstrates, given an adequate length of time, a donor can maximize the total benefit (i.e., the combination of the net present value of the income and remainder interests) by selecting the lowest possible payout rate.

If the projected measuring term of the trust is less than the period illustrated in this analysis (as would be the case with older life income recipients), the payout rate will need to be increased in order to maximize the total benefit of the trust.

J. Power to Distribute Excess Income or Principal to Charity

Even though a charitable remainder trust can distribute only the annuity or unitrust amount to a noncharitable income recipient, the regulations do permit the transfer of trust principal or excess income to the charitable remainderman prior to the conclusion of the measuring term of the trust.

1.   Gift of Entire Income Interest

Regarding the deductibility of advance payments, Rev. Rul. 86-60 provides that an income recipient's contribution of their *entire* annuity or unitrust income interest to charity qualifies for income and gift tax deductions.[43]

2.   Gift of Partial Income Interest

In a 1988 letter ruling, an individual created a charitable remainder unitrust from which a 5 percent unitrust amount was payable for his life and thereafter for the life of his spouse. The trustor reserved the right, exercisable by will, to revoke his spouse's income interest. It was trustor's original intent to keep the trust in operation throughout his lifetime; however, during the initial years following its creation, the trust appreciated greatly in value. The trustor then decided to accelerate a portion of the remainder interest to the charitable remainderman. In his request for ruling, the trustor asked (a) Will the transfer of a portion of the trustor's entire interest and a portion of the contingent recipient's entire interest in the trust qualify for a charitable contribution deduction? (b) Will the proposed transaction cause a merger of the income and remainder interests thereby disqualifying the trust? (c) How will the charitable contribution deduction, if allowed, be calculated?

In response to the first question, the Service ruled that a deduction would be allowable only for the trustor's component of the transfer. A deduction for the portion of the transfer attributable to the spouse's contingent interest was disallowed because the trustor's reserved right of revocation could be exercised, leaving the surviving spouse with nothing to give. With respect to the second question, in interpreting state law, the Service ruled that, although a merger would exist on the accelerated portion, the trust would not be disqualified provided it continued to pay the 5 percent unitrust amount to the noncharitable income recipient from the remaining trust assets. Finally, the amount of the income tax charitable deduction would be calculated by multiplying the amount being transferred by the quantity 1.00000 minus the present value of remainder interest factor based on the trustor's age (on the date of transfer).[44]

Another trustor approached this issue differently. Through a reformation, the trustor divided one unitrust and its assets into two separate (but identical) unitrusts. The trustor then contributed his retained unitrust income interest in the newly formed trust to charity while retaining the income interest from the original trust.[45]

3.   Distributing Excess Income

In a 1994 letter ruling, the IRS approved an arrangement whereby a special independent trustee of a 10 percent charitable remainder unitrust was given the

---

[43]   Rev. Rul. 86-60, 1986-1 C.B. 302; Ltr. Rul. 9721014

[44]   Ltr. Rul. 8805024; Ltr. Rul. 9529039 held that, under a similar fact pattern, a charitable contribution gift tax deduction was allowed. *See also* Ltr. Rul. 9550026

[45]   Ltr. Rul. 9817010

discretionary power to distribute income that exceeded the 5 percent unitrust amount to the charitable remainderman.[46] The trustors also retained the right to transfer all or a portion of trust corpus to the remainderman at any time during the measuring term of the trust. Although the issue was not specifically addressed, it is assumed that no income or gift tax deduction accompanied the contributions of the excess income. Likewise, it is assumed that payments to the charitable remainderman are not considered to be taxable to the grantors. The ruling also provided that, in the case of distributions in kind, the adjusted basis of the property distributed would be fairly representative of the adjusted basis of the property available for payment on the date of payment.

K. Use of Unitrust Assets to Collateralize Loans to Remaindermen

The Service approved a provision in a charitable remainder unitrust that granted authority to the trustees to pledge, with the consent of the income recipients, trust assets as collateral to third party lenders for loans made to the charitable remaindermen of the trust.[47] Note that a unitrust was the subject of the ruling. The Service has not ruled on the application of this type of provision to an annuity trust.

L. Trust Measuring Terms

The rules concerning the payment period or measuring term of a charitable remainder trust offer great theoretical flexibility in designing a trust's operational life. However, flexibility often breeds complexity and the possibility of producing undesired tax consequences. Therefore, this section should be read with consideration to the marital deduction, gift tax, and estate tax consequences of various measuring term formats.[48]

Following is an overview of measuring term rules as described in Reg. §§1.664-2(a)(5) and 1.664-3(a)(5):

- The obligation to pay the annuity or unitrust amount begins the day the trust is created (i.e., funded) and continues either for the life of one or more named individuals or for a term of years not to exceed 20 years. The obligation generally ends with the regular payment next preceding the end of the measuring term.

- Only an individual or an organization described in IRC §170(c) may be named as the income recipient of a trust payable for the life of an individual. If an individual receives an amount for life, it must be solely for his life.

- In the case of an amount payable for a term of years, the length of the term must be ascertainable with certainty at the time of creation of the trust. However, the term may be terminated by the death of the recipient or by the trustor's exercise by will of a retained power to revoke or terminate the interest of any recipient other than an organization described in IRC §170(c). Thus, the term of years may not be

---

[46]   Ltr. Rul. 9423020; Reg. §1.664-2(a)(4); *See also* Ltr. Rul. 9323039

[47]   Ltr. Rul. 8807082

[48]   *See also* Chapter 5 - Gift and Estate Tax Considerations.

conditioned on the happening of an event such as income paid to *A* for his life followed by a term of years for *B*. On the other hand, *A* may receive income for life followed by income to *B* for a term of years which begins when the trust is created.[49]

The following are common forms of measuring terms:

- **Life Only -** The trust makes payments to one or more persons as long as one individual is alive.

- **Term of Years -** The trust makes payments to one or more persons for a period not to exceed twenty years.

- **Life and Concurrent Term of Years (the longer of)** The trust makes payments for a guaranteed term of years that is concurrent with the lives of one or more individuals. For example, the trust could pay income to an individual as long as an individual is alive, or for a period of ten years, *whichever is longer*. If the individual dies within the first ten years, income will be distributed to the individual's estate, named individuals or a named class of individuals for the balance of the ten-year period.[50]

- **Life and Concurrent Term of Years (the shorter of)** The trust makes payments for *the shorter of* a term of years (not to exceed twenty) or the life (or lives) of the measuring life. For example, the trust could pay income to an individual for a period of twenty years. If the individual dies during the twenty-year period, however, all payments stop and the remainder interest passes to the charitable beneficiary.

- **Life and Consecutive Term of Years (measured by other lives) -** The trust makes payments to named recipients for the balance of their lives. At their deaths, the trust continues to make income payments to a new group of recipients whose income term is measured by *the shorter of* their lives or a term of years not to exceed twenty (which begins at the death(s) of the life recipients). If the second class of recipients dies within the term of years (in this example, twenty), the trust terminates.

---

[49]   Reg. §§1.664-2(a)(5); 1.664-3(a)(5)
[50]   Ltr. Rul. 9331043

Income Options

Trust Stops =

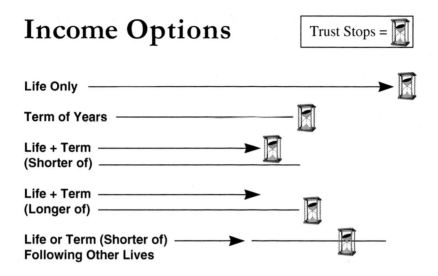

A study conducted by the *National Committee on Planned Giving* reported that 94 percent of charitable remainder trusts are measured by the life of the last surviving income recipient; 4 percent provide payments for a fixed term of years; and only 2 percent include a combination of the two.[51]

1. Children as Successor Life Income Recipients

The Service approved a structure whereby a husband and wife established a trust that would pay a unitrust amount to them for their joint lifetimes, then for the life of the survivor. Upon the survivor's death, the trust would pay the unitrust amount to their two children in equal amounts for their joint lifetimes, and then pay all income to the survivor.[52]

> **Comment:** While this format was allowed as a qualified charitable remainder trust, the ruling did not consider the loss of the marital deduction on the income interest passing to the surviving spouse. See the discussion of the marital deduction in Chapter 5.

2. Changing Recipient Order Disqualifies Trust

A trustor established a charitable remainder trust with income payable to himself for life, then to his sister for her life (if she survives him), then to his wife for her life (if she survives them both). The trustor proposed to change the order of income distributions by changing positions with his sister. The change was to be made with the consent of the income recipients and the charitable remainderman.

Section 1.664-3(a)(4) of the regulations provides, "The trust may not be subject to a power to invade, alter, amend, or revoke for the beneficial use of a person other than an

---

[51] *Charitable Remainder Trusts: Characteristics of Selected CRTs Established in 1992.* National Committee on Planned Giving.

[52] Ltr. Rul. 9326049

organization described in section 170(c)." The Service considered the proposed change a prohibited power that would disqualify the trust under IRC §664(d)(2).[53]

M. Terminating an Income Recipient s Interest

Can a trustor retain the right to terminate an income recipient's interest prior to the term stated within the trust? Yes, in two ways.

First, the regulations permit a trustor to reserve a power to revoke non-trustor income recipient's interest. This power must be included within the trust instrument and is exercisable solely by the trustor's will.[54] As will be discussed in Chapter 5, a retained power of revocation can provide gift and estate planning opportunities.

The second method in which a trustor can terminate an income recipient's interest is the *qualified contingency*. Reg. §1.664-3(a)(5)(i) requires that a trust that is measured by life must be measured solely by the life of the income recipient(s). However, IRC §664(f) allows a trustor to terminate a charitable remainder trust prior to its stated measuring life based on the happening of a qualified contingency. IRC §664(f)(3) defines a qualified contingency as, "any provision of a trust which provides that, upon the happening of a contingency, the unitrust or annuity trust payments will terminate no later than such payments would otherwise terminate under the trust." This language grants great latitude in defining the contingency.

A established a testamentary charitable remainder unitrust that named *B* as the sole income recipient. *A*'s will provided the trust term would end upon the death of *B* or *C*, whichever occurred sooner. The Service concluded that the death of *C* was a qualified contingency that met the requirements of a qualified charitable remainder trust.[55]

Can a trustor, who establishes a charitable remainder trust naming a non-spouse as the sole income recipient of the trust, retain the power to revoke the recipient's income interest by will or through use of a qualified contingency?

The answer seems to be yes on both counts. It is clear that a power of revocation can be used in the case where the trustor is a life income recipient. Further, the IRS has allowed a right of revocation exercisable by will for a charitable remainder trust measured by a *term of years* in which the trustor was not an income recipient.[56] In the case where the trust is measured by the life of the non-trustor recipient, however, a question arises. The regulations require a trust that is measured by life to be measured solely by the life of the income recipient(s).[57] Although this requirement seems to prevent a non-income recipient trustor from terminating the trust by will, IRC §664(f) allows a trustor to terminate a charitable remainder trust prior to its stated measuring life for virtually any reason.[58]

---

53   Ltr. Rul. 9143030

54   Reg. §§1.664-2(a)(4); 1.664-3(a)(4)

55   Ltr. Rul. 9322031

56   Ltr. Rul. 8949061

57   Reg. §1.664-3(a)(5)(i)

58   See Ltr. Rul. 9322031; Ltr. Rul. 9829017 terminates an individual's income interest upon her remarriage.

N. Permissible Income Recipients

The annuity or unitrust amount must be payable *to* or *for the use of* a person or persons, at least one of which is not an organization described in IRC §170(c). The term *person* includes:

- an individual

- trust or estate

- partnership

- association

- company, or

- corporation[59]

If the annuity or unitrust amount is to be paid to an individual or individuals for their lifetime, they must be living at the time of creation of the trust. A named person or persons may include members of a named class provided that, in the case of a class which includes any individual, all such individuals must be living and ascertainable at the time of the creation of the trust unless the annuity or unitrust amount is to be paid to such class consists solely of a term of years. For example, in the case of a testamentary trust, the testator's will can provide that an amount shall be paid to his children who are living at the time of his death.[60]

1. Noncharitable Trust as Income Recipient

Can a noncharitable trust be named as the income recipient of a charitable remainder trust that is measured by the life of an individual?

In Rev. Rul. 76-270, a charitable remainder trust was established for the lifetime of an individual who was incompetent.[61] Because of the income recipient's incompetence, the unitrust paid the unitrust amount over to a second trust, which provided for payments of a designated portion of the unitrust amount to the income recipient for his lifetime. The trustee of the second trust could pay additional amounts for the care, support, and maintenance of the income recipient, if the amounts provided were insufficient. Any amounts remaining in the second trust at the income recipient's death would be payable to his estate. The Service ruled the arrangement would qualify and would be treated as though the unitrust payments were made directly to the income recipient of the second trust.[62]

In a similar ruling, the IRS allowed a provision that enabled the trustee of a charitable remainder trust, in its sole discretion, to make payments for the benefit of the recipient if, in the opinion of the trustee, the recipient was without legal capacity. Payments were to be

---

[59]   IRC §7701(a)(1)

[60]   Reg. §§1.664-2(a)(3)(i); 1.664-3(a)(3)(i)

[61]   Rev. Rul. 76-270, 1976-2 C.B. 194

[62]   Ltr. Rul. 9232019

deposited in a bank account in the name of the recipient, or to a legal guardian or conservator for the recipient.[63]

It is important to note that these two rulings dealt with income recipients who lacked the legal capacity to accept payments from a charitable remainder trust. What if the income recipient *is* competent? Can payments still be made to a trust for his or her benefit?

Two grantors proposed to create three residuary charitable remainder trusts from their estates.[64] Upon the death of the surviving grantor, the trustee would create two separate charitable remainder annuity trusts and one charitable remainder unitrust. The payments from all three trusts would be made to a fourth (noncharitable) trust established for the purpose of making distributions to separate trusts for the benefit of the grantors' relatives. The measuring terms of the charitable remainder trusts ranged from five to twenty years.[65] The Service approved the arrangements.

In a subsequent and unrelated request for ruling, a parent proposed to establish a charitable remainder unitrust that named a noncharitable trust as its sole income recipient. The charitable remainder trust was measured by the life of the grantor's son. The son was the sole beneficiary of the noncharitable trust and had the absolute and unqualified right to withdraw, except in the case of disability or incapacity, all or any part of the trust account. Further, the son had a general power of appointment, exercisable by will, over the trust account.

The Service approved the proposed arrangements based on the facts the son would retain a power to withdraw principal and income from the noncharitable trust under IRC §678(a) and, further, would be treated as the owner of the noncharitable trust for income tax purposes under IRC §671.[66] However, the Service subsequently had a change of heart and has revoked this ruling.

In a telephone call to the grantor's authorized representative, the Service stated that it was revoking 9619044 because, "it is not in accord with the current views of the Service." In response, the grantor requested that the transaction subject to the original ruling be excluded from the retroactive revocation. In subsequent rulings, the Service permitted the grantor to rely on the holdings of the original ruling.[67]

In Ltr. Rul. 9718030, the Service announced that it is revoking Ltr. Rul. 9101010 in which it had ruled that a charitable remainder unitrust could distribute the unitrust payments to a trust established to benefit the donor's daughter. The trustee of the noncharitable trust could in its sole discretion distribute principal and income to the daughter. On the daughter's death, the remaining principal and income would be distributed to her estate.

---

[63]   Ltr. Rul. 9339018

[64]   Ltr. Rul. 9328041

[65]   See also Ltr. Rul. 9253055

[66]   Ltr. Ruls. 9619042; 9619043; and 9619044

[67]   Ltr. Ruls. 9710008, 9710009, and 9710010

The Service stated, "Under section 664(d)(2), an otherwise qualifying charitable remainder trust that makes distributions for the life of a named individual to a second trust (whose only function is to receive and administer those distributions for the benefit of the named individual beneficiary) will not qualify as a charitable remainder unitrust, unless the named individual is incompetent."[68]

The key to the Service's current position on this issue seems to be the measuring term of the trust. If the charitable remainder trust is measured by a term of years, it can make distributions to a trust without restriction. If, however, the charitable remainder trust is measured by the life of an individual, payments to a trust on that individual's behalf will be allowed only when that individual is incompetent.

2. Living Trust as Trustor and Income Recipient

In a private ruling, the beneficiary of a living trust held a lifetime limited power to appoint any part or all of the trust principal to or for the benefit of his heirs or charitable organizations. The beneficiary proposed to appoint the trust principal to a charitable remainder unitrust with the unitrust amount payable to the living trust for a term of twenty years. The Service approved the arrangement stating, "There is nothing in section 664 or the applicable regulations that prohibits a trust from being a permissible donor to an otherwise qualified charitable remainder trust."[69] Again, the key to this ruling most likely rests in the fixed measuring term. A life measuring term might have produced a different result.

3. Multiple Grantor Income Recipients Deemed Association

There is no limit to the number of income recipients a charitable remainder trust can have. However, there may be a limit to the number of trustors if they are also the income recipients. In Letter Ruling 9547004 a husband, wife, and their six grandchildren proposed to make contributions to one charitable remainder unitrust. Under the terms of the trust instrument, the husband and wife would be entitled to the entire unitrust amount during their lives, after which, the grandchildren, as a class, would receive the unitrust amount.

In determining whether the trust was a qualified charitable remainder trust, the Service first address whether the trust was classified as a trust for federal income tax purposes.

Procedure and Administration Regulation §301.7701-2(a)(1) sets forth six characteristics to be considered in determining whether an organization is properly classified as an association taxable as a corporation, a partnership, or a trust:

- associates

- an objective to carry on business and divide the gains therefrom

---

[68]   TAM 9831004 also confirms this interpretation.

[69]   Ltr. Rul. 9821029

- continuity of life

- centralization of management

- limited liability

- free transferability of interests

Reg. §301.7701-2(a)(2) provides that characteristics common to trusts and corporations are not material in attempting to distinguish between a trust and an association.

If an entity, the Service said, has both associates and a business purpose, it cannot be classified as a trust for federal income tax purposes. In the present situation, eight individuals will each contribute their own funds to the proposed trust. As the recipients of the unitrust amount, the grantors will share in the profits derived from the joint investment of their assets held by the proposed trust. Thus, the grantors are associates and have pooled their assets with an object to carry on business and divide the gains from it. The arrangement, the Service concluded, is not a trust for federal income tax purposes. Therefore, it is not a qualified charitable remainder trust.

Notwithstanding this issue, as will be discussed, the presence of additional income recipients (other than the trustor's or spouse) may also cause adverse income, gift, and estate tax consequences.

4. Pets as Income Recipients

Many people consider their pets to be more human than some people they know. Charitable remainder trusts that name animals as income recipients may, depending on local law, be deemed valid and enforceable, valid but unenforceable, or void from inception.

Not only is a charitable income tax deduction unavailable in all three cases, but the transfer may also be subject to gift or estate tax.[70] After all, there are no valuation tables based on the nine lives of a cat!

O. Sprinkling Powers

The trustee of a charitable remainder trust may be given the power to allocate or *sprinkle* income among named recipients or a named class of recipients. Because an individual cannot receive an income interest measured by the life of another, trusts containing sprinkling powers must either have a measuring term that ends with the death of the last surviving income recipient or one that is based on a term not to exceed twenty years. As previously stated, in the event the measuring term is based on the life of an individual or individuals, the individuals must be alive when the trust is created. Alternatively, a trust that is established

---

[70]   Rev. Rul. 55-335, 1955-1 C.B. 455; Rev. Rul. 78-105, 1978-1 C.B. 295

based solely on a term of years can provide for distributions to be made to a named class of individuals not yet in being (e.g., the children of the trustor).[71]

In order to avoid treatment as a grantor trust, a trustee that is granted sprinkling powers must be *independent* as described in Reg. §1.674(c)-1.[72]

P. Testamentary Charitable Remainder Trusts

The regulations provide that when a decedent establishes a testamentary charitable remainder trust, the trust is deemed created on the date of death of the decedent (even though the trust is not funded until the end of a reasonable period of administration or settlement).[73]

The obligation to pay the annuity or unitrust amount must commence with the date of death. If permitted by applicable local law or authorized by the provisions of the governing instrument, payment of the annuity or unitrust amount may be deferred from the date of death until the end of the taxable year of the trust in which complete funding of the trust occurs.[74]

Because the regulation includes the phrase, "may be deferred," in reference to the payment of the annuity or unitrust amount, the decedent's estate can make distributions to the income recipients during the course of estate administration or settlement and in advance of the funding of the trust. These advance payments are, therefore, estimates which may differ from the amounts that are ultimately determined when actual funding of the trust occurs.

Within a reasonable time after the end of the taxable year in which the complete funding of the trust occurs, the trustee must pay to the recipient (in the case of an underpayment) or must receive from the recipient (in the case of an overpayment) the difference between:

(a) any annuity or unitrust amounts *actually paid*, plus interest on such amounts, computed at the rate of interest specified in Reg. §1.664-1(a)(5)(iv), compounded annually,[75] and

(b) the unitrust amounts *payable*, plus interest on such amounts, computed at the rate of interest specified in Reg. §1.664-1(a)(5)(iv), compounded annually.

The amounts payable are retroactively determined by using the taxable year, valuation method, and valuation dates ultimately adopted by the charitable remainder trust.[76] In the case of a unitrust (funded by residuary bequest, for example), it may be difficult to determine the amount the income recipient would have received, plus interest, had the trust been funded and operational on the date of the decedent's death. An alternative method of determining the amount is, accordingly, provided in Reg. §1.664-1(a)(5)(ii).

---

[71] Reg. §1.664-3(a)(3)

[72] See Chapter 7 - Selecting a Trustee

[73] Reg. §1.664-1(a)(5)(i)

[74] *Ibid.*

[75] For valuation dates on or after April 30, 1984, the rate of interest specified in section 7520 for the month in which the valuation date occurs (or one of the prior two months if elected under section 1.7520-2(b)) is used. See the regulations for rules applicable to valuation dates occurring prior to April 30, 1984.

[76] Reg. §1.664-1(a)(5)(i)

Revenue Rulings 88-81[77] and 82-165[78] erroneously indicate that interest should be added to the amount determined under the formula in Reg. §1.664-1(a)(5)(ii). Revenue Ruling 92-57[79] properly interprets the regulation stating the interest component is included in the computation; thus, no additional interest is required.[80]

The sample provisions in Rev. Proc. 90-30[81] and Rev. Proc. 90-31[82] correctly apply section 1.664-1(a)(5)(ii) and may be used.[83]

Q. Permissible Charitable Remaindermen

Following the termination of payments to the income recipient(s), the remainder interest in the trust must be transferred to, or for the use of, an organization described in IRC §170(c) or can be retained by the trust for such use.[84] In the latter case, in the absence of a noncharitable income recipient, the trust is treated as a private non-operating foundation.

1.   Income, Gift, and Estate Tax Considerations

As discussed in the next chapter, the choice of charitable remainderman may adversely affect the grantor's charitable contribution income tax deduction. For example, the selection of a private non-operating foundation as remainderman might cause the deduction to be computed based on the lesser of (a) the fair market value, and (b) the adjusted cost basis of the contributed assets, whereas the choice of a public charity as remainderman will enable the deduction to be computed based on the possibly higher fair market value. In contrast, the selection of the charitable remainderman will have no effect on deductions for gift and estate tax purposes.

The trust agreement may include multiple remaindermen by fractional interest or by a combination of a fractional interest, fixed amount, or residuary interest.

2.   Mandatory Provision to Name Alternate Remainderman

The trust instrument must contain a provision that, in the event a named charity does not exist or is not qualified at the time the interest is to be transferred to the charity, the trustor or trustee must select an alternate qualified organization. Caution must be taken in drafting this provision to ensure that the alternate organization is of the same tax-exempt status. For example, if the originally named organization is a 50 percent-type public charity, but the document allows the trustee to select any organization as described under section 170(c), the possibility exists that the trustee could select a 30 percent-type private

[77]   Rev. Rul. 88-81, 1988-2 C.B. 127

[78]   Rev. Rul. 82-165, 1982-2 C.B. 117

[79]   Rev. Rul. 92-57, 1992-2 C.B. 123

[80]   See also Ltr. Rul. 9617036

[81]   Rev. Proc. 90-30, 1990-1 C.B. 534

[82]   Rev. Proc. 90-31, 1990-1 C.B. 539

[83]   For further discussion, see James M. Crowley, J.D., *Testamentary CRTs: Opportunities and Issues in Lifetime Planning and Post Mortem Administration*, Proceedings: Eighth National Conference on Planned Giving, National Committee on Planned Giving, 1995.

[84]   IRC §§664(d)(1)(C); 664(d)(2)(C)

foundation as an alternate remainderman. The IRS would then base the trustor's income tax deduction on the assumption that the 30 percent-type organization would be the recipient.

3. Power of Substitution

In Rev. Rul. 76-8 the Service considered the case of a charitable remainder trust in which the governing instrument permitted the grantor to, at any time, designate, in lieu of the charitable organization named in the trust instrument as remainderman, another organization satisfying the requirements of sections 170(c), 2055(a), and 2522(a) of the Code.[85] The ruling concluded that such a reserved power will not disqualify the trust. The power of substitution is accomplished by written notice delivered to the trustee on an inter vivos or testamentary basis.[86] The Service subsequently issued letter rulings granting non-trustor and successor income recipients the power to substitute the charitable remaindermen.[87]

4. Power to Designate Use of Proceeds

A trustor can designate the specific use to which the charitable remaindermen places the remainder interest. Examples typically include maintaining the remainder interest in an endowment for a general or specific purpose or limiting the use of the funds for a specific purpose within the organization. If such a restriction is desired, it can be accomplished by including a provision in the governing instrument. In the absence of such a provision, the use of the proceeds is unrestricted.

A recent letter ruling permitted the estate of a decedent trustor to claim a charitable contribution estate tax deduction for a charitable remainder trust that restricted the use of the trust proceeds to funding scholarships for students with specific surnames.[88]

---

[85]   Rev. Rul. 76-8, 1976-1 C.B. 179

[86]   Ltr. Ruls. 9331043; 9204036; 9629009

[87]   Ltr. Ruls. 9252023; 9445010; 9517020; 9707027

[88]   Ltr. Rul. 9527026

Chapter Four

Charitable Contribution Deduction

I. Distinguishing Income, Gift, and Estate Tax Deductions

Generally, no deduction is allowed for other than a donor's entire interest in property for income, gift, and estate tax purposes unless the contribution takes the form of qualified trust. Specifically, a qualified trust must be a charitable remainder annuity trust, charitable remainder unitrust, or pooled income fund.[89]

A. Calculating the Present Value of Remainder Interest

The deductible portion of a transfer to a charitable remainder trust for income, gift, and estate tax purposes is based on the present value of the remainder interest. This amount is calculated from unisex Treasury tables that discount the net fair market value of the transfer by the present value of income distributable to the income recipients over the anticipated measuring term of the trust.[90] The computation is generally based on eight factors:

- the net fair market value of the property transferred

- the annuity or unitrust format

- the annuity rate or payout rate

- the measuring term of the trust (term of years, lives of income recipients or a combination)

- the payment frequency

- in the case of the unitrust, the number of months between the valuation date and the first payment

- in the case of the annuity trust, whether the payment is at the beginning or end of the payment period, and

- the Applicable Federal Mid-term Rate (AFMR)

---

[89] Referred to as the *partial interest rule*. IRC §§170(f)(2)(A); 2522(c)(2); 2055(e)(2)

[90] Reg. §1.664-2(c); Reg. §1.664-4(a)

The amount of deduction a trustor can claim for gift and estate tax purposes is unlimited. The amount a trustor can claim for income tax purposes is subject to reduction and percentage limitation rules discussed in Chapter 4.

B. Valuation Tables

Effective for trusts created after April 30, 1989, the discount rate and payment frequency adjustments by which remainder interest amounts are calculated is based on 120 percent of the Applicable Federal Mid-term Rate (AFMR) rounded to the nearest two-tenths of 1 percent. Further, 1980 mortality tables are effective for gifts after April 30, 1989.

When calculating the deduction, the trustor may use the AFMR applicable to the month of contribution or the rate applicable to either of the two previous months. This *lookback* feature applies to the applicable rate in effect in the selected month, and it includes the mortality table in effect in the selected month.[91]

C. Exceptions to Standard Valuation Methods

The Treasury has issued final regulations that provide examples of situations in which the standard actuarial tables and discount assumption rules do not apply. In general, the rules are applicable when, in the case of a charitable remainder trust, the income recipient is not given an interest having a degree of beneficial enjoyment consistent with the traditional character of such an interest under local law.[92] The tables are not used, for example, when a person who is a measuring life of a trust is terminally ill at the time of transfer.[93] A second and more perplexing component of the new regulations involves the transfer of non-income or low-income producing property to a trust in which the income recipient has no power to require the trustee to convert the property to produce income. In such cases, the tables cannot be used. How are such interests valued? How do the regulations apply to net income unitrusts? Unfortunately, the regulations do not provide examples of alternative valuation methods. Reg. §1.664-4(a) should override this rule based on the assumption the unitrust or annuity amount will be paid.

D. Ten Percent Minimum Present Value Requirement

As was discussed in the previous chapter, The Taxpayer Relief Act of 1997 contained a provision that now requires that the present value of the charitable remainder with respect

---

[91] IRC §7520; Rev. Rul. 89-34, 1989-1 C.B. 263 7; Notice 89-60, 1989-1 C.B. 700

[92] T.D. 8630, 12/12/95

[93] A terminally ill person is one who is known to have an incurable illness and has a 50 percent probability of death within one year. If the person survives at least eighteen months, however, the Service takes the position they were not terminally ill at the time of transfer.

According to Rev. Rul. 96-3, 1996-1 C.B. 348, "Rev. Rul. 80-80, 1980-1 C.B. 194, and Rev. Rul. 66-307, 1966-2 C.B. 429 hold that the valuation tables in the regulations for valuing annuities, interests for life or a term of years, and remainder or reversionary interests are not to be used if the individual, who is the measuring life, is known to be terminally ill at the time of the transfer. These revenue rulings have been superseded by section 20.7520-3(b)(3) of the Estate Tax Regulations, effective with respect to estates of decedents dying after December 13, 1995. Similar provisions are set forth in sections 1.7520-3(b)(3) of the Income Tax Regulations and 25.7520-3(b)(3) of the Gift Tax Regulations. Section 1.7520-3(b)(3) is effective with respect to transactions after December 13, 1995 and section 25.7520-3(b)(3) is effective with respect to gifts made after December 13, 1995."

to any transfer to a qualified charitable remainder annuity trust or charitable remainder unitrust be at least 10 percent of the net fair market value of such property transferred in trust on the date of the contribution to the trust.

E. Sample Unitrust Deduction Computation

Mr. and Mrs. Smith are both age 60. On January 15, 1996, they contributed $1,000,000 of long-term capital gain stock with a zero cost basis to a charitable remainder unitrust naming a public charity as remainderman. The Smiths elected to receive a 6 percent unitrust amount payable at the end of each calendar quarter. The measuring term of the trust is their joint lives.

The steps for the computation as outlined in Reg. §1.664-4 are as follows:

Charitable Remainder Unitrust
Deduction Calculation

A. Input Assumptions

Date of transfer	01/15/1996
Fair market value of property transferred	$1,000,000.00
Unitrust payout rate	6.00%
Payment sequence	Quarterly
Number of months between the valuation date and the first payout for the first full taxable year of the trust	3
IRC Sec. 7520(a) election to use 11/95 discount rate of	7.40%
The mortality table is based on the census taken in	1980
Jim's nearest age on the date of the gift is	60
Jane's nearest age on the date of the gift is	60

B. Calculation of Present Value of Remainder Interest Factor

(Interpolation of Table U factor for Number of Lives)

1.	Factor from Table F based on the payment period, the number of months between the valuation date and the first payment date, and the discount rate	0.956552
2.	Adjusted payout rate (Table F factor times payout rate)	5.74%
3.	The nearest usable payout rate less than the Line 2 rate	5.60%
4.	Line 2 minus Line 3	0.14%
5.	Line 4 divided by .20 percent	0.69656
6.	Factor from Table U at the Line 3 rate	0.25428
7.	Factor from Table U at the rate .20 percent higher than the Line 3 rate	0.24283
8.	Line 6 minus Line 7	0.01145
9.	Line 8 times Line 5 (interpolation adjustment)	0.00798
10.	Present value of remainder interest factor for number of lives (Line 6 minus Line 9)	0.2463

C. Calculation of Tax Deduction for Charitable Remainder Unitrust

1.	Fair market value of property transferred	$1,000,000.00
2.	Present value of remainder interest in unitrust factor (from section B)	0.2463
3.	Present value of remainder interest = the tax deduction (Line 1 times Line 2)	$246,300.00

F. Sample Annuity Trust Deduction Computation

Had the Smiths selected a charitable remainder annuity trust bearing a 6 percent annuity rate, the present value of remainder interest would have been calculated as follows:

Charitable Remainder Annuity Trust
Deduction Calculation

A. Input Assumptions

Date of transfer	01/15/1996
Fair market value of property transferred	$1,000,000.00
Annual annuity rate	6.00%
Payment sequence	Quarterly
Is payment at beginning or end of payment period	End
IRC Sec. 7520(a) election to use 11/95 discount rate of	7.40%
The mortality table is based on the census taken in	1980
Jim's nearest age on the date of the gift is	60
Jane's nearest age on the date of the gift is	60

B. Calculation of Tax Deduction

(for Number of Lives)

1.	Fair market value of property transferred	$1,000,000.00
2.	Annual annuity rate	6.00%
3.	Annuity amount payable on an annual basis	$60,000.00
4.	Line 2 minus Line 3	
	(a) Factor from Table R(2) (for remainder interest)	0.18964
	(b) 1.00000 minus Line 4(a) (factor for life estate)	0.81036
	(c) Line 4(b) divided by AFMR (factor for annuity)	10.9508
5.	Line 3 annuity amount times Line 4(c) factor	$657,048.00
6.	Adjustment factor for payment sequence (from Table K)	1.0273
7.	Adjusted annuity value (Line 5 times Line 6)	$674,985.41
8.	Amount of first annuity payment if payment is made at beginning of payment sequence (otherwise 0)	0.00
9.	Present value of annuity interest (Line 7 plus Line 8)	$674,985.41
10.	Minimum value of annuity interest (lesser of Line 1 and Line 9)	$674,985.41
11.	Present value of remainder interest = the tax deduction (Line 1 minus Line 10)	$325,014.59

G. Five Percent Probability Test

A gift to a charitable remainder annuity trust will not qualify for income, gift, and estate tax deduction purposes if the probability exceeds 5 percent that trust assets will be exhausted prior to charity receiving the remainder interest. The test does not apply to annuity trusts measured by a term of years. Nor does it apply to charitable remainder unitrusts (due to the *theoretical* impossibility that principal can be exhausted).[94]

Five Percent Probability Test

		(a) At Creation of Trust	(b) At Exhaustion of Trust
1.	Fair market value of property transferred		1,000,000.00
2.	Annuity amount payable on an annual basis		60,000.00
3.	Adjustment factor for payment sequence (from Table K)		1.0273
4.	Adjusted annuity amount (Line 2 * Line 3)		61,638.00
5.	Line 1 divided by Line 4		16.223758
6.	Present worth of annuity (based on Table B) next higher than or equal to factor on Line 5		13.5083
7.	Estimated number of years until trust will be exhausted (years from Table B opposite factor on Line 6)		110
8.1	Age of first annuitant.	60	170
8.2	Age of second annuitant	60	170
9.1	First annuitant's mortality table factor.	83,726	0
9.2	Second annuitant's mortality table factor	83,726	0
10.1	Probability of first annuitant dying before exhaustion of trust (1.0000 - Line 9.1(b) / Line 9.1(a))		100.0000%
10.2	Probability of second annuitant dying before exhaustion of trust (1.0000 - Line 9.2(b) / Line 9.2(a))		100.0000%
11.	Probability of all annuitants dying before exhaustion of trust (product of all Line 10 probabilities)		100.0000%
12.	Probability that at least one annuitant will survive to the exhaustion of the fund (1.0000 minus Line 11).		0.0000%
13.	The probability of exhausting the trust fund is less than 5%. This trust passes the 5% probability test.		

In an interesting letter ruling, a decedent created a testamentary trust in which the grandniece and grandnephew were to receive an annuity of 8 percent annually for their lives with the remainder passing to charity. Based on the ages of the income recipients, the annuity rate and the prevailing applicable federal mid-term rate, the trust failed the 5 percent probability test. Thus, no deduction was allowed for federal estate tax purposes. Many practitioners were surprised that even though no estate tax deduction was allowed, the Service ruled the trust

[94]   Rev. Rul. 77-374, 1977-2 C.B. 329

was still a qualified charitable remainder annuity trust under IRC §2652(c).[95] The Service also concluded, because the charitable organization would have an interest in the trust and would be considered a non-skip person, the trust would not be a skip person for purposes of IRC §2613 (which determine the application of the generation-skipping transfer tax), and that distributions from the trust would be taxable distributions for purpose of IRC §2612(b).

In a new ruling, the Service reversed itself stating that under Reg. §1.664-1(a)(1)(iii)(a), the term, *charitable remainder trust* means a trust with respect to which a deduction is allowable under sections 170, 2055, 2106, or 2522, and which meets the description of a charitable remainder annuity trust or charitable remainder unitrust. "Thus, our original conclusion that the trust would qualify as a charitable remainder trust was in error … because no estate tax charitable deduction is allowable to the trust," the Service said. The Service also held that the initial funding of the trust (in the absence of qualification under IRC §2652(c)) was a direct skip and should have been taxed for generation-skipping transfer tax purposes. Subsequent distribution would, however, not be taxable as set forth in the previous ruling.

In a show of good faith, the Service compromised by allowing the trust to operate as a qualified charitable remainder trust on the conditions the generation-skipping transfer tax was paid currently and the trust continued to be treated as a charitable remainder annuity trust for income tax purposes.

H. Effect of Design Variables on Deduction Computations

The prior sample computations assumed a fixed set of design assumptions. What effect does changing those assumptions have on the deduction computation?

1. Annuity Trust or Unitrust Format

Annuity trusts and unitrusts with identical design factors do not produce identical deductions. Furthermore, the relationship of one to the other is not linear. In general, a charitable remainder annuity trust measured by the life of one or more individuals produces larger deductions at higher annuity rates and at younger ages than a unitrust with similar payout rates and ages. The deductions, however, crossover as a function of these two variables. Specifically, as the annuity rate and unitrust payout rate approach the Applicable Federal Mid-term Rate, and as the income recipient's age advances, the annuity trust and unitrust deductions merge until the deduction for the unitrust exceeds that of the annuity trust. This can be seen graphically in the following charts and graphs. The first table and chart use a 5 percent payout/annuity rate and the second use a 10 percent payout/annuity rate. The 10 percent payout/annuity rate produces unitrust and annuity trust deductions that are almost identical regardless of age. Results can vary based on other payment frequencies.

---

[95]   Ltr. Rul. 9440010. In a subsequent ruling, which addressed the use of assignable call options as trust investments, the Service ruled a unitrust did not qualify under IRC §664 because the contribution of the option did not generate either an income, gift, or estate tax deduction. See Ltr. Ruls. 9240017 and 9501004 and the discussion of options beginning on page 116.

Comparison of Deduction Factors - 5% Payout

Age	CRU 5%	CRA 5%
30	0.09134	0.504970
35	0.11427	0.507735
40	0.14267	0.511990
45	0.17739	0.518360
50	0.21913	0.527640
55	0.26835	0.540745
60	0.32540	0.558765
65	0.38970	0.582565
70	0.46087	0.613250
75	0.53693	0.651060
80	0.61606	0.696140
85	0.69074	0.743880
90	0.75553	0.789420
95	0.80663	0.828275
100	0.83980	0.854375

Comparison of Deduction Factors - 5% Payout

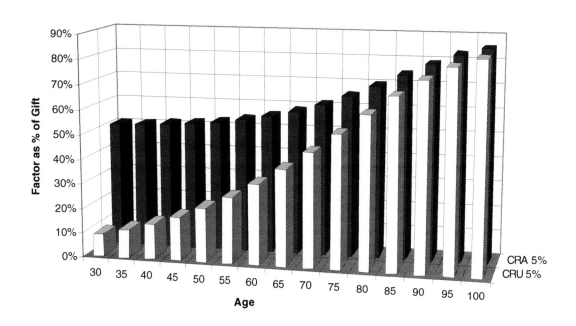

Figure 11 This table and chart illustrate the difference between the deduction factors for a 5 percent annuity trust and 5 percent unitrust as a function of the varying age of the income recipient. The Applicable Federal Mid-term Rate used in this calculation was 7.4 percent.

Comparison of Deduction Factors - 10% Payout

Age	CRU 10%	CRA 10%
30	0.00996	0.00994
35	0.01549	0.01547
40	0.02399	0.02398
45	0.03674	0.03672
50	0.05531	0.05528
55	0.08151	0.08149
60	0.11756	0.11753
65	0.16516	0.16513
70	0.22653	0.22650
75	0.30214	0.30212
80	0.39230	0.39228
85	0.48777	0.48776
90	0.57885	0.57884
95	0.65655	0.65655
100	0.70875	0.70875

Comparison of Deduction Factors - 10% Payout

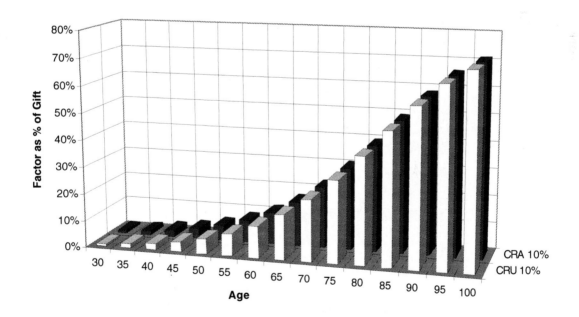

Figure 12   This table and chart illustrate the difference between the deduction factors for a 10 percent annuity trust and 10 percent unitrust as a function of the varying age of the income recipient. The Applicable Federal Mid-term Rate used in this calculation was 7.4 percent.

2. Payout or Annuity Rate

A charitable remainder trust can be compared to a teeter-totter with the income recipient at one end and charitable remainderman at the other. The higher the annuity or payout rate, the lower the charitable deduction. Conversely, the lower the rate, the greater the deduction.

Comparison of Deduction - 5% to 10% Payouts

Payout Rate	Deduction Factor	Deduction Amount
5.00%	0.38970	$38,970
6.00%	0.32589	$32,589
7.00%	0.27346	$27,346
8.00%	0.23032	$23,032
9.00%	0.19465	$19,465
10.00%	0.16516	$16,516

Comparison of Deduction - 5% to 10% Payouts

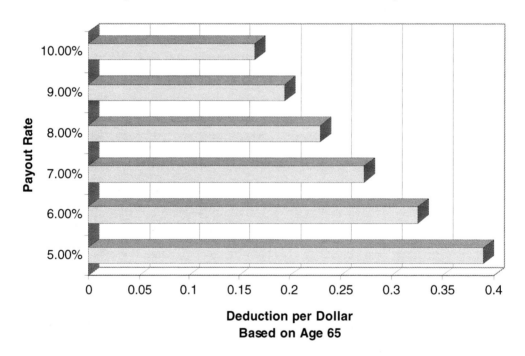

Figure 13   This table and chart show the impact of an increasing payout rate on the deduction of a $100,000 unitrust.

3.   Measuring Term

Back to the teeter-totter. If the trust is measured by the life of the income recipient, the remainder interest is based on the recipient's actuarial life expectancy. Therefore, the older the income recipient, the greater the charitable deduction, and vice versa. In the case of a trust measured by a term of years, the shorter the term, the larger the deduction. In fact, a twenty-year term of years trust produces roughly the same deduction as a trust measured by the lifetime of a sixty-five year old income recipient.

4.   Number of Income Recipients

In the case of a trust measured by a term of years, the number of income recipients is irrelevant when calculating the present value of remainder interest. In the case of a trust measured by the life of its income recipients, adding income recipients always decreases the deduction. The amount of reduction depends on the age of the added recipient and his or her age relationship to the primary recipient.

For example, grandfather is considering creating a charitable remainder trust in which he is the sole life income recipient. If he adds his granddaughter as a successor income recipient, his income tax deduction will plummet. On the other hand, if granddaughter creates a charitable remainder trust naming herself as the primary income recipient and grandfather as the successor income recipient, the reduction in an already small income tax deduction will be negligible.

5.   Payment Frequency

Trusts that provide for one payment at the end of each trust year generate the highest deduction compared to those that call for one annual payment at the beginning of the year. The reason is that undistributed income remains invested and adds to the value of the remainder interest. All other combinations of payment frequencies fall between these two limits. The overall effect on the deduction is, however, rather small.

6.   Applicable Federal Mid-term Rate

For unitrusts, the payout rate is used as the discount rate for determining the present value of the remainder interest. The AFMR is not involved in the computation, other than for the payment frequency adjustment factor (Table F). If the unitrust payment frequency is annual with zero months until the first payment, the AFMR has no effect on the deduction.

For annuity trusts, the AFMR (rather than the annuity rate) is used as the discount rate for the purpose of determining the present value of the annuity interest. Further, the AFMR also affects the payment frequency adjustment factor (Table F). If payments are made annually at the beginning of the period, the AFMR has no effect on the adjustment factor.

Effect of AFMR on Deduction

AFMR	Unitrust	Annuity Trust
10%	26.12%	19.86%
9%	26.43%	26.43%
8%	26.74%	32.15%
7%	27.04%	37.15%
6%	27.35%	41.56%

Affect of AFR on Deduction

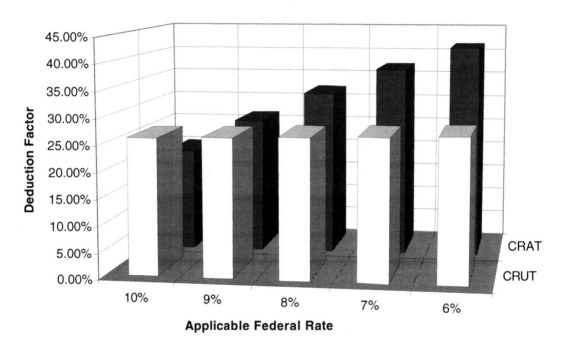

Figure 14 As can be seen the impact of the AFMR on the present value of the remainder interest of a unitrust is barely visible. With respect to an annuity trust, however, the lower the AFMR, the higher the resulting deduction. These trusts assume a payout or annuity rate of 7 percent and trustor ages of 65/65.

II. Determining the Trustor s Allowable Charitable Income Tax Deduction

Once the present value of the remainder interest has been calculated, the planner must determine to what extent the remainder interest is deductible for income tax purposes, subject to the reduction and annual percentage limitation rules applicable to charitable contributions under IRC §170. The rules for gifts of remainder interests are the same, with few exceptions, as are the rules for direct transfers.

Prior to immersion in the deduction limitation rules, the following Tax Court and Court of Appeals excerpts should set the tone:

In deciding the percentage deduction limitation applicable to a gift of property to a veteran's organization (in favor of the government), Judge Swift stated:

Trying to understand the various exempt organization provisions of the Internal Revenue Code is as difficult as capturing a drop of mercury under your thumb. There are currently 23 categories of exempt organizations under section 501(c) and five categories of organizations recognized as qualifying donees of tax deductible contributions under section 170(c).

Weingarden v. Comm r, 86 T.C. 669

On appeal, Circuit Judge Merrit opined:

"Although we believe that the taxpayer's argument of the technical interpretation of the statute is more persuasive than the Commissioner's, it is obvious that at best the statutory scheme is ambiguous. The general canon of construction is that statutes imposing a tax are interpreted liberally (in favor of the taxpayer). But provisions granting a deduction or exemption are matters of legislative "grace" and are construed strictly (in favor of the government). A special rule applies to charitable deductions, however, because these provisions are an expression of "public policy" rather than legislative grace. Provisions regarding charitable deductions should therefore be liberally construed in favor of the taxpayer. Given this rule of interpretation, we construe the hopeless ambiguity created by this statutory scheme in favor of the taxpayer."

A. Overview of Deduction Limitations

The amount of income tax charitable contribution deduction a trustor can claim in any tax year for a transfer to a charitable remainder trust is based on the five following factors:

- the statutory limitation

- the type of organization named as remainderman

- the type of property being contributed

- whether the gift is to or for the use of the remainderman, and

- the carryover provisions

The facts of each contribution are applied against these criteria with the smallest applicable percentage limitation governing the use of the deduction.

1. Statutory Limitation

The Code imposes a ceiling on the amount of charitable contribution deduction that may be claimed in any tax year.

An individual may deduct charitable contributions to the extent of 50 percent of trustor's contribution base in any tax year.[96] The term, *contribution base* means adjusted gross income without regard to any net operating loss carryback to the taxable year.

For C-corporations, deductible contributions are limited to 10 percent of taxable income.[97] S-corporations can pass deductions through to shareholders subject to the limitations of IRC §1366(d)(1).[98]

2. Type of Charitable Organization

The 50 percent statutory ceiling can be reduced depending on the type of organization receiving the gift. In the case of a charitable remainder trust, the status of the charitable remainderman governs.

Contributions to charitable remainder trusts that name as remaindermen public charities, *supporting organizations*, *private operating foundations*, *pass-through foundations*, and *common fund private foundations* are deductible to the extent of 50 percent of the trustor's contribution base in any tax year. These organizations are referred to as *50 percent-Type Organizations*.[99]

Contributions to charitable remainder trusts that name as remaindermen *private non-operating foundations* are deductible to the extent of 30 percent of the trustor's contribution base in any tax year. These organizations are referred to as *30 percent-Type Organizations*.[100]

3. Type of Property Being Contributed

Further limitations are imposed on deductible contributions based on the type of property being contributed. The rules are complex in that not only are there three categories of percentage limitations (50 percent, 30 percent, and 20 percent), there are also rules that reduce the amount of the deductible portion of the gift property itself. These limitations and corresponding reduction rules are most easily described on an integrated basis as follows:

a. Transfers to 50 Percent-Type Organizations Named as Remaindermen

1) Cash

Contributions of cash are deductible to the extent of 50 percent of trustor's contribution base.

---

96   Reg. §1.170A-8(b)

97   IRC §170(b)

98   See Chapter 6 - S-Corporations

99   IRC §§170(b)(1)(A); 509(a)(3); 4942(j)(3); 509(a); 170(b)(1)(E)(iii); Reg. §1.170A-9(h); Ltr. Rul. 8212009

100   IRC §170(b)(1)(B)

2) Ordinary Income Property

Ordinary income property includes short-term capital gain property, inventory in a business, property subject to depreciation recapture, IRC §306 stock, original issue discount debt instruments, market discount obligations, listed options, and other property, the sale of any of which would produce ordinary income to the trustor.

In determining the present value of the remainder interest, the net fair market value of the property is reduced by the amount of gain that would *not* have been long-term capital gain had the property been sold at its fair market value on the date of contribution. The remaining amount is deductible to the extent of 50 percent of trustor's contribution base.[101]

3) Long-Term Capital Gain Property

The full fair market value of long-term capital gain property is deductible to the extent of 30 percent of trustor's contribution base.[102]

Special Election: An individual may elect to have all 30 percent limitation capital gain property contributions and carryover contributions into the election year treated as being IRC §170(e)(1)(B) property subject to the 50 percent limitation. However, the cost of this election is the reduction of the deduction from fair market value to the lesser of fair market value and adjusted cost basis.[103]

4) Tangible Personal Property

The deductibility of transfers of tangible personal property to a charitable remainder trust presents special issues.

a) Future Interest Rule

Payment of a charitable contribution that consists of a future interest in tangible personal property is treated as made only when all intervening interests in, and rights to the actual possession or enjoyment of, the property have expired or are held by persons other than the taxpayer or those standing in a relationship to the taxpayer described in IRC §§267(b) or 707(b).[104]

When does an intervening interest in tangible personal property held by a charitable remainder trust expire? Arguably, because the life interest is retained in the trust and not the tangible property, the interest should expire when the trust sells the property to an unrelated party. This argument has finally been validated by the Service in a letter ruling.[105] Other commentators believe the deduction should be permitted at the time the property is

---

[101] IRC §170(e)(1)(A)

[102] IRC §170(b)(1)(C)

[103] IRC §170(b)(1)(D)(iii); Reg. §1.170A-8(d)(2)

[104] IRC §170(a)(3)

[105] Ltr. Rul. 9452026

transferred to the trust based on the fact that the self-dealing rules prohibit the use of the property by the donor after it is transferred to the trust.

b) Related Use Look-Through Rule

The amount of the available charitable contribution and the percentage limitation applicable to its use depends on the relation of the tangible personal property to the tax-exempt purpose of the charitable remainderman.

The use by a trust of tangible personal property contributed to it for the benefit of a charitable organization is an unrelated use if the use by the trust is one that would have been unrelated if made by the charitable organization.[106]

Presumably, because a charitable remainder trust will not place the property to a related use but, rather, will most likely sell it in due course, such a use normally falls outside the tax-exempt purpose of most organizations.

If property is considered *related*, the deduction is based on fair market value and available to the extent of 30 percent of the trustor's contribution base. The deduction is delayed, however, until the property is sold from the trust.

If property is considered *unrelated*, the deduction is based on the lesser of its fair market value and its cost basis, and is available to the extent of 50 percent of trustor's contribution base. Again, the deduction is delayed until the tangible personal property is sold from the trust.[107]

Safe Harbor for Museums? If artwork is transferred to a trust that names a museum that normally retains the type of property being transferred, would the sale of such property fall within the definition of that organization's tax-exempt status and could it be deemed a related use? The Service has not ruled on this question.

Special Rule: A charitable contribution income tax deduction may not be available if the charitable remainderman purchases tangible property from the trust and a related individual or entity as described in IRC §267 has direct or indirect control of the recipient tax-exempt organization.[108]

c) Inventory

Inventory is not a capital asset but, rather, is property held by a taxpayer primarily for sale to customers in the ordinary course of a trade or business.[109]

If inventory property is transferred to a charitable remainder trust, the present value of the remainder interest is based on the lesser of fair market value and the cost of goods sold (ordinary income property). The resulting amount is

---

[106]   Reg. §1.170A-4(b)(3)(i)

[107]   IRC §170(e)(1)(B)

[108]   IRC §§170(a)(3); 267(b)(9); Reg. §1.267(b)-1(a)(3)

[109]   IRC §1221(1)

deductible to the extent of 50 percent of the trustor's contribution base. Further, the sale of property transferred by its creator (e.g., an artist transferring artwork) or dealer might cause the trust to have unrelated business income.

b. Transfers to 30 Percent-Type Organizations Named as Remaindermen

1) Cash or Ordinary Income Property

The deduction is based on the lesser of fair market value and adjusted cost basis. The resulting amount is deductible to the extent of 30 percent of trustor's contribution base.

2) Long-Term Capital Gain Property

The deduction for a gift of long-term capital gain property is based on the lesser of fair market value of the property and its adjusted cost basis. The resulting deduction is available against 20 percent of trustor's contribution base.

Note: Under IRC §170(e)(5), a full fair market value deduction was provided for gifts of "qualified stock" to private non-operating foundations. However, the deduction phased-out on June 30, 1998.

3) Related Use Long-Term Tangible Personal Property

The deduction for gifts of related use tangible personal property is based on the lesser of fair market value of the property and its adjusted cost basis. The deduction is available against 20 percent of trustor's contribution base.

Special Rule: Charitable deduction may not be available if charitable remainderman purchases tangible property from trust and a related individual or entity as described in IRC §267 has direct or indirect control of the recipient tax-exempt organization.[110]

4) Unrelated Use Tangible Personal Property

The deduction tangible personal property that is unrelated to the charitable remainderman's tax-exempt purpose is limited to the lesser of fair market value and adjusted cost basis. The deduction is available against 30 percent of trustor's contribution base.[111]

4. Gifts For The Use Of Charity

A gift of a remainder interest to charity is considered a gift *to* the organization unless, upon termination of the trust's measuring term, the remainder interest is to be held in

---

[110] IRC §§170(a)(3); 267(b)(9); Reg. §1.267(b)-1(a)(3)

[111] Ltr. Rul. 9452026

trust for the benefit of the organization.[112] The latter alternative is treated as a gift *for the use of* charity.

Gifts *to* 50 percent-type organizations are subject to the 50 percent limitation. Gifts *for the use of* 50 percent-type organizations are subject to the 30 percent limitation.

Gifts *to* 30 percent-type organizations are subject to the 30 percent limitation. Gifts *for the use of* 30 percent-type organizations are subject to the 20 percent limitation.

B. Carryover of Excess Charitable Deductions

Contributions *to* or *for the use of* charity in excess of the applicable percentage limitation in the year of contribution are treated as being made in the five years following the year of contribution.[113] In other words, to the extent the donor cannot, by virtue of the percentage limitations, deduct the entire amount of the gift in the year of contribution, any remaining deduction can be carried forward up to an additional five years, if needed.

Whether carryovers can be used by the trustor depends on the trustor's additional charitable contributions in those subsequent five years. Excess contribution carryovers are subordinated to current year contributions in determining a trustor's current year allowable contribution deductions. See IRS Publication 561.

Carryover Deductions for Qualified Stock: Section 170(b)(1)(D)(ii) provides, in part, that to the extent the donor's contributions of capital gain property to a private non-operating foundation exceed the percentage limitation under section 170(b)(1)(D)(i), the excess shall be treated as a charitable contribution of capital gain property in each of the five succeeding taxable years in order of time.

The Service has ruled privately that carryovers of excess charitable contributions for gifts of qualified stock originating prior to January 1, 1995 are deductible at fair market value even though a deduction is not otherwise allowable for the capital gain element of the gift if it is made after December 31, 1994.[114]

III. Effect of Itemized Deduction Reduction on Charitable Contributions

Taxpayers with adjusted gross incomes exceeding a specified minimum floor must reduce the amount of their claimed itemized deductions by 3 percent of adjusted gross income that exceeds the limitation floor.[115] Many contributors, however, do not feel the effect of the reduction on the charitable contribution deduction because they have other fixed deductions such as home mortgage interest, or state and local taxes that bear the brunt of any reduction each year. Under

---

[112]   Reg. §1.170A-8(a)(2)

[113]   IRC §170(d)(1)

[114]   Ltr. Rul. 9424040

[115]   The limitation floor for the 1995 tax year is $114,700 for individual taxpayers or $57,350 for married taxpayers filing separate returns.

these circumstances the charitable deduction will not be reduced unless the donor has a combination of high income and large charitable contributions in relation to other itemized deductions.

IV. Impact of Alternative Minimum Tax on Charitable Remainder Trusts

The Revenue Reconciliation Act of 1993 permanently repealed for Federal Income Tax purposes the Alternative Minimum Tax treatment for gifts of appreciated property. Under prior law, the appreciation element of long-term capital gain real, personal, or intangible property transferred to charity after December 31, 1986 was considered a tax preference item for purposes of the AMT computation.[116] A limited exception to this rule was granted for gifts of tangible personal property made between January 1, 1991 and July 1, 1992.

Current law eliminates the treatment of contributions by individuals of appreciated property of all types as a tax preference for AMT purposes. In addition, the bill provides that no adjustment related to the earnings and profits of any charitable contribution by a corporation shall be made in computing the ACE component of the corporate AMT.

The new rules are effective for gifts of tangible personal property made after June 30, 1992, and contributions of other property made after December 31, 1992. Regarding the effect of the new law on carryovers of excess contributions deduction generated on gifts made prior the repeal, the conferees specifically stated that the relief provided in the provision does not apply to any contribution made prior to the applicable effective date.[117]

Because of the possibility a taxpayer may have carryovers of excess contribution deduction generated on gifts made prior to the effective date, the following is a review of the AMT computation. Examples of carryovers of the charitable preference into future tax years, computation of preference amounts for split interest trusts, and a sample tax analysis are provided. Furthermore, many states include a charitable preference item for the computation of state alternative minimum tax.

A. Overview of AMT Computation
The computation of the AMT, as described in IRC §55, follows:

---

[116]   Tax Reform Act of 1986

[117]   Revenue Reconciliation Act of 1993, Section 13171 of the Conference Agreement, footnote /5/

Start with	Taxable income
Add or Subtract	Certain adjustments
Add	Preference items
Subtract	AMT net operating loss
Equals	**Alternative Minimum Taxable Income**
Subtract	Exemption amount
Equals	**Amount subject to AMT**
Multiply by	26% for amounts up to $175,000
	28% for amounts exceeding $175,000
Subtract	AMT Foreign Tax Credits
Equals	**Tentative Minimum Tax**

B. Effect of Regular Tax Itemized Deduction Reduction on AMT

The IRC §68 reductions for certain itemized deductions does not apply for purposes of the AMT limitation on deductions. For purposes of the alternative minimum tax, itemized deductions that are otherwise allowed in computing AMTI are not reduced by the provision (i.e., the cutback amount determined for regular tax purposes is disregarded in calculating AMTI). This is accomplished via a negative adjustment within the computation of AMTI by the amount reduced under IRC §68.[118]

C. Charitable Preference Item for Pre-January 1, 1993 Transfers

IRC §57(a)(6) was repealed under the 1993 Act; however, it is reproduced here for historical perspective in the event the taxpayer may have excess carryover contributions.

(6) Appreciated property charitable deduction.--
(A) In general.--The amount by which the deduction allowable under section 170 or 642(c) would be reduced if all capital gain property were taken into account at its cost basis.
(B) Capital gain property.--For purposes of subparagraph (A), the term "capital gain property" has the meaning given to such term by section 170(b)(1)(C)(iv). Such term shall not include any property to which an election under section 170(b)(1)(C)(iii) applies. In the *case of any taxable year beginning in 1991, such term shall not include any tangible personal property.*

If an asset was contributed to a charitable remainder trust between January 1, 1987 and December 31, 1992 (subject to the exception for tangible personal property), the amount of the trustor's contribution deduction *and the amount of tax preference* was based on the value actually conveyed to charity rather than the entire gain attributable to the property (i.e., the preference is allocable to the present value of remainder interest).

Example

Suppose a taxpayer donates $100,000 of stock with an adjusted basis of $30,000 to a charitable remainder unitrust in 1991. The trustor will receive a 5 percent annual life income, after which the trust will terminate and distribute its corpus to charity.

---

[118]   1990 OBRA Conference and Senate Committee Report

The trustor receives a deduction (calculated from Treasury tables) in the amount of $40,000. What is the amount of tax preference?

The answer to this question is most easily obtained by determining the ratio of gain to fair market value and multiplying this ratio by the amount of the gross charitable contribution deduction.

In this case the capital gain ratio of the gift property is 70 percent ($70,000/$100,000). When multiplied by the deduction amount of $40,000, this yields a gross preference amount of $28,000.

Preference Calculations

D. Allocating Preference Amounts when Carryovers Occur

After passage of TRA '86, many practitioners speculated that, in cases that resulted in excess contribution carryovers, the basis in the charitable contribution would be allocated in direct proportion to the amount of charitable contribution deduction actually claimed by the taxpayer in a given year.

Under prior law, the Joint Committee explanation offered a more favorable result for taxpayers in that the entire basis attributable to the trustor's charitable deduction was applied first, with the appreciation element carried forward. This delayed the effect of the AMT as long as possible. However, under the new law, such deferral can result in the payment of tax at higher marginal AMT rates.

E. TRA 6 Joint Committee Bluebook Explanation of Charitable Preference

[Pages 444 and 445]

Charitable contributions of appreciated property

In the case of a taxpayer who makes one or more charitable contributions of appreciated capital gain property, an amount equal to the regular tax deduction claimed with respect to such appreciation is treated as a minimum tax preference. Thus, the charitable contribution deduction is generally limited to the taxpayer's adjusted basis in the property. For purposes of this rule, capital gain property has the same meaning as under the rules relating to charitable deductions.

In the case of a contribution of less than the taxpayer's entire interest in appreciated property, the preference shall be computed by applying the principles applicable under section 170(e), relating to contributions of ordinary income property (see Treas. Reg. §1.170A-4(c).

The amount of the preference is determined by disregarding any amount that is carried forward to another taxable year for purposes of the regular tax. Thus, when a portion of a charitable deduction is carried forward because it exceeds the applicable percentage limitation on such contributions, the portion so carried forward cannot increase the amount of the minimum tax preference until it is allowed as a deduction for regular tax purposes.

Where a taxpayer makes charitable contributions in excess of those for which a regular tax charitable deduction is allowed during the taxable year, the minimum tax consequences require determining which contributions (or portions thereof) are deducted, and which are carried forward. The minimum tax charitable deduction (net of preference) is computed by in effect using basis in place of fair market value. Thus, no preference should apply unless the relevant basis in the property contributed is less than the amount of the regular tax deduction.

Example:

For example, assume that in year 1 a taxpayer with an adjusted gross income of $100,000 is allowed a charitable deduction of $30,000. The taxpayer has made a charitable contribution of property having an adjusted basis of $50,000 and fair market value of $150,000. In year 1, the taxpayer's minimum tax deduction (net of the preference) equals $30,000 since the basis of the contributed property exceeds the amount deductible for regular tax purposes. In year 2, if the taxpayer again is allowed to deduct $30,000 for regular tax purposes and has made no additional charitable contributions, the deduction for minimum tax purposes is limited to $20,000.

The preference does not apply with respect to charitable contributions made before August 16, 1986. In the case of a contribution made on or after August 16, 1986, and before the beginning of the first taxable year beginning after December 31, 1986, the preference applies only with respect to amounts carried forward to taxable years beginning after December 31, 1986. Thus, for example, in the case of a calendar year taxpayer, the preference applies, with respect to a contribution made on or after August 16, 1986, and before January 1, 1987, to amounts carried forward to the 1987 taxable year and thereafter. In the case of gifts made before 1986, the gifts shall be treated as deductible in the order made in determining the character of carryovers to 1987 and later years. Thus, for example, if a calendar year taxpayer made a charitable contribution of property having an adjusted basis of $50,000 and a fair market value of $100,000 in April of 1986, and made a similar contribution in October 1986, and was allowed to deduct only $175,000 in light of adjusted gross income, the $25,000 carryover to 1987 is treated as being attributable to appreciation on the October contribution and therefore is a tax preference in 1987 assuming that the $25,000 is deductible in that year.

Continuing with the example, assuming the trustor has an adjusted gross income of $50,000, he will be able to deduct $15,000 (30 percent of $50,000) in the year of transfer. For AMT purposes, the preference is $3,000 ($15,000 deduction - $12,000 basis). In the following year, AGI remaining constant, the AMT preference will be $15,000 ($15,000 - $0) where $0 is the remaining basis. In the third year, the taxpayer will have $10,000 of deduction remaining for regular tax purposes. With all cost basis having been allocated in the first year, the preference will be $10,000.

In conclusion, the transfer of $100,000 of stock resulted in (a) the avoidance of $50,000 of long-term capital gain, (b) the production of a $40,000 charitable contribution deduction, and (c) a tax preference of only $28,000. The avoidance of capital gain is absolute. However, the ultimate tax benefit of the charitable deduction will depend on the other elements of the taxpayer's tax structure.

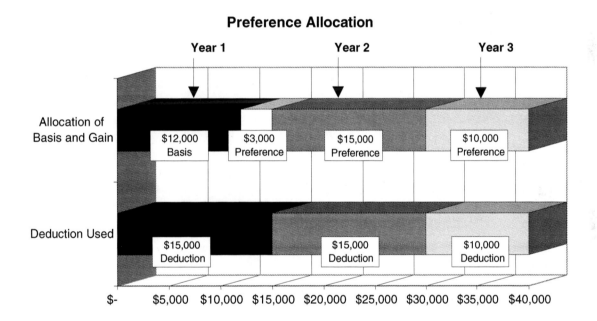

F. AMT Exclusion for Gifts of Tangible Personal Property

OBRA '90 created a special exclusion from AMT for gifts of tangible personal property to related use organizations. With respect to the exclusion for tangible personal property, the Senate Explanation stated, "Although it is appropriate to adopt a general limitation on itemized deductions applicable to upper-income individuals, the Committee believes there is a special need to encourage donations to charitable and educational institutions of tangible articles with unique cultural or educational value (such as works of art and manuscripts). If a taxpayer makes a charitable contribution of tangible personal property (other than inventory or other ordinary income property, or short-term capital gain property), the use of which is related to the donee's tax exempt purpose, the taxpayer is entitled to claim a deduction for both regular tax and alternative minimum tax in the amount of the property's fair market value (subject to present law limitations)."

The original Conference Report stated that the tax preference exclusion would be available only for contributions made in 1991.[119] The exemption was later extended until June 30, 1992 and then extended permanently into the new law.[120] Carryovers of excess contributions from gifts of tangible personal property made in 1991 are, however, considered exempt from tax preference.[121]

G. AMT Credit

The AMT credit is produced in years in which the taxpayer is subject to AMT and is used to reduce the taxpayer's tax liability in any subsequent year in which the taxpayer is subject to the regular tax. The credit is equal to the amount by which the AMT (calculated without regard to *deferral* preferences) exceeds the regular tax. This amount is referred to as the Net Minimum Tax. However, the credit cannot reduce the taxpayer's regular tax liability below the taxpayer's Alternative Minimum Tax.

The net result of the AMT credit is the exposure of *deferral* preferences to the regular tax rate over time. The AMT effectively accelerates the payment of the regular tax. Further, in cases in which the AMT credit arises solely from *deferral* preferences, any charitable contributions will have the effect of increasing the *Net Minimum Tax* and, therefore, the credit. Therefore, all charitable contributions will have a value of between 26 percent and 28 percent in the deduction year with up to a 10 percent credit against the regular tax in subsequent years.

When a carryover deduction is claimed for the transfer of LTCG property prior to the AMT exemption effective date, the value of taxpayer's tax benefit will depend on the mix of *deferral* and *exclusion* preferences that comprise the AMT computation and their effect on the AMT credit. Under the best of circumstances, the taxpayer may receive a tax benefit of 36 percent of the property's fair market value. At the other extreme, the taxpayer may only realize a tax benefit equal to 26 percent of the property's adjusted cost basis.

H. Summary of AMT

During the period in which a gift of appreciated property produced a tax preference item, under the worst case scenario a trustor transferring property with a zero adjusted cost basis could realize zero tax benefit from their charitable contribution deduction. Under the best case scenario, they could have realized savings equal to the charitable deduction multiplied by the trustor's highest applicable regular tax bracket.

---

[119]   OBRA '90, P.L. 101-508, 11-5-90

[120]   P.L. 102-227; Section 13171 Conference Report OBRA '93

[121]   Rev. Rul. 90-111, 1990-2 C.B. 30

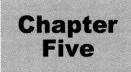

Chapter Five

Gift and Estate Tax Considerations

I. Taxable Transfers

A charitable remainder trust consists of a gift of remainder interest with a retained income interest. Gifts made to charity via a charitable remainder trust qualify for unlimited gift and estate tax deductions for the present value of the remainder interest. However, a gift or estate tax can be generated on the value of the retained income interest if it is transferred to someone other than the trustor, the trustor's spouse, or charity. Further, a charitable remainder trust that is disqualified can produce a transfer tax.

A. Trustor as Sole Income Recipient

A trustor establishes a charitable remainder trust naming herself as the trust's sole life income recipient. The transfer qualifies for the charitable gift tax deduction in an amount equal to the present value of the remainder interest in the year the trust is created.[122] Because the trustor retains the income interest, there are no further gift tax consequences. Upon her death, the full value of the trust is includible in her estate.[123] However, the full value of the trust will be deducted from her taxable estate via the estate tax charitable deduction.[124]

B. Non-Trustor as Income Recipient

When a trustor creates a charitable remainder trust naming another person as an income recipient, the trustor has made a potentially taxable gift of an income interest to the income recipient.

1. Computation of Taxable Gift when Non-Trustor is Sole Income Recipient

When one or more non-trustors are the sole income recipients of a charitable remainder trust, the amount of the taxable gift is equal to the present value of the annuity or unitrust interest. It is equal to the amount transferred minus the present value of the remainder interest. The computation of the present value of remainder interest is identical to that

---

[122]   IRC §2522(c)(2)

[123]   IRC §2036(a)

[124]   IRC §2055(e)(2)

used for income tax deduction purposes; however, the reduction rules of section 170 of the Code do not apply.[125]

Example: A father, age 70, transfers $1,000,000 to a charitable remainder annuity trust that names his son, age 40, as the trust's sole life income recipient. The trust will pay a 5 percent annuity amount in quarterly installments. The AFMR is 8 percent.[126] Based on these assumptions, the present value of the son's annuity interest and, therefore, the taxable gift is $577,385.

2. Computation of Taxable Gift with Trustor and Non-Trustor Income Recipients

If the trustor and non-trustor are co-income recipients, the amount of the taxable gift depends on whether the non-trustor income recipient has a concurrent or successive income interest.

a. Non-Trustor as Primary Life Income Recipient and Trustor as Successor Life Income Recipient

When a non-trustor is the primary income recipient for life followed by the trustor, the amount of the taxable gift is equal to the present value of the income interest based on the non-trustor's life. In other words, the presence of the trustor as a successor income recipient has no impact on the non-trustor's enjoyment of the income interest. The computation of the taxable gift is, therefore, no different than if the non-trustor is the sole income recipient of the trust.

b. Trustor as Primary Life Income Recipient and Non-Trustor as Successor Life Income Recipient

When the trustor is the primary income recipient followed by the non-trustor as successor income recipient, the taxable gift is equal to the present value of the non-trustor's survivor annuity or unitrust interest. It is equal to the difference between the present value of the annuity or unitrust interest based on the trustor's and non-trustor's joint lives and the present value of the annuity or unitrust interest based solely on the life of the primary income recipient (trustor).

Example: Continuing with the previous example, suppose the father names himself as the primary income recipient and his son as the successor. The computation of the value of the son's successor income interest is as follows:

	PV of annuity interest based on joint lives	$586,326
Minus:	PV of annuity interest based on father's life	$371,598
Equals:	PV of son's successor annuity interest - gift	$214,728

---

[125] Refer to Chapter 4 for detailed examples of present value calculations.

[126] Technically, 120 percent of the Applicable Federal Mid-term Rate.

c. Trustor and Non-Trustor Joint and Survivor Life Income Recipients

When the annuity or unitrust amount is payable to the trustor and non-trustor in equal shares for each of their lives with the decedent's portion payable to the survivor, the trustor has, in essence, made two gifts: (a) the present value of the non-trustor's right to receive a survivor income interest from one-half of the trust, and (b) the present value of income interest for the income recipients' joint lives from the remaining one-half of the trust.

Example: Suppose the father names himself and his son as joint and survivor income recipients of the trust. While they are both living, each will receive one-half of the annuity amount. When either dies, the survivor will receive the entire annuity amount for their lifetime. The computation of the taxable gift is as follows:

Gift 1 Computation

	PV of annuity interest based on joint lives	$586,326
Minus:	PV of annuity interest based on father's life	$371,598
Equals:	PV of son's successor annuity interest	$214,728
Times:	.50	
Equals:	Gift 1 amount	**$107,364**

Gift 2 Computation

	PV of annuity interest based on father's life	$371,598
Plus:	PV of annuity interest based on son's life	$577,385
Minus:	PV of annuity interest based on joint lives	$586,326
Equals:		$362,657
Times:	.50	
Equals:	Gift 2 amount	**$181,329**
	Combined gift amount from 1 and 2	**$288,693**

C. Marital Deduction

If an income recipient is the trustor's spouse at the time of transfer, the transfer will qualify for the unlimited gift tax marital deduction (provided the spouse or both spouses are the sole noncharitable recipients of the trust).[127] The estate tax marital deduction will not be available, however, if the couple divorces during the term of the trust.

Caution: The marital deduction is available only if married trustors are the sole income recipients of the trust. For example, a trust that has a term measured by the longer of the lifetime of the trustor and spouse, or a term of years, will not qualify for the marital gift or estate tax deduction because the possibility exists that persons other than the trustor or spouse will receive income.

---

[127] IRC §§2056(b)(8); 2523(g); 2523(i); 1981 ERTA Sec. 403(d)

D. Noncitizen Spouses

A question arises regarding the availability of the marital deduction when the trustor's spouse is not a U.S. citizen. The repeal of the *all income* provision for Qualified Domestic Trusts (QDT), as provided by the 1989 Revenue Reconciliation Act, means that a charitable remainder trust that is entitled to a marital deduction under IRC §2056(b)(8) may also be a QDT.

The IRS has ruled privately that a properly structured charitable remainder trust will qualify as a QDT, thereby qualifying for the unlimited gift tax marital deduction, and will qualify for the unlimited estate tax charitable deduction upon termination. The Service also concluded, the grantor's reserved right to revoke the noncitizen spouse's successor life estate made the creation of the interest an incomplete gift.[128]

E. Availability of Annual Gift Tax Exclusion

If all or part of the income interest is given to someone other than a spouse, the $10,000 annual gift tax exclusion is available only if the non-trustor recipient has a concurrent (present) rather than consecutive (future) income interest. This presumes the trust does not contain sprinkling provisions that provide the trustee with discretion in determining which non-trustor income recipients receive distributions. If the non-trustor income recipient is not the trustor's spouse, the annual gift exclusion can be increased to $20,000 with the consent of the trustor's spouse. Any remaining taxable gifts can be further offset by the trustor's unified gift tax credit.[129]

F. Testamentary Power to Revoke Income Recipient s Interest

As mentioned in Chapter 3, a trustor can forestall the recognition of a taxable transfer to a non-spouse income recipient by reserving the power in the trust instrument to revoke the non-trustor recipient's income interest, thereby making the transfer incomplete for gift tax purposes. This power must be exercisable solely by the trustor's will.[130]

1.   Taxable Gifts Accrue as Income is Received

For trusts containing the power to revoke a recipient's income interest, taxable gifts are deemed made by the trustor as income payments are actually received by the recipient. Such amounts are considered gifts of a present interest and, accordingly, qualify for the $10,000 annual exclusion.[131]

2.   Estate Tax Consequences when Right of Revocation is Unexercised

A trustor established a charitable remainder trust that named her children as the sole joint life income recipients. The trustor also reserved the right, exercisable solely by will, to revoke the children's income interests. The trustor predeceased her children, failing to

---

[128]   Ltr. Rul. 9244013

[129]   IRC §§2503(b); 2505(a)

[130]   Reg. §§1.664-2(a)(4); 1.664-3(a)(4)

[131]   IRC §2503(b)

revoke. The entire value of the trust was includible in her gross estate under IRC §2038(a). The present value of the charitable remainder interest was calculated based on the fair market value of the trust and the ages of the life income recipients on the date of the trustor's death. The present value of the remainder interest qualified for the estate tax charitable deduction under IRC §2055(a).[132]

3.   Estate Tax Consequences when Right of Revocation is Absent

If the trustor had not reserved the right to revoke her children's interests, the gifts would have become complete at the time the trust was created. Furthermore, the value of the trust would not have been includible in her estate. In that case, the trustor would file a gift tax return for the value of the income interest that exceeded the $10,000 annual exclusion per recipient (assuming the trust did not contain sprinkling provisions). The trustor's unified gift tax credit would be applied to the balance of any gift tax due. When the trustor died, the value of the original taxable gift would be included in the calculation of her estate tax, with any prior gift taxes paid or unified credit used, credited against her tentative estate tax liability.

4.   Trustor s Intervening Income Interest

If the trustor had included herself as the primary income recipient and named her children as successor income recipients, the full value of the trust would have been includible in her estate regardless of the absence of a retained right of revocation.[133] As before, the present value of the remainder interest (based on the fair market value of the trust and the successor income recipients' ages on the date of her death) would qualify as an estate tax charitable deduction. If the trustor did not retain the right to revoke and incurred gift tax in the year the trust was created, her estate would receive a credit for any previous gift taxes paid or unified gift tax credit used.

5.   Planning Considerations Regarding Retained Rights of Revocation

When should a trustor retain a right of revocation? From a non-tax standpoint, there may be many reasons a trustor might desire to maintain the discretionary right to terminate an income recipient's interest. From a tax planning standpoint, however, there may be some compelling reasons to include or exclude the right.

a.   Potential Loss of Marital Deduction

Some commentators have stated, in the presence of an unlimited marital deduction, a right of revocation is not necessary for a married couple who establish a charitable remainder trust. Consider the following scenario, however.

---

132   Lober v. United States, 346 U.S. 335 (1953)

133   IRC §2036(a)

A married couple establishes a charitable remainder trust and then subsequently divorces. The ex-husband remarries and dies of happiness shortly after completing a new estate plan that leaves his entire estate to his new wife.

As a result, the transfer of the decedent ex-husband's income interest to the surviving ex-wife no longer qualifies for the marital deduction. The ex-husband's estate (i.e., now intended for the new spouse) must pay any estate tax attributable to the transfer of the income interest to the ex-wife. Because the estate tax cannot be paid from the trust itself, the full burden falls upon the estate.

The exercise of a right of revocation would have accelerated one-half the remainder interest to the charitable remaindermen upon the death of the husband and would have eliminated any taxable transfer. The charitable remainder trust would continue to operate with one-half of its assets for the life of the surviving ex-wife.

b. Marital Deduction Planning

In private letter ruling 9827017, two trusts qualify as valid charitable remainder unitrusts under IRC §664(d)(2) despite the fact that all interests in the trusts are incomplete gifts for federal gift tax purposes.

A husband and wife each established a unitrust. The husband's trust provides that a unitrust amount of 11 percent will be paid to him semi-annually. At his death, the unitrust amount will be paid to his wife and at her death, to another individual. At the death of the survivor of the three individuals, the remainder of the trust will pass to three charities. The husband is the trustee of his trust and an independent trustee is appointed to value assets that do not have ascertainable values. The husband retains the power exercisable only by his will to revoke or terminate the successive interests of his wife and the other individual. The husband also reserves the power to add or substitute other charitable beneficiaries and/or to change the percentages to be received by each charity. If any charity is not qualified under IRC §§170(b)(1)(A), 170(c), 2055(a) and 2522(a), then the trustee is to distribute such charity's share to one or more charities, which are so qualified.

The wife's trust is substantially similar to the husband's trust except that the wife receives the initial unitrust amount from her trust, she is the initial trustee of her trust, and she retains the testamentary power to revoke the interests of her husband and the other individual beneficiary. We assume that the wife also retained the power to change the charities or the percentages going to the charities under her trust. (There are some apparent typographical errors in the ruling as it pertains to the provisions of the wife's trust.)

The Service held that the husband and wife made incomplete gifts via their respective trusts. The trusts qualify as charitable remainder unitrusts for purposes of IRC §664(d)(2) with respect to transfers made to them prior to July 28, 1997. The IRS did not rule on qualification with respect to any transfers after that date (for transfers after July 28, 1997, the value of the remainder interest in a charitable remainder trust must be equal to at least 10 percent of the value of the assets transferred to the trust).

This ruling raises interesting issues and planning opportunities. If the interest of the non-spouse individual beneficiary is not revoked, then in all likelihood, the unitrust interest passing from the deceased spouse's trust to the surviving spouse at the death of the first spouse to die will not qualify for the federal estate tax marital deduction. Perhaps the plan contemplated for the non-spouse individual beneficiary to disclaim his or her interest in the trust created by the spouse who dies first and keep his or her interest in the trust created by the spouse who dies last. This scenario would avoid gift taxes, postpone estate taxes until both spouses die, and avoid estate taxes with respect to one charitable remainder trust.

c. Paying Gift Tax Now to Save Estate Tax Later
Can the trustor receive any tax benefit by not retaining a right of revocation? Perhaps.

Example: A mother, age 75, transfers $5,000,000 to a charitable remainder unitrust. The trust will pay a 7 percent unitrust amount in quarterly installments for her life and then to her daughter, age 50, for her life. The balance of the mother's estate is valued at $4,000,000, placing it in the 55 percent marginal federal estate tax bracket. She has not used any of her unified gift or estate tax credit.

In the event the mother does not retain a right of revocation, a gift to the daughter of the successor income interest will be complete when the trust is created. Based on the previous assumptions, the gift is valued at $1,757,100. The gift tax on this amount is $671,495. The mother will use her $202,050 unified gift tax credit[134], leaving a net tax payable of $474,845.

Suppose the mother dies five months later (having already paid the gift tax). Along with her other assets, the entire value of the unitrust will be includible in her estate. Assuming no change in the value of the assets, the mother's gross estate will be $8,521,305.[135] The present value of the remainder interest of the unitrust based on the daughter's successor life income interest is $1,017,850. This amount is permitted as an estate tax charitable deduction. This leaves a net taxable estate of $7,503,455. In calculating the estate tax, the mother's estate will receive a credit for the gift tax previously paid. The net estate tax is calculated to be $3,092,355. In this example, the combined gift and estate taxes total $3,567,200.

Will the total amount of transfer taxes paid change if the mother retains the right to revoke her daughter's interest? In such case, there will be no gift tax payable when the trust is created; therefore, the mother's gross estate will be increased to $9,000,000. The present value of the remainder interest from the unitrust will remain unchanged

---

[134] Assumes transfer is completed in 1998.

[135] $5,000,000 + $4,000,000 - $478,695 = $8,521,305

at $1,017,850. Based on a net taxable estate of $7,982,150, the gross estate tax is $4,030,983. Applying the mother's unused unified estate tax credit of $202,050, the net tax is $3,834,333.

The transfer taxes attributable to the two scenarios differ by $263,283. Why? Under the first scenario, a gift tax in the amount of $474,845 was paid. The mother's taxable estate was reduced by this amount. Under the second scenario, no gift tax was paid. The difference in taxes paid is equal to the gift tax paid under the first scenario multiplied by the mother's marginal estate tax bracket.[136]

If the taxable gift was small enough to be absorbed entirely by the mother's unified gift tax credit, there would have been no difference in the amount of tax paid under either scenario.

The previous example does not, however, take into consideration any change in the value of the trust's assets between the time of creation and the trustor's death, nor does it consider the period of time between these events and its effect on the income and remainder interest calculations. Furthermore, it does not consider the investment opportunity cost incurred by paying the tax up front. Discounted cash flow analysis, based on the specific facts and circumstances of the donor, should assist the planner in evaluating the efficacy of a retained right of revocation.

G. Planning with Qualified Terminable Interest Property

The Economic Recovery Tax Act of 1982 introduced the concept of *qualified terminable interest property* as a method whereby a decedent spouse can preserve the estate tax marital deduction for the transfer of property to a surviving spouse while retaining control of the ultimate distribution of the property. Section 2056(b)(7) of the Code defines QTIP property as property:

- that passes from the decedent only to the surviving spouse;

- in which the surviving spouse is entitled to all the income from the property, payable annually or at more frequent interval, or has a use for life in the property; and

- for which an election has been made by the executor of the decedent's estate.

A charitable remainder trust presumably cannot qualify as a QTIP trust because of a conflict with the *all income* provision under section 2056(b)(7). However, a charitable remainder trust, in which the spouse of a decedent is the only noncharitable recipient, will be entitled to a marital deduction.[137] Further, an individual who desires to provide a surviving spouse with a life income with the remainder to specified charitable organizations can do so through the use of a QTIP trust. In addition to providing all income to the surviving spouse and the use of trust assets, the trust can allow for invasions of principal, if necessary. The transfer will qualify

---

[136] $478,695 x 55% = $263,283

[137]   IRC §2056(b)(8)

for the unlimited marital deduction in the first spouse's estate and will qualify for the estate tax charitable deduction in the estate of the surviving spouse.[138]

Some people have used a blend of QTIP trusts and CRT's. A taxpayer proposed an arrangement whereby a portion of her estate will fund a testamentary charitable remainder annuity that will pay the greater of $1,000,000 or 5 percent of its initial value to the surviving spouse for his life with the remainder to charity. The balance of her estate will be transferred to a QTIP trust for the benefit of her surviving spouse with the remainder to charity. The Service ruled that, (a) the transfer to the QTIP trust will qualify under section 2056(a) for the marital deduction in the decedent's estate, (b) the property remaining in the trust upon the death of the surviving spouse will be includible in his estate under section 2044(a), and (c) the transfer will qualify for the estate tax charitable deduction under section 2055(a) if it is distributed to qualified charitable organizations. The charitable remainder annuity trust will also qualify for the marital and charitable estate tax deductions.[139]

The Service has also ruled that naming a charitable remainder trust as the remainderman of a QTIP trust also qualifies. In this case, the QTIP trust will pay income for the life of the surviving spouse. The surviving spouse will be granted a limited testamentary power of appointment for the remainder of the trust to her daughter. If she fails to make the election, the remainder will be paid over to a charitable remainder annuity trust that presumably names the daughter as the income recipient.[140]

II. Payment of Estate Taxes

Revenue Ruling 82-128 specifically prohibits the payment of federal estate tax attributable to a charitable remainder trust from trust corpus. This ruling makes the creation of charitable remainder trusts with non-trustor income recipients a potentially risky proposition because a possible tax must be paid from other estate assets. In the absence of such assets, the IRS might attempt to attach the income of the trust.

In a letter ruling, donors *A* and *B* establish a charitable remainder trust naming *A* and *B*, who are presumably unmarried, as joint and survivor life income recipients. *A* and *B* propose to amend the trust to provide that, upon the death of the first donor, no estate or inheritance taxes will be allocated to, or recoverable from the trust. As an alternative, the lifetime unitrust interest of the surviving donor will continue in effect upon the death of the first donor to die only if the surviving donor furnishes the funds to pay those taxes for which the trustee may be liable upon the death of the first donor to die. The Service approved the arrangement.[141]

---

[138]   See Ltr. Ruls. 9036040; 9028008; 9020831

[139]   Ltr. Rul. 9323039

[140]   Ltr. Rul. 9144016

[141]   Ltr. Rul. 930929

A. Provision Requiring Payment of Estate Taxes by Successor Income Recipient Permitted

A donor proposed to include a provision in a charitable remainder trust that, in the event the trust became liable for death taxes attributable to a successor income recipient, the recipient's interest would continue or take effect only if the recipient furnished the funds for payment of all taxes attributable to the recipient's interest. Finally, the trust provided that, if the recipient failed to furnish all such funds, such recipient would be deemed to have predeceased the donor.

Because there can be no invasion of the trust's assets to pay federal estate or state death taxes upon the grantor's death, and thus no interference with the charity's remainder interest, the Service ruled the trust will be qualified under IRC §664(d)(2)(B).[142]

B. Who Pays the Estate Tax?

How is the amount of the estate tax charitable deduction computed in the case of a transfer to a charitable remainder unitrust if, under applicable state law, federal estate taxes with respect to the trust are to be apportioned entirely to trust principal?

An individual died in 1991. At the time of her death, she was the life income beneficiary of a marital trust created by her husband that was includible in her gross estate.[143] Upon her death, the trust corpus was to be distributed to a charitable remainder unitrust that named the decedent's son as life income recipient with the remainder to a designated charity.

Under IRC §2207A and the decedent's will, the marital trust was burdened with the estate taxes generated by the inclusion of the marital trust in the decedent's gross estate. The trust instrument contains no provision regarding the apportionment of federal estate taxes to be paid by the trust. The applicable state apportionment statute provides that, if both a present interest and a future interest in property are involved, a tax shall be apportioned entirely to principal. This shall be the case even if the future interest qualifies for an estate tax charitable deduction, even if the holder of the present interest also has rights in the principal, and even if the principal is otherwise exempt from apportionment.

On the federal estate tax return, the estate claimed a charitable deduction for the present value of the charitable remainder interest. The deduction was computed by determining the net amount passing to the unitrust (before payment of estate taxes), subtracting from that amount the federal estate taxes payable with respect to the unitrust, and multiplying the difference by the appropriate unitrust remainder factor.

Upon audit of the return, the district office took the position that, pursuant to the estate's methodology, because the estate tax liability was paid *off the top* of trust corpus, the lifetime recipient's unitrust interest (which is the lesser of trust income or percentage of the value of the trust) was necessarily reduced proportionately. Thus, the estate's method for apportioning

---

[142]   Ltr. Rul. 9512016

[143]   IRC §2044

the estate tax effectively placed the burden of a portion of the estate tax liability generated by the unitrust on the interest of the lifetime unitrust recipient.

The district office argued this approach conflicted with the state's statute which specifically provides that any estate tax is to be apportioned "entirely to the principal." The district office contended that, under the statute, the unitrust/income recipient is exonerated from paying any tax, and that the entire tax burden is borne by the beneficiary of the trust principal—the charitable remainderman. This result could be obtained (even though the taxes are paid currently) if, for example, the lifetime recipient received an additional payment each month (i.e., from the charitable remainderman) to compensate for the reduced unitrust/income payment resulting from the tax payment. The charitable deduction would be computed by subtracting the value of the unitrust interest from the value of the trust corpus and from the amount so obtained, and then subtracting the estate taxes allocable to the trust. The balance is the amount of the charitable deduction.

Fortunately for the charitable remainderman, the Service ruled in technical advice that the estate's approach in computing the allowable charitable deduction is correct.[144]

C. Interrelated Estate Tax Computations

In determining the taxable estate of a decedent, a deduction is allowed for qualified gifts to charity. If the value of the property to be transferred to charity is burdened with the payment of any death taxes, the amount of the charitable deduction is reduced by the amount used to pay the taxes. In essence, the computation of the estate tax is dependent on the charitable deduction, which is dependent on the estate tax. The computation therefore *chases its own tail*. The computation of death taxes attributable to a charitable interest requires an interrelated computation. Formulas and examples of interrelated computations are provided in IRS Publication 904.

With respect to planning a testamentary charitable remainder trust, the interrelated computation can be avoided altogether by providing a specific amount to the trust and allocating any death taxes attributable to the noncharitable income interest to other estate assets. Funding a charitable remainder trust on a residuary basis or apportioning estate taxes to the amount used to fund the trust will trigger the interrelated computation, which may cause a significant reduction in the amount of the charitable interest.

Example: Mr. Jones' adjusted gross estate is valued at $5,000,000. His estate plan provides for the payment of specific bequests in the amount of $1,000,000 with the remainder of his estate, net of estate taxes and miscellaneous deductions, to be paid to a charitable remainder trust for the benefit of family members. The following computation calculates the amount of estate tax due and the amount transferred to a charitable remainder trust.

---

[144]   Ltr. Rul. 9419006 Technical Advice Memorandum

Assumptions:

E	= Adjusted Gross Estate	$5,000,000
D	= Estate Deductions	$250,000
f	= Charitable Remainder Trust Deduction Factor	.25000
S	= Specific Bequests to Non-Charitable Recipients	$1,000,000

The estate tax and residuary funding amount can be calculated as follows:[145]

Step 1 Calculate the estimated range of the taxable estate:

$$R = (E-D) - ((E-D-S) * f)$$
$$R = \$3,812,500$$

Step 2 Select the *a* slope and *b* intercept corresponding to R from the following table:

Estimated Taxable Estate			a Slope	b Intercept
$600,000	-	$700,000	.37	-222,000
$750,000	-	$1,000,000	.39	-237,000
$1,000,000	-	$1,250,000	.41	-257,000
$1,250,000	-	$1,500,000	.43	-282,000
$1,500,000	-	$2,000,000	.45	-312,000
$2,000,000	-	$2,500,000	.49	-392,000
$2,500,000	-	$3,000,000	.53	-492,000
$3,000,000	-	$10,000,000	.55	-552,000
$10,000,000	-	$21,040,000	.60	-1,052,000

Step 3 Once the *a* and *b* parameters are identified, the following formula can be used to calculate the estate tax:

$$X = (aT - afT + afS + b) / (1- af)$$
$$X = \$1,791,159$$

where:

$$T = (E-D)$$

Step 4 Calculate the amount to be transferred to the charitable remainder trust:

	Adjusted Gross Estate	$5,000,000
Less:	Estate Deductions	$250,000
Less:	Specific Bequests	$1,000,000
Less:	Estate Tax	$1,791,159
Equals:	Amount to Charitable Remainder Trust	$1,958,841

---

[145] Formula provided by Stanley L. Klein, Ph.D.

Gift and Estate Tax Summary

	Trustor creates trust paying income to:	Taxable Gift?	$10,000 Exclusion?	Marital Deduction?	Included in Trustor's Estate?
1	self for life	No	N/A	N/A	Yes, but 100% charitable deduction
2	spouse for life with retained right of revocation	No	N/A	Yes	Yes, but 100% charitable and marital deductions
3	spouse for life without retained right of revocation	No	N/A	Yes	Yes, but 100% charitable and marital deductions
4	self and spouse for life	No	N/A	Yes	Yes, but 100% charitable and marital deductions
5	spouse and non-spouse for life with retained right of revocation	Yes, as payments are received by non-spouse	Yes, as payments are received by non-spouse	No	Yes
6	spouse and non-spouse for life without retained right of revocation	Yes	Yes	No	No
7	non-spouse for life or term of years with retained right of revocation	Yes, as payments received by non-spouse	Yes, as payments received by non-spouse	N/A	Yes
8	non-spouse for life or term of years without retained right of revocation	Yes	Yes	N/A	No
9	self for life, then to non-spouse with retained right of revocation	No	No	N/A	Yes
10	self for life, then to non-spouse without retained right of revocation	Yes	No	N/A	Yes
11	self and non-spouse as joint and surviving income recipients with retained right of revocation	Yes, as payments are received by non-spouse	Yes, as payments are received by non-spouse	N/A	Yes
12	self and non-spouse as joint and surviving income recipients without retained right of revocation	Yes	Yes	N/A	Yes

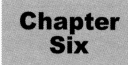

Chapter Six

Suitable Gift Assets

I. Suitable Assets

- Cash

- Publicly Traded Securities

- Closely-Held Stock

- Certain Real Property

- Certain Intangible Property

- Tangible Personal Property

II. Potential Problem Assets

- Sole Proprietorships

- Partnership Interests

- Professional Corporations

- Certain Real Property

- UBTI Assets

- Debt encumbered Assets

- Certain Intangible Property

III. Discussion of Asset Types

There are many types of assets that are ideally suited for transfer to a charitable remainder trust. Others are accompanied by more complexity, less benefit, or should be avoided completely.

A. Cash

Although cash represents the least complicated asset for transfer to a charitable remainder trust, it is often overlooked because there is no capital gains leverage to be achieved by its use. However, cash is often used to purchase tax-exempt bonds that are then used to fund a charitable remainder annuity trust. Under this scenario, income distributions will be tax-free to the recipients (provided the trust generates no short or long-term capital gains).[146] Some individuals become aware of a charitable remainder trust after they have sold appreciated property and incurred a tax. They can transfer cash or tax-exempt bonds to a charitable remainder trust and use the resulting charitable contribution deduction to mitigate their capital gains tax liability.

B. Publicly Traded Securities

Publicly traded stock is an ideal asset for transfer to a charitable remainder trust. It is often highly appreciated, is easily transferred and valued, and produces only modest income. Other suitable securities are government, municipal, and corporate debt instruments, mutual fund shares, and warrants.

1.   Original Issue Discount and Market Discount Obligations

IRC sections 1271 through 1275 deal with the income tax rules associated with OIDs and market discount obligations. The specifics are beyond the scope of this treatise. However, the relevant point is that these instruments often produce ordinary income upon sale or redemption. The ordinary income element is not deductible. However, neither is it recognized upon transfer and sale.

2.   U.S. Savings Bonds

If Series EE or HH savings bonds are transferred to a charitable remainder trust, the trustor may claim a charitable contribution deduction for their fair market value. However, all unrealized income will be taxed to the trustor on the date of contribution.[147]

3.   Restricted Securities

Securities that are restricted under SEC Rule 144 or 145 can be transferred to a charitable remainder trust. The trustee is, however, bound by the holding period and volume sales limitations that were applicable to the trustor at the time of the transfer. Because of these restrictions, the securities may not have a readily ascertainable fair market value (even though market quotations may be available).

Under the substantiation rules of Reg. §1.170A-13(c), a taxpayer making a contribution of publicly traded securities is not generally required to obtain a qualified appraisal to determine their value. If, however, the securities are subject to any restrictions that

---

[146]   See Chapter 8 - The Four-Tier System

[147]   Ltr. Rul. 8010082

materially affect their value to the donor or prevent the securities from being freely traded, the taxpayer is required to obtain a qualified appraisal.[148]

In separate rulings the Service has also held that, (a) restricted securities are not considered *qualified stock*[149] if the securities cannot be sold at the time of contribution due to hold period requirements,[150] and (b) an individual's *initial* gift of restricted securities to a charitable remainder trust will not constitute a prohibited act of self-dealing if the individual's status as a disqualified person arises solely as a result of his contribution to the trust.[151]

4. Stock Subect to Right of First Refusal

In Rev. Rul. 80-83, a transfer of stock of a publicly held corporation subject to a first right of refusal by the corporation to a charitable remainder unitrust which named the trustor as trustee qualified for a charitable gift tax deduction under IRC §2522. The right required any shareholder desiring to sell stock to first offer the shares to the corporation at the same price and terms as offered to any other buyer.[152]

Comment: Such agreements should be reviewed to confirm that a transfer to a charitable remainder trust is permitted.

5. Listed Options

Listed options are any options to which the *mark-to-market* rules apply. They are referred to technically as *Section 1256 Contracts* and include all listed equity and non-equity options (including stock index futures and foreign currency contracts).

The holding period for such contracts is irrelevant. All capital gains and losses from section 1256 contracts must be reported annually according to the *60-40 Rule*. Gains and losses are allocated 60 percent long-term capital gain or loss and 40 percent short-term capital gain or loss, respectively. The contribution of such contracts to a charitable remainder trust will trigger application of the reduction rules applicable to the short-term capital gain (ordinary income) element.

A listed option may be a suitable asset for transfer to a charitable remainder trust provided the trustee does not intend to hold it for investment purposes. Such contracts have been identified as being a potential *jeopardizing investment* under IRC §4944.

---

[148] Reg. §1.170A-13(c)(7)(xi)(C)(1); Ltr. Ruls. 9623018 and 9247018; Rev. Rul. 77-287, 1977-2 C.B. 319

[149] For purposes of the percentage deduction limitations applicable to gifts to private non-operating foundations under IRC §170(e)(5), as limited by IRC §170(e)(5)(D).

[150] Ltr. Ruls. 9247018 and 9435007

[151] Ltr. Rul. 9623018

[152] See also Ltr. Rul. 9452020

6.   Real Estate Investment Trusts

A real estate investment trust (REIT), as defined in IRC §856, may not be a suitable investment asset for a charitable remainder trust because it may produce unrelated business income. Refer to the prospectus of the REIT under consideration.

7.   Publicly Traded Master Limited Partnerships

Master limited partnerships (MLPs) may or may not be a suitable contribution or investment asset for a charitable remainder trust. Under prior law, the decision was clear. For partnerships acquired after December 17, 1987, the gross income from such partnership interests was treated as unrelated business income to the tax-exempt partner regardless of the nature of the underlying income. Section 13145(a)(1) of the Revenue Reconciliation Act of 1993, however, repeals IRC §512(c)(2)(A). Therefore, MLP distributions are subject to the same classifications as other types of partnerships. The transfer of an MLP to a charitable remainder trust should be considered only after a thorough examination of the partnership prospectus and with specific attention given to possible unrelated business income from acquisition indebtedness or the partnership's business activities.

C. Selling a C-Corporation

Stock in a C-corporation (which may also be closely-held[153]) presents several unique planning opportunities and challenges in connection with charitable remainder trusts.

The TRA '86 repeal of the *General Utilities Doctrine* makes the sale of corporate assets a two-edged sword resulting in potential taxation of sale proceeds at both corporate and shareholder levels. Can these taxes be mitigated or avoided?

1.   Stock Sale

The transfer of stock to a charitable remainder trust followed by a sale of such stock can result in complete avoidance of capital gain at both stockholder and corporate levels. However, this is achieved at the expense of the buyer losing a stepped-up basis on the corporate assets and bearing potential liability for prior business operations.

---

[153]   A closely-held corporation is any corporation other than an S-corporation of which at least 50 percent of the total outstanding stock is owned by or for less than five shareholders. Reg. §1.170A-13; IRC §542(a)(2)

Sale of closely held stock

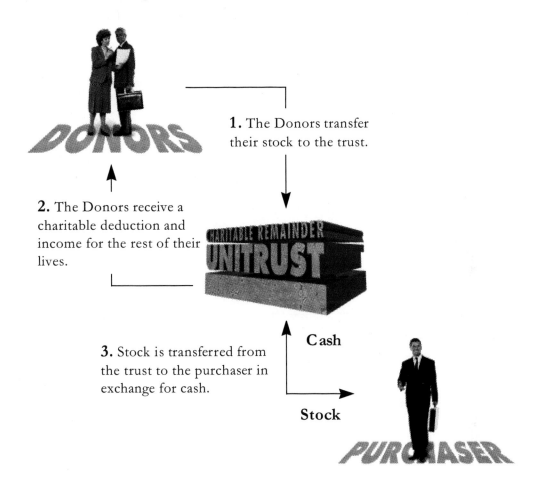

1. The Donors transfer their stock to the trust.

2. The Donors receive a charitable deduction and income for the rest of their lives.

3. Stock is transferred from the trust to the purchaser in exchange for cash.

Cash

Stock

2.   Asset Sale Followed by Liquidation

In the event stock is transferred to a charitable remainder trust followed by an asset sale and a subsequent corporate liquidation, the trust will have no effect on the tax paid by the corporation on the sale of corporate assets. However, the capital gains tax will be avoided upon liquidation and distribution of the net proceeds to the shareholder (because the trust is a tax-exempt trust).

Even though tax might not be avoided at the corporate level, the impact of the tax can be mitigated by the tax savings created by the charitable contribution deduction received by the trustor outside the trust.

Asset sale followed by liquidation

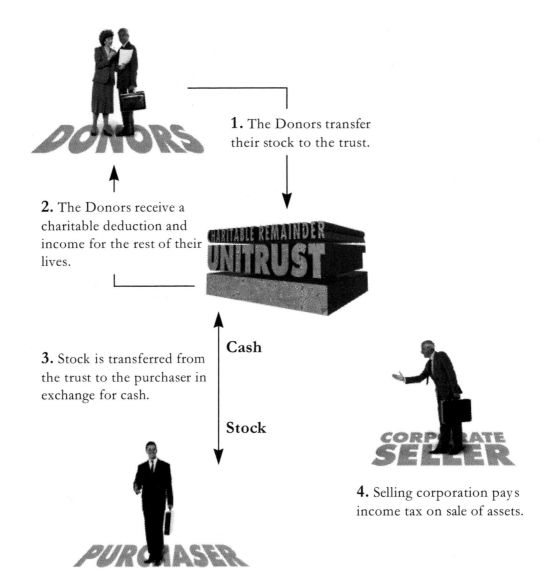

1. The Donors transfer their stock to the trust.

2. The Donors receive a charitable deduction and income for the rest of their lives.

3. Stock is transferred from the trust to the purchaser in exchange for cash.

Cash

Stock

4. Selling corporation pays income tax on sale of assets.

Case Study

Selling a C-Corporation

Mr. and Mrs. Williams, both age 60, own 100% of the stock of a C-corporation. The stock is worth $3,000,000. They intend to sell the company to an independent party.

The Williams have three questions:

1. What are the income tax consequences to the corporation and the Williams if the corporation sells its assets followed by a complete corporate liquidation?

2. What are the income tax consequences to the Williams if they sell the stock personally?

3. Are there any creative alternatives to paying all these taxes that can also help them accomplish their financial, estate, and philanthropic planning objectives?

The Williams started the company with $50,000 twenty years ago. Accordingly, the cost basis of their stock is $50,000. The assets of the corporation itself have an adjusted basis of $750,000.

The Williams' personal adjusted gross income is $350,000. For purposes of the following analysis, it is assumed they are subject to tax on ordinary income at a rate of 39% and at a rate of 28% for long-term capital gains. These rates include state income tax; therefore, the projections contained in this analysis will vary depending on the state of the taxpayer's domicile.

It is further assumed that for purposes of projecting cash flows, the net proceeds from the sale of the corporation are reinvested at a rate of 10% that is taxable as ordinary income. The term of the analysis is 26 years. Finally, the total value of the Williams' estate places them in the 55% estate tax bracket.

The analysis that appears on the following page compares four planning scenarios:

• The first scenario assumes the corporation sells its assets for $3,000,000 followed by a complete liquidation and distribution of the corporate assets to the Williams.

• The second scenario assumes the Williams sell the stock of the corporation for $3,000,000.

• The third scenario is similar to the first; however, it assumes the Williams transfer their stock to a charitable remainder unitrust (bearing a 7.5% payout rate) prior to the sale of the corporate assets and subsequent liquidation.

• The final scenario is similar to the second scenario; however, it assumes the stock is transferred to a charitable remainder unitrust prior to the sale of the stock.

Comparison of Sales Methods

	Option 1	Option 2	Option 3	Option 4
	Asset Sale/ Liquidation	Stock Sale	Gift to CRT/Asset Sale/ Liquidation	Gift to CRT/Stock Sale
Asset Sale				
Sales Proceeds	3,000,000	N/A	3,000,000	N/A
Basis	750,000	*	750,000	*
Gain	2,225,000	*	2,225,000	*
		*		*
Corporate Tax		No Corporate		No Corporate
Federal (34%)	(765,000)	Tax	(765,000)	Tax
State (6%)	(135,000)	*	(135,000)	*
Total Tax	(900,000)	*	(900,000)	*
		*		*
Net Proceeds	**2,100,000**	**N/A**	**2,100,000**	**N/A**
Liquidation/Sale	**Liquidation**	**Sale**	**Liquidation**	**Sale**
Sales or Distribution Proceeds	2,100,000	3,000,000	2,100,000	3,000,000
Basis	(50,000)	(50,000)	(50,000)	(50,000)
Gain	2,050,000	2,950,000	2,050,000	2,950,000
Individual Tax (F&S @ 28%)	574,000	826,000	0	0
Net Proceeds	**1,526,000**	**2,174,000**	**2,100,000**	**3,000,000**
Charitable Deduction Tax Savings	0	0	137,617	196,595
Total Income Tax Erosion	49.1%	27.5%	25.4%	-6.6%
Net Cash Flow During Life	2,334,435	3,325,729	3,470,366	4,957,666
Optional: Life Insurance Premiums	0	0	582,949	582,949
Net Income During Life	**2,334,435**	**3,325,729**	**2,887,417**	**4,375,000**
Estate Taxes (55%)	839,300	1,195,700	0	0
Net to Heirs (Year 26)	**686,700**	**978,300**	**3,000,000**	**3,000,000**
Net to Charity (Year 26)	**0**	**0**	**3,719,046**	**5,312,923**

3. Charitable Stock Redemptions

One of the more creative uses of a charitable remainder trust involves the transfer of stock in a C-corporation followed by a redemption by the corporation of the shares held by the trust. The transaction can be likened to a partial redemption on a partially deductible basis and may be an excellent method of transferring excess retained earnings from the corporation.

The Service has ruled privately that a provision that grants an independent trustee with the power to accept any offer for the redemption of shares of the company stock and to value said stock will not disqualify the trust.[154]

Corporate redemption

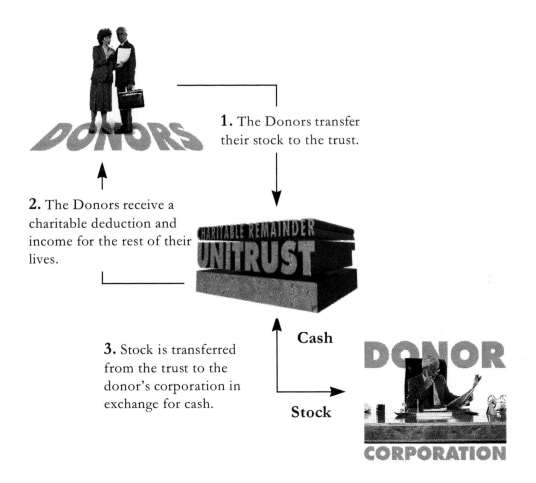

1. The Donors transfer their stock to the trust.

2. The Donors receive a charitable deduction and income for the rest of their lives.

3. Stock is transferred from the trust to the donor's corporation in exchange for cash.

Cash

Stock

4.   Palmer v. Commissioner

Palmer had voting control of both a corporation and a private foundation. He contributed stock in the corporation to the foundation and then directed the corporation to redeem the stock from the foundation the very next day. The Service argued that, in substance, the corporation had redeemed the shares directly from Palmer followed by a contribution by Palmer of the proceeds to the foundation.

---

[154]   Ltr. Rul. 9339018

The Tax Court found for Palmer.[155] In its acquiescence to the decision the IRS stated, "The Service will treat the proceeds of a redemption of stock under the facts similar to those in Palmer as income to the donor only if the donee is legally bound, or can be compelled by the corporation, to surrender the shares for redemption."[156]

5.   Self-Dealing Rules and Corporate Stock Redemptions

Charitable remainder trusts are subject to private foundation excise taxes imposed on acts of self-dealing between the trustee and a disqualified person (the trustor). Normally, a transfer of stock to a charitable remainder trust by an owner of more than 35 percent of the voting stock of the corporation followed by a corporate redemption is a prohibited act of self-dealing. However, a special exception applies.

Who disqualified persons are and the acts they are prohibited from committing are discussed in detail in Chapter 7.[157] For purposes of this discussion, however, it is important to note that a redemption of stock from a charitable remainder trust will *not* be considered an act of self-dealing under the following condition:

[IRC §4941(d)(2)(F)]

(a) any transaction between a private foundation and a corporation which is a disqualified person (as defined in section 4946(a)), pursuant to any liquidation, merger, recapitalization, or other corporate adjustment, organization, or reorganization, shall not be an act of self-dealing if all of the securities of the same class as that held by the foundation are subject to the same terms and such terms provide for receipt by the foundation of no less than fair market value;

The phrase, *subject to the same terms* means the corporation makes a bona fide offer on a uniform basis to the foundation and every other person who holds such securities.[158] Furthermore, the exception appears to require an all-cash transaction. Any loan would, in and of itself, arguably appear to constitute a separate act of self-dealing.

In Ltr. Rul. 9015055, a private foundation owned 100 percent of the issued and outstanding 6 percent cumulative preferred stock of a for-profit corporation. The foundation received the stock under the wills of a husband and wife, who formed the foundation, and who owned and controlled the corporation until their deaths. The founding couple's daughter and her husband currently manage the foundation and run the corporation. The husband holds 99.99 percent of the company's common stock for the benefit of his wife for life, with the remainder to the daughter's children. The corporation proposed to redeem all outstanding preferred stock at fair market value as determined by an independent appraisal and by a previous IRS appraisal (made for estate tax value purposes).

The Service ruled the corporation is a disqualified person with respect to the foundation and the proposed redemption of the corporation's preferred stock constitutes an act of self-dealing. However, the redemption will not be subject to the self-dealing excise tax

---

155   Palmer v. C.I.R. 62 T.C. 684, acq., aff'd (CA-8, 1975), F.2nd 1308, 36 AFTR 2d 75-5942

156   Rev. Rul. 78-197, 1978-1 C.B. 83

157   See Chapter 7 - Private Foundation Excise Taxes.

158   Reg. §53.4941(d)-3(d)(1)

because, under IRC §4941(d)(2)(F), all of the shares subject to the redemption will be treated alike.[159]

6. The Charitable ESOP or CHESOP

A charitable remainder trust can be a very effective tool in effectuating the sale of a closely-held business interest to employees via an Employee Stock Ownership Plan (ESOP). Under the rules of IRC §1042, a noncorporate shareholder can sell employer securities to an ESOP on a tax-free basis, provided (a) the individual held the securities for at least three years prior to the sale, (b) the individual purchases "qualified replacement property" (QRP) within 15 months of the date of sale, and (c) the ESOP meets percentage stock ownership tests and consents to being subject to certain excise taxes.[160]

Generally, a disposition of QRP will cause recapture of capital gain. Therefore, a seller who purchases QRP will be *locked in* if they wish to avoid recognition of gain. Enter the charitable remainder trust.

The Code provides several exceptions to the recapture provisions. Included within these exceptions is a gift of replacement securities.[161] The term "gift" is not defined in section 1042 or the regulations, however. Furthermore, a transfer to a charitable remainder trust is a gift of only a remainder interest. Therefore, the transfer attributable to the retained income interest might not qualify.

The IRS has ruled privately that a taxpayer does not avoid recognition of capital gain upon the transfer of appreciated property to a charitable trust due to any specific non-recognition provision of the Code. Rather, it is because an irrevocable trust assumes the holding period and cost basis of assets transferred to it and, therefore, does not realize gain at all. The ruling concluded the transfer of QRP constitutes a disposition of property within the meaning of IRC §1042(e). However, no gain is realized by the trustors upon the transfer of QRP to a charitable remainder trust. Thus, no recapture of gain is triggered on the original sale by the trustor to ESOP.[162]

Regarding the financing of the purchase, a bank, an insurance company, or other lending institution may exclude from gross income 50 percent of the interest received with respect to a securities acquisition loan. Therefore, the ESOP may be able to borrow the cash needed to purchase the shares on favorable terms. Further, the ESOP could service the debt by receiving tax deductible contributions from the corporation (generally subject to a limit of 15 percent of participating employee payroll).[163] As an alternative, if any portion of the sale could not be paid for in cash, the shareholder could contribute this portion of the stock to the charitable remainder trust. The trust could then sell the gifted securities to the ESOP in exchange for a note. The trust

---

[159] See also Ltr. Ruls. 9338046 and 9347035

[160] Temp. Reg. §1.1042-1T

[161] IRC §1042(e)(3)

[162] Ltr. Ruls. 9234023; 9438012; 9515002; 9547022; 9547023

[163] IRC §409

permits financing, while the tax-free exchange rules of IRC §1042 do not.[164] In all events, the planner should pay particular attention to valuation issues pertaining to both closely-held stock and promissory notes as discussed *supra*.

---

[164]   A loan from a private foundation to a disqualified person is a prohibited act of self-dealing. The self-dealing rules are discussed on page 157.

The Charitable ESOP or CHESOP

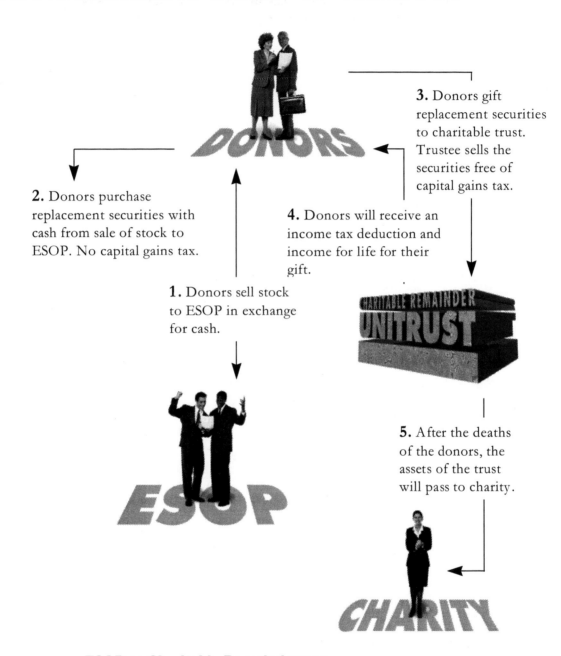

3. Donors gift replacement securities to charitable trust. Trustee sells the securities free of capital gains tax.

2. Donors purchase replacement securities with cash from sale of stock to ESOP. No capital gains tax.

4. Donors will receive an income tax deduction and income for life for their gift.

1. Donors sell stock to ESOP in exchange for cash.

5. After the deaths of the donors, the assets of the trust will pass to charity.

a. ESOP as Charitable Remainderman

Can an ESOP be named as the charitable remainderman of a charitable remainder trust? Apparently so.

The IRS has ruled privately that a charitable remainder trust was qualified because any distribution to an ESOP could be made only in the event the ESOP was a qualified charitable organization to which the remainder interest could be transferred. The trust also provided, in the event the ESOP did not qualify, that trust assets would be distributed to another qualified organization.[165]

b. ESOP as Disqualified Person

Is an ESOP a disqualified person for purposes of the self-dealing rules. Rev. Rul. 81-76[166] holds that an ESOP described in Section 4975(e) of the Code is not treated as the owner of stock in a corporation where the stock is allocated to participating employees and thus is not a disqualified person.

7. Retained Vote

If the trustor retains voting rights in a non-fiduciary capacity (other than as trustee), the trust will be disqualified.[167] Further, the transfer of stock with retained voting rights is considered a non-qualified gift of a partial interest.[168] As will be discussed, the trustor should not be the sole trustee of a trust that holds a *hard-to-value* asset such as closely-held stock.

. Stock in a Professional Corporation

Stock in professional corporations such as incorporated legal, accounting, medical, or dental practices may or may not be allowed for transfer to a charitable remainder trust. Determination of suitability will depend on the licensing authority in the state of the corporation's situs. A transfer may be permissible if the trust is only a transitory holder, pending the sale or other disposition of the practice, or if the trustee holds a professional license compatible with the type of stock being contributed.

9. Section 306 Stock

Preferred stock issued as a nontaxable stock dividend is considered "tainted" under IRC §306. Such stock is considered ordinary income property to the extent of the corporation's retained earnings. Therefore, the trustor's deduction is based on the lesser of fair market value and adjusted cost basis.

10. Valuation

In order to claim a charitable contribution deduction (for amounts exceeding $10,000), the value of a closely-held business interest must be determined by qualified appraisal. Without a qualified appraisal, no deduction is allowed.

In general, when less than a majority interest is transferred to trust, the valuation must reflect the lack of voting control that accompanies a minority position. By contrast, a

---

[165]   Ltr. Rul. 9244001

[166]   Rev. Rul. 81-76, 1981-1 C.B. 516; See additional discussion on page 157.

[167]   Reg. §1.664-1(a)(4)

[168]   Rev. Rul. 81-282, 1981-2 C.B. 78

majority position may command a control premium. In either case, closely-held stock may be subject to a discount for lack of marketability.

A key planning consideration in securing an appraisal on closely-held stock is cost. This is particularly critical because the entire corporation must be valued first before the fractional interest being contributed can be valued. Further, if the trustee of a *unitrust* plans on retaining such stock, the annual valuation requirement might at additional expense.[169]

11. Excess Business Holdings and Jeopardizing Investment Concerns

A charitable remainder trust will not be subject to the excess business holdings or jeopardizing investment rules unless it includes as income recipient an IRC §170(c) organization.[170] Specimen trusts published by the IRS include these two prohibitions (most likely in an effort to cover the possibility that charity will be an income recipient). Thus, a trustor who transfers stock to a specimen trust that does not include a charitable income recipient might unwittingly and unnecessarily subject the trust to the excess business holdings and jeopardizing investment rules.

The jeopardizing investment rules could come into play if the trustee decides to hold the one issue of stock for investment purposes (due to lack of diversification). Regarding excess business holdings, the trustee has five years to dispose of the stock (with a possible five-year extension).[171] Accordingly, if the transfer is followed by a sale, these two problems should disappear. Letter Ruling 9210005 confirms that charitable remainder trusts are exempt from the excess business holdings and jeopardizing investment rules per IRC §4947(b)(3)(B).

12. Unrelated Business Income

If a charitable remainder trust owns more than 80 percent of the combined total voting power of all classes of stock in a corporation and at least 80 percent of all other classes of shares, the corporation will be considered a *controlled organization.*[172]

Interest, annuities, royalties, and rents derived by the trust from the controlled organization are included as an item of gross income of the trust. However, a trust will not usually receive this type of income from a corporation. The key is that dividends are excluded. Accordingly, even though a charitable remainder trust may own 100 percent of the stock in a closely-held corporation, the issuance of a dividend will not cause the trust to have unrelated business income.[173]

---

[169] Methods of valuing closely-held stock are discussed in Rev. Rul. 59-60; Rev Rul. 77-287 and 83-120. See Chapter 7 - Valuation and Appraisal Requirements.

[170] IRC §4947(b)(3)(B)

[171] IRC §4943(c)(6),(7)

[172] IRC §368(c)

[173] IRC §512(a)(13)

13. C-Corporation as Trustor

Can a C-Corporation establish a charitable remainder trust? Yes. Like the S-Corporation, a C-Corporation can create a charitable remainder trust provided the measuring term of the trust consists of a term of years not to exceed twenty. The IRS has ruled privately that in a case where the trust was funded with publicly traded stock and which named a private foundation as remainderman, the trust qualified. The corporation would be allowed a charitable income tax deduction based on the fair market value of the stock provided the amount contributed did not exceed 10 percent of the gift corporation's outstanding stock. If the amount contributed to a private foundation exceeded the 10 percent limit, the deduction on any excess would be based on the lesser of the stock's fair market value and its adjusted cost basis.[174]

D. S-Corporations

Can stock in an S-corporation be transferred to a charitable remainder trust? Yes, but not if the shareholder wishes to retain S-corporation status. A charitable remainder trust is not a qualified S-corporation trust.

The Service has stated that IRC §§664 and 1361 contemplate two distinct systems of taxation and are mutually exclusive. It further noted that a beneficiary electing under IRC §1361(d) to be treated as the owner of the portion of the trust consisting of stock, agrees to be taxed on all items of income relating to that stock. Under IRC §664(b) it said, the recipient of an income interest in a charitable remainder unitrust is only taxable on the unitrust amount. Therefore, the transfer of even one share of stock to a charitable remainder trust will terminate S-corporation status.[175] Rev. Rul. 92-48[176] cements the IRS's opinion. However, the corporation may qualify for relief under the inadvertent termination rules of IRC §1362(f).

In 1996, Congress enacted The Small Business Job Protection Act.[177] Although the Act permits a charitable organization to be an eligible shareholder of an S corporation beginning January 1, 1998, that privilege does not extend to charitable remainder trusts.

1.   S-Corporation as Trustor

Can an S-Corporation establish a charitable remainder trust? Yes. Like a C-Corporation, an S-corporation will be the trustor and income recipient of the trust. Income distributions will pass through to shareholders according to their pro rata share holdings. However, because an S-corporation is other than an individual or a qualified charitable organization, the trust term is limited to a term of years not to exceed twenty.[178]

---

[174]   Ltr. Rul. 9205031

[175]   Ltr. Rul. 8922014

[176]   Rev. Rul. 92-48, 1992-1 C.B. 301

[177]   Public Law 104-188; signed into law on August 20, 1996

[178]   Ltr. Rul. 9340043

2. Pass-Through of Charitable Deduction to Shareholders

Can an S-Corporation that establishes a charitable remainder trust pass the charitable contribution deduction through to its shareholders? According to Ltr. Rul. 9340043, it can.[179]

Section 1366(a)(1)(A) of the Code provides that a shareholder in an S-corporation determines his liability by assuming his prorata share of items of income, loss, deduction, or credit that if separately stated and given separate treatment would effect his individual income tax liability. Items of loss include charitable contributions.[180]

The amount of the shareholder's contribution deduction is the present value of the remainder interest in the gift reduced in accordance with the applicable provisions of section 170(e) of the Code. Under that section, the amount of a contribution of property is reduced by the amount of gain that would not have been long-term capital gain (i.e., short-term capital gain or ordinary income) had the property been sold at its fair market value. Under section 170(e)(1)(B), however, the amount of the contribution is reduced by the amount of gain that would have been long-term capital gain if (a) the property is tangible personal property unrelated the exempt organization's purpose, or (b) the contribution is *to* or *for the use of* a private non-operating foundation.

Regarding the percentage limitation placed on the use of the deduction, the Service's position was favorable to the taxpayer, but at the same time perplexing. Section 1366(d)(1) of the Code provides that the aggregate amount of losses and deductions assumed by any shareholder shall not exceed the sum of the adjusted basis of the shareholder's stock in the S-corporation and the shareholder's adjusted basis of any indebtedness.[181] The Service, however, made no reference to that section in its ruling, stating simply, "The limitations applicable to individuals set forth in section 170(b) apply in determining the shareholder's allowable deduction for the charitable deduction." Finally, when the net charitable deduction is passed through to the shareholder, the shareholder's basis in his stock is decreased (but not below zero) by the amount of the deduction.[182]

3. S-Corporation Without Built-In Gains

Stock in an S-corporation that has no built-in gains (resulting from a conversion from a C-corporation), that would otherwise cause tax at the corporate level in the event of an asset sale / liquidation, may not be suitable for transfer to a charitable remainder trust if an asset sale / liquidation is anticipated.

An asset sale / liquidation outside the charitable remainder trust will result in a taxable event only at the shareholder level. By contrast, the transfer of stock in an S-corporation to a charitable remainder trust will terminate S-corporation status. Therefore, a subsequent asset sale (within the trust) will result in a taxable event at the C-corporation

---

[179]   *Ibid.*

[180]   IRC §702(a)(4)

[181]   IRC §1366(d)(1)

[182]   IRC §§1367(a)(2)(B); 1366(a)(1)(A)

level. The subsequent liquidation will avoid tax at the shareholder (trust) level. However, the damage has already been done. Even though the corporation is owned by a tax-exempt entity, the tax will remain the obligation of the corporation. Accordingly, the net tax result of both alternatives may be roughly the same with the only difference caused by the marginal tax bracket applicable to the shareholder verses the corporation and the charitable contribution deduction generated to the trustor.

As an alternative, the S-corporation itself should consider becoming the trustor and income recipient.

E. Using Options to Transfer Incompatible Assets

In 1992, the IRS published a letter ruling that offered a unique solution to a traditional problem; how to liquidate an incompatible asset via a charitable remainder trust. An incompatible asset is one that will either terminate the tax-exempt status of a charitable remainder trust or that will adversely effect qualification of the asset itself. Examples of incompatible assets include stock in an S-corporation, stock in a professional corporation, and real property that generates unrelated business income or that may contain toxic waste.

The solution called for the creation and transfer to the trust of an assignable call option in place of the incompatible asset. The following case study illustrates how such a strategy operates.

The Facts

Mr. Smith owns unencumbered real property that he wants to sell to Mr. Jones for $2,000,000. Smith would like to sell the property via a charitable remainder unitrust and, in the process, avoid a $1,500,000 capital gain. The property is unencumbered; however, Smith has been advised that his property produces unrelated business income that will jeopardize the tax-exempt status of the trust.

An Exotic Solution - Creating a Charitable Option.

Step 1. Smith creates an assignable three-year option that allows the holder to purchase the property for $100,000.

Step 2. Smith transfers option to a charitable remainder trust.

Step 3. Trustee sells option to Jones for $1,900,000 (the difference between market value and exercise price).

Step 4. Jones exercises the option to buy paying Ping $100,000.

Result

Because the trust never owned the property , the unrelated business income produced by the property could not taint the trust. Smith will recognize capital gain allocable to the $100,000 received upon exercise of the option. Gain attributable to the remaining $1,900,000 will be recognized by the trust.[183]

1.   IRS Rules on Option with Unencumbered Property

In Letter Ruling 9240017, the IRS concluded that, under facts similar to those presented above, the trustee's contractual right to acquire a fee interest in the property for an amount below the fair market value of the property is an asset of the trust for purposes of meeting the requirements of IRC §664(d)(2). In addition, the trustee's contract right to acquire a fee interest in real property with substantial value ($2,000,000) for an amount substantially lower ($100,000) has substantial fair market value. This substantial fair market value must be included each year in determining the net fair market value of the trust's assets and the resulting unitrust amount payable to the income recipient.

Regarding the availability and sequencing of the trustor's charitable income tax deduction, the IRS's opinion was disappointing, but logical. Rev. Rul. 82-197[184] provides, an individual who grants an option on real property to charity is allowed a charitable deduction for the year in which the charitable organization exercises the option in an amount equal to the excess of fair market value of the property on the date the option is exercised over the exercise price.[185] The IRS concluded that the trustor is not entitled to a deduction for the remainder interest, either when the purported option is granted or when the charitable remainder trust sells it. The trustor is, however, entitled to a deduction for the remainder interest only if and when he sells the property to the trust or to another charitable organization exercising the option. The deduction is based on the spread between the fair market value and the exercise price ($1,900,000).

2.   IRS Rescinds Ltr. Rul. 9240017

One month after receiving a favorable ruling regarding the use of an option with unencumbered real property, the same taxpayer requested a new ruling on the use of the same technique with encumbered property. This triggered an unanticipated result. The Service responded by immediately issuing a ruling that rescinded the 1992 ruling stating only that it was reconsidering the issues raised in the original ruling.

3.   IRS Rules on Use of Options for Unencumbered and Encumbered Assets

In September of 1994, the Service responded to the second ruling request. There were two questions at issue. First, was the trust a qualified charitable remainder trust? Second,

---

[183]   The trust, however, will not pay any tax unless it has unrelated business taxable income.

[184]   Rev. Rul. 82-197, 1982-2 C.B. 72

[185]   Ltr. Ruls. 8714013; 8825069; 8826008

would the taxpayer (trustor) be treated as the owner of the trust, thereby causing the gain realized by the trust on the sale of the option to be recognized by the taxpayer?

With respect to the first issue, the Service first stated,

> To qualify as a charitable remainder trust within the meaning of section 664 of the Code and the regulations thereunder, a trust must be one with respect to which a deduction is allowable under one of the specified sections—section 170, 2055, 2106, or 2522. Further, the trust must be a charitable remainder trust in every respect and must meet the definition of and function exclusively as a charitable remainder trust from its creation. The requirements of being a charitable remainder trust in every respect and functioning exclusively as a charitable remainder trust from its creation cannot be met unless each transfer to the trust during its life qualifies for a charitable deduction under one of the applicable sections (IRC §§170, 2055, 2106, or 2522).

This being an inter vivos trust, the Service then focused its attention on the qualification for income tax deduction under section 170 and qualification for gift tax deduction under section 2522.

With respect to qualification for an income tax deduction, the IRS concluded,

> The transfer to a charitable organization of an option by the option writer is similar to the transfer of a note or pledge by the maker. In the noted situation there is a promise to pay money at a future date. In the pledge situation there is a promise to pay money or transfer other property, or to do both, at a future date. And in the option situation there is a promise to sell property at a future date. Although the promise may be enforceable, a promise to pay money or to sell property in the future is not itself a 'payment' for purposes of deducting a contribution under section 170 of the Code. Thus, the grant of the option to [the charitable organization] in this case is not a contribution for which a deduction is allowable under section 170.

With respect to the availability of the gift tax charitable deduction under section 2522, the IRS cited Rev. Rul. 80-186[186] in its primary argument, which concludes that the transfer of an option to purchase real property for a specified period is a completed gift under section 2511 of the Code on the date the option is transferred, if, under state law, the option is binding and enforceable on the date of the transfer. In the instant case, under local law, the purported option is not binding on a taxpayer when granted. Accordingly, the proposed transfer of the purported option to the trust would not be a completed gift on the date of transfer under section 25.2511-2(b), because taxpayer would not have made a binding offer on that date.

With respect to the second issue (i.e., whether the grantor would be treated as the owner of the trust and, accordingly, be taxable on the gain from the sale of the option), the IRS's conclusion was obvious. If the trust is not a qualified charitable remainder trust, it must be a grantor trust the income from which, including gain from the sale of trust assets, is taxable to the grantor.[187]

---

[186]   Rev. Rul. 80-186, 1980-2 C.B. 280

[187]   Ltr. Rul. 9501004

F. Employee Stock Options

An employee stock option is an offer made by a corporation to an employee to sell stock in the corporation to the employee at a bargain price for a stated period of time.

Employee stock options fall into two general categories: (a) nonstatutory options, and (b) statutory options.

1.   Nonstatutory Options

The taxation of nonstatutory (i.e., nonqualified) options is governed by IRC §83. Generally, such options are not taxable to an employee when granted unless they have a readily ascertainable value (i.e., they are actively traded on an established market) at the time of the grant. However, compensation will be realized when the option is exercised *or otherwise disposed of*.[188] The regulations further state that, "Section 83 applies to a transfer to or from a trust or under an annuity plan for the benefit of employees, independent contractors, or their beneficiaries (except as provided by exceptions none of which apply to charitable remainder trusts).[189]

Therefore, the transfer of an unexercised, nonqualified stock option to a charitable remainder trust will not protect the employee from realization of compensation.

2.   Statutory Options

Statutory options include incentive stock options, employee stock purchase plans, qualified stock options, and restricted stock options.[190]

Incentive stock options and employee stock purchase plans are described in IRC §§422 and 423. Qualified stock options and restricted stock options were repealed by OBRA '90 and occupied former IRC §§422 and 424.

Among other requirements, the employee (optionee) will not be taxed upon the *grant* or *exercise* of a statutory stock option provided the option:

- is in writing,

- is not transferable by the optionee (other than by will or by laws of descent and distribution), and

- is exercisable only during the lifetime of the optionee.[191]

These rules prevent the transfer of an unexercised statutory option to a charitable remainder trust without triggering realization of compensation.

---

[188]   Reg. §1.83-7

[189]   Reg. §1.83-8

[190]   IRC §421

[191]   Reg. §1.421-7(b); IRC §§422(b)(6); 423(b)(9)

3. Effect of Disqualifying Dispositions

Statutory options are subject to holding period requirements relating to disposition of exercised shares. An optionee will avoid recognition of income provided the stock is disposed of:

- in the case of incentive stock, employee stock purchase plan, or restricted stock option, after the latter of two years from the date of grant or one year from the date of exercise; or

- in the case of a qualified stock option, more than three years from the date of exercise.

The meaning of the term *disposition* includes a sale, exchange, *gift*, or any transfer of legal title (subject to exceptions, none of which include a transfer to charity or a charitable remainder trust).[192] Accordingly, the transfer of exercised shares to a charitable remainder trust prior to the expiration of the applicable holding period would most likely be deemed a disqualifying disposition within the meaning of IRC §421(b).

One taxpayer proposed to exercise an incentive stock option that had been held for longer than two years, then transfer the stock into a charitable remainder trust within one year after exercise. The Service ruled that such a transfer causes the taxpayer to recognize compensation in the amount equal to the difference between the exercise price and the fair market value of the stock on the date of exercise. The Service further stated that if the taxpayer transfers the stock after the one-year holding period, no compensation is recognized.[193]

4. Summary of Employee Stock Options and Charitable Remainder Trusts

To summarize, the transfer of a statutory or nonstatutory employee stock option to a charitable remainder trust will cause realization of compensation to the transferor. However, the transfer of stock received subject to the exercise of a *statutory* employee stock option (which has met applicable holding period requirements) to a charitable remainder trust will enable the transferor to avoid realization of compensation upon the subsequent disposition of the stock by the trustee.

G. Real Property

Real property can include raw land, residential property, commercial real estate, condominiums, agricultural property, or stock in a cooperative housing corporation.[194]

Real property adds complexity that requires thorough examination prior to transfer.

---

[192] Reg. §1.425-1(a)(8)(c)

[193] Ltr. Rul. 9308021

[194] Some states may treat stock in a cooperative as personal property rather than real property. Tax treatment can vary per IRC §216 (e.g., 80 percent test).

- Is the property marketable?

- Does the donor possess clear title?

- Can a qualified appraisal be obtained?

- Does the property produce income to meet its operating expenses?

- Who will manage the property?

- Does a disqualified person occupy or use the property?

- Does the property produce UBTI?

- Does the property have a potential toxic hazard?

- Is there a binding obligation to sell or is the property subject to a purchase option?

- Can the trust pass depreciation deductions through to income recipients?

- Can a donor retain mineral rights?

- Will the transfer trigger a revaluation for property tax purposes?

- Is the property debt-encumbered?

1.   Marketability

Real property is best transferred to a charitable remainder trust with the intention of an immediate sale. If, however, the only means of disposition available to the owner is to give the property away, it is probably not a suitable candidate for a charitable remainder trust. It has been said, a potential trustee should *always look a gift house in the mouth* and understand the donor's true intentions prior to accepting a transfer.

2.   Obtaining Clear Title and Transferability

Will a preliminary title report or opinion show the property to be free and clear of all encumbrances? Have the reconveyances been recorded? Do any covenants or other agreements made by the trustor prevent the transfer and sale of the property? Has the property just been declared a wetland or adversely zoned? Is the property in compliance with building codes and free of any material defects that would result in a delay of sale? Are there any easements on the land that might affect its future use or sale?

3. Obtaining a Qualified Appraisal

A qualified appraisal will not only establish a valuation for charitable deduction purposes, but will also help the trustee set the sales price. Accordingly, the appraisal is usually performed close to the transfer date.[195]

4. Potential Lack of Income

Does the property produce enough income to meet its operating expenses, property taxes, and the unitrust or annuity amount? If not, the trustor should consider a net income unitrust or, if a standard unitrust is selected, be willing to make additional cash contributions as long as necessary to make up any shortfalls.

5. Property Management and Maintenance

Who will maintain the property during the period in which the trust holds it? Can the trustor manage the property? Yes, provided compensation reflects market rates.[196]

6. Self-Dealing Considerations

If the property is occupied or used by a disqualified person (i.e., the trustor or a family member), are they prepared to vacate the property or terminate its use prior to transfer to the trust?[197]

7. Unrelated Business Taxable Income Considerations

The production of any unrelated business *taxable* income by the subject property will cause a charitable remainder trust to lose its tax-exempt status for the year in which such income is earned. If this occurs in the same year a highly appreciated asset (such as that frequently contributed to a charitable remainder trust) is sold by the trust, the gain on sale will be taxed.

Unrelated business income can arise from operations or due to the property being subject to indebtedness. For example, can a mobile home park be transferred to a charitable remainder trust? The answer is a definite maybe. Income from a recreational vehicle park that rents space on a daily use basis is most likely UBI. However, income from a mobile home park that rents or leases space on terms similar to the operation of apartment should arguably qualify for exception.

A thorough UBI *audit* should be performed on the operations of any subject property. For example, does the owner operate a convenience store or other retail operation on the property? Are utilities centrally metered with the owner billing such utilities to renters at a profit? What percentage of income is derived from the rental of personal property? Does the owner maintain a coin operated laundry or other enterprise?

---

[195]   See detailed discussion of appraisal requirements beginning on page 145.

[196]   IRC §4941(d)(2)(E)

[197]   Refer to page 157 for a complete discussion of the self-dealing rules.

▪ Environmental Hazards

According to the Comprehensive Environmental Response, Compensation and Liability Act (CERCLA), an owner of property within the boundaries of a "Superfund" site may be held liable for the costs of cleaning up the site. State law may also apply.

As originally drafted, the liability was joint and several. Thus, a charitable organization or fiduciary accepting property could be subject to liability for the entire cost of cleanup even though they played no role in contaminating the property. The remediation expense frequently exceeded the value of the contributed property.

In 1996, Congress enacted the Asset Conservation, Lender Liability, and Deposit Insurance Protection Act. The Act amended the fiduciary liability rules under CERCLA to limit liability to the property itself and protect fiduciaries against personal liability. However, the safe harbor rule does not limit the liability of a fiduciary whose negligence causes or contributes to a release or threatened release.

When even a remote possibility of an environmental hazard exists, a potential trustee should require an environmental audit prior to accepting the property. A *Phase 1* review researches prior owners and uses of the property. If the findings are suspect, a *Phase 2* review includes physical inspection and core sampling.

9. Binding Obligation to Sell

Gain on the sale of an appreciated asset is not considered attributable to the trustor so long as the asset is given away before sale. However, this rule is inapplicable if the trustor retains direct or indirect control over the asset or there is an express or implied prearranged obligation on the part of the trustee to sell the property. In such case, the trustor may be taxed on the subsequent sale on one of three theories.[198]

Most practitioners agree that, in the case of real property, the obligation to sell arises upon the opening of a sale escrow.[199]

10. Property Subject to a Purchase Option

The IRS has ruled privately that, in the case of property transferred to a charitable remainder unitrust subject to a lease with a purchase option at fair market value, the exercise of such option would not defeat the interest of charity. The effect of the transaction would be to substitute one interest for another of equal value.

The Service also noted that, the lease and option to purchase are factors to be considered in arriving at the fair market value of the property (for purposes of determining the charitable contribution deduction and establishing the annuity or unitrust amount).[200]

---

[198] Reg. §1.664-1(a)(3); Rev. Rul. 60-370 1960-2 C.B. 203

[199] See the discussion on selling transferred assets beginning on page 147.

[200] Ltr. Rul. 8312005

11. Depreciation Pass-Through

Charitable remainder trusts can invest in depreciable property. Depreciation deductions are generally apportioned between income recipient and trustee on the basis of trust income allocable to each, unless the governing instrument (or local law) requires or permits the trustee to maintain a reserve for depreciation. In the latter case, the deduction is allocated to the trustee to the extent of the depreciation reserve with any excess being apportioned between income recipient and trustee according to trust income allocable to each.[201]

The Service has ruled that a depreciation reserve is not required for a standard unitrust (and presumably an annuity trust), whereas one is required for a net income unitrust.[202]

12. Property with Retained Mineral Rights

May an individual transfer property to charity (or a charitable remainder trust) while retaining the right to minerals *in place*? Rev. Rul. 76-331 says no.[203] Retaining such a right was compared to the retention of voting rights on stock. Therefore, the transfer was deemed a nonqualified gift of a partial interest.[204]

13. Property Tax Considerations

Will transferring the title to real property to a charitable remainder trust trigger a revaluation for property tax purposes? The answer depends on the county in which the property is situated. Refer to local law.

H. Property Subject to Indebtedness

The transfer of debt-encumbered property to a charitable remainder trust raises more questions than any other issue. If there was ever a need for the Service to provide clear guidance via a Revenue Ruling, this is it. In the absence of such authority, however, two letter rulings can be used as guides to the issues.

In Letter Ruling 9533014, an individual owned a 70 percent interest in a partnership. The sole asset of the partnership was an apartment building that was subject to nonrecourse mortgage debt. The debt was incurred in 1970 and refinanced (with no increase in the amount of original debt) in 1993. All income from the partnership qualified as rents from real property, excluded from treatment as unrelated business income.[205] None of the partners had any personal liability with respect to the partnership debt. Each partner would, however, remain liable for any future cash calls by the partnership.

The taxpayer proposed to transfer between 50 percent and 100 percent of his partnership interest to a charitable remainder unitrust, after which, he would indemnify and hold the trust

---

[201] Reg. §1.167(h)-1(b)

[202] See also Ltr. Ruls. 8931019 and 8931020.

[203] Rev. Rul. 76-331, 1976-2 C.B. 52

[204] See discussion regarding royalty interests beginning on page 132.

[205] IRC §513(b)(3)

harmless from and against all expenses, losses, payments, or obligations that might arise from the partnership.

The taxpayer also provided management services, through a wholly-owned company, on behalf of the property for a fee equal to 2 percent of gross revenues. The donor agreed to waive any management fees due from the trust.

The taxpayer proposed the following:

- The proposed gift will not violate the regulations regarding restrictions on investments.

- The gift will not violate the prohibition against other payments from a charitable remainder trust.

- The transfer will not constitute a prohibited act of self-dealing.

- The trust's distributive share of income or sale from the partnership will not be unrelated debt-financed income for a period of ten years following the date of the gift.

- Upon completion of the gift, continued payment of reasonable management fees by the partnership to the donor's management company (less the trust's portion of the fees) will not constitute self-dealing.

1.   Restrictions on Investments
The regulations provide that a trust is not a charitable remainder trust if it includes a provision that restricts the trustee from investing the trust assets in a manner which could result in the annual realization of a reasonable amount of income or gain from the sale or disposition of assets. [206] The Service found no provision that violated the rule.

2.   Prohibitions against Other Payments
The regulations provide in part that, (a) no amount other than the unitrust amount may be paid to or for the use of any person other than an organization described in section 170(c); (b) an amount is not paid to or for the use of any person other than an organization described in section 170(c) if the amount is transferred for full and adequate consideration; and (c) the trust may not be subject to a power to invade, alter, amend, or revoke for the beneficial use of a person other than an organization described in section 170(c). [207]

Although it is not specifically stated in the ruling, it is implied that the partnership (as compared to the trustor or trustee) will make the payments on the indebtedness and that the partners will remain personally responsible for any cash calls. The Service concluded

[206]   Reg. §1.664-1(a)(3)
[207]   Reg. §1.664-3(a)(4)

that, because the taxpayer agreed to remain solely liable for any obligation arising under the partnership for which the trust would otherwise be liable, the proposed gift would not violate the prohibition against other payments.

3. Self-Dealing

The Code provides that a transfer of real or personal property by a disqualified person to a private foundation shall be treated as a sale or exchange if (a) the property is subject to a mortgage or similar lien which the private foundation assumes, or (b) it is subject to a mortgage or similar lien which a disqualified person placed on the property within the 10-year period ending on the date of transfer (to the trust).[208]

A charitable remainder trust is treated as a private foundation for purposes of the rules against self-dealing.[209] As a substantial contributor and creator of the trust, the donor is a disqualified person with respect to the trust.[210] The regulations provide, however, that the donor's status as a substantial contributor is disregarded in determining whether the transfer to the charitable remainder trust is self-dealing, because the donor's stature as a substantial contributor arises only as a result of the transfer.[211] In this case, the donor's status as a disqualified person arises not as a result of making the gift but, rather, out of the donor's decision to serve as trustee.

According to the Service, the threshold question was whether the partnership interest was transferred *subject to* the mortgage. Without deciding that question, the Service found that the transfer was not treatable as a sale or exchange; that the charitable remainder trust would not assume the mortgage; and that no disqualified person placed the mortgage on the property within 10-years of the gift. In making the latter decision, the Service disregarded the refinancing because it did not increase the amount of the outstanding debt.[212]

4. Acquisition Indebtedness

If the trustee of a charitable remainder trust accepts property subject to an indebtedness or places indebtedness on the property after its contribution to the trust, the trust will have acquisition indebtedness. Therefore, income from the property and gain upon sale will be included within the computation of unrelated business *taxable* income.

When a charitable remainder trust acquires mortgaged property by gift, the debt secured by the mortgage will not be treated as acquisition indebtedness during the 10 years following the date of acquisition as long as:

---

[208] IRC §4941(d)(2)(A)

[209] IRC §4947(a)(2)

[210] IRC §§507(d)(2)(A); 4946(a)(1) and 4946(b)

[211] Reg. §53.4941(d)-1(a)

[212] Reg. §1.514(c)-1(c)

- the mortgage was placed on the property more than five years prior to the gift, and

- the property was held by the donor for more than five years prior to the gift.

However, this exception is inapplicable if the trust assumes any part of the debt secured by the mortgage.[213] The trust must, therefore, take property subject to the indebtedness in order for the exception to apply.

It is important to distinguish the agreements between the original obligor on the note (original borrower) and a transferee who assumes the debt, and any rights that a lender may have against a borrower.

A transferee may acquire property by taking it *subject to* an existing indebtedness, in which case such transferee has no obligation either to the lender or to the transferor (original borrower). Alternatively, the transferee may assume the indebtedness by contractually agreeing to pay the obligation and relieving the transferor of any responsibility or risk. Note, however, that unless the lender consents to this and releases the original borrower from liability, such assumption is merely an agreement between transferor and transferee.

Some obligations are deemed *recourse* debts and others are classified as *nonrecourse* debts. In the case of recourse indebtedness, the borrower remains personally liable for any amount by which the debt remains unpaid after foreclosure and sale of the property. In the case of nonrecourse indebtedness, a lender's ability to recover the loan amount is limited to the property itself. Laws vary by state. In California, for example, deficiency judgments against borrowers (i.e., personal liability) are prohibited under a purchase money deed of trust or mortgage for a personal residence or four-unit or less structure in which the borrower resides. Commercial properties may be subject to recourse debts, however.

In Letter Ruling 9533014, the Service ruled that under Rev. Rul. 74-197, a charitable remainder trust's interest in a partnership than incurs acquisition indebtedness is debt-financed property. Therefore, a portion of the trust's share of the net income derived by the partnership from the rental or sale of property is UBTI, unless an exception applies.[214] In this case, it did. Because the mortgage was placed on the property more than five years prior to the gift, and the property was held by the trustor for more than five years prior to the gift, the debt secured by the mortgage will not be treated as acquisition indebtedness during the 10-years following the date of the gift.

5. Bargain Sale and Related Issues

In the present ruling, the Service noted other consequences of the transaction. These included the application of the bargain sale rules, determination of the charitable contribution deduction, and determination of the unitrust amount.

---

[213]   IRC §514(c)(2)(B)

[214]   Rev. Rul. 74-197, 1974-1 C.B. 143

If property subject to indebtedness is transferred to *charity*, the donor is treated as having been relieved of the indebtedness under the bargain sale rules of IRC §1011(b). In such case, the amount of indebtedness is treated as an amount realized by the donor, even though the transferee does not agree to assume or pay the indebtedness.[215]

Applying this rule to the charitable remainder trust, the Service concluded that the adjusted basis in contributed property subject to nonrecourse indebtedness is allocated to the indebtedness in the same ratio the basis bears to the entire property. The gain attributable to the indebtedness is recognized by the trustor.[216] If any portion of the gain would have been treated as ordinary income under section 751 of the Code (because of unrealized receivables of substantially appreciated inventory items), such gain must also be apportioned to the amount recognized.[217]

In determining whether a charitable contribution deduction is allowable, the Service stated that if section 751 applies, the amount of the charitable contribution deduction might be reduced under section 170(e)(5). Finally, although the liability was nonrecourse, the fair market value of the property must be reduced by the liability in determining the annual unitrust amount.

The Service then made an interesting qualifying statement. It said, "Otherwise, we express no opinion as to the tax consequences of the above-described transaction under the cited provisions of the Code or under any other provisions of the Code. Specifically, no opinion is expressed or implied concerning whether the trust qualifies as a charitable remainder trust under the Code." The Service then offered to provide the taxpayer with additional information relating to the issues under sections 170, 664, 751, and 1011 of the Code. Had the taxpayer asked all of the relevant questions? Is this really a positive ruling?

6.   Grantor Trust Rules

The grantor trust rules of sections 671 through 677 of the Code contain provisions that tax the income of a trust to the grantor or another person even though he or she may not be a beneficiary. Sections 673 through 677 define the circumstances under which income is taxed to a grantor. These circumstances are in general as follows:

- The grantor has retained a reversionary interest in the trust, within specified time limits (section 673).

- The grantor or a nonadverse party has certain powers over the beneficial interests under the trust (section 674).

- Certain administrative powers over the trust exist under which the grantor can, or does, benefit (section 675).

---

[215]   IRC §1011(b); Reg. §1.1011-2(a)(3)

[216]   Ltr. Rul. 9533014

[217]   Presumably, the recapture rules of IRC §§1245 and 1250 would also apply.

- The grantor or a nonadverse party has the power to revoke the trust or return the trust to the grantor (section 676).

- The grantor or a nonadverse party has the power to distribute income to or for the benefit of the grantor or the grantor's spouse (section 677).

Regulation §1.671-1(d) provides that, the provisions of Subpart E (the grantor trust rules) are not applicable with respect to a pooled income fund as defined in paragraph (5) of section 642(c) and the regulations thereunder, a charitable remainder annuity trust as defined in paragraph (1) section 664(d), or a charitable remainder unitrust as described in paragraph (2) of section 664(d). At first glance, one might conclude that all charitable remainder trusts are exempt from the grantor trust rules. This is not the case, however, if the trust contains any provision that would otherwise cause the grantor to be treated as the owner of the trust.

The regulations describe several additional situations that will cause the grantor to realize income. They include:

- an assignment of future income, whether or not the assignment is in trust;

- the rules applicable to family partnerships, even though the partnership may be held in trust;

- the right of a grantor to deductions for payments to a trust under a transfer and leaseback arrangement; and

- the income of a trust when it is used to discharge a legal obligation of a grantor.

The following discussion illustrates the application of the fourth situation to the contribution of debt-encumbered property to a charitable remainder trust.

In Letter Ruling 9015049, a taxpayer proposed to fund a charitable remainder unitrust with income-producing real property that was encumbered by a mortgage liability for which the taxpayer was to remain personally liable following transfer. Further, the trust would make the mortgage payments.

The Service ruled that under such circumstances the trust would be subject to Reg. §1.677(a)-1(d) which provides that a trustor is, in general, treated as the owner of a portion of a trust whose income is, or in the discretion of the trustor or a non-adverse party or both, may be applied in discharge of a legal obligation of the trustor. Accordingly, the taxpayer will be treated as owner of the entire trust under IRC §677. Therefore, the trust is not a charitable remainder trust under IRC §664. The IRS did rule beyond this issue.

It is interesting to note that in Letter Ruling 9533014 there is no mention of application of the grantor trust rules to the transaction. Perhaps the differentiating fact (and explanation of the Service's silence) between the rulings is the presence of nonrecourse (as opposed to recourse) financing.[218] What seems to be an obvious missed opportunity on the part of the Service to apply the grantor trust rules however is the trustor's intent to serve as the trustee for a hard-to-value asset (i.e., a partnership interest).[219]

7. Possible Solutions to Debt-Encumbrance Problems

a. Retire Debt Prior to Transfer

Although paying off the debt is the *cleanest* alternative, many people cannot afford this option. As an alternative, it may be possible, depending on the lender, to re-hypothecate the debt to other property in the trustor's portfolio.

b. Short-Term Swing Loan

Suppose Mr. Brown owns a commercial building worth $1,000,000 with an adjusted basis of $200,000. In addition the property is encumbered by a $200,000 mortgage that is one year old. Brown would like to sell the property via a charitable remainder trust. However, transferring the property subject to a fresh loan will cause the trust to have acquisition indebtedness. In addition, Brown owns a $500,000 bungalow that is free-and-clear.

Step 1. As an alternative, Brown will borrow $200,000, secured by his bungalow.

Step 2. Brown pays off the loan on the building (and records the reconveyance).

Step 3. Brown transfers an undivided fractional interest of 80 percent of the building to a charitable remainder unitrust.

Step 4. Brown and the trustee each sell their respective interests to a third party buyer.

Step 5. Brown uses his $200,000 of sales proceeds to pay off the loan against his bungalow.

To summarize, Brown will incur a capital gain of $180,000 on the sale of his retained interest ($200,000 - $20,000 allocable basis). However, the gain can be partially offset by the charitable contribution deduction.

---

218   It may also be distinguishable that the 1990 ruling the was issued by the Pass-Throughs and Special Industries Branch of the Internal Revenue Service while the 1995 ruling was issued by the Exempt Organizations Technical Branch. Differences of opinion or interpretation are not the exclusive domain of the private sector.

219   See the discussion of hard-to-value assets on page 153.

> **Caution:** IRS has suggested that a transfer of an undivided fractional interest in property to a charitable remainder trust with a retained interest by the trustor (a disqualified person) may constitute a prohibited act of self-dealing.[220] Until the Service reverses its stand on the self-dealing issue surrounding gifts of fractional interests, this technique may not be advisable. *See Chapter 7 - Self-Dealing Rules - for a detailed discussion.*

c. Charity Purchases a Fractional Interest in Property Equal to Debt and Joins in Sale

In the previous example, the charitable remainderman might have participated as the lender. Such transactions are usually structured *at arms length* with an independent trustee. As an alternative, the trustor can avoid a potential self-dealing problem by having the charity purchase an undivided fractional interest in the property from the trustor in an amount equal to or greater than the indebtedness. The sale proceeds are used to retire the indebtedness, and then the free-and-clear remaining interest is transferred to the charitable remainder trust. The trustor and charity then join in the sale of their respective interests.

Because the seller is transferring his *entire* interest in the property, no self-dealing issue should be raised. Gain recognized on the taxable sale to the charity can be mitigated by the charitable contribution deduction generated upon transfer of the retained interest to the trust.

d. Trustor Holds Trustee Harmless for Debt Obligation

The issues of bargain sale, unrelated debt-financed income, and grantor trust implications all assume the trustor is relieved of the mortgage obligation. Several legal commentators have speculated that, if the trustor indemnifies the trustee against liability for the debt, there is no such relief of indebtedness.

However, because the lender would most likely not reduce its security by releasing any portion of the property transferred to the trust, the trustor would retain an undivided fractional interest in the property. When the property is ultimately sold, the trustor will have the proceeds necessary to retire the debt.

> **Comment:** Again, the potential self-dealing problem may discourage use of this technique. The problem is, proceeds paid on the sale of the property owned by the trust will not relieve the trustor of the personal liability unless the trustor pays off the debt outside the trust.

I. Intangible Assets

Certain intangible personal property such as copyrights, royalty interests, patents, oil and gas interests, installment obligations, life insurance contracts, and partnership interests are often considered for transfer to charitable remainder trusts.

---

[220]   Ltr. Rul. 9114025

1. Copyrights

A copyright owned by an individual whose personal efforts created the copyrighted work (or given to the individual by the work's creator) is considered ordinary income property.[221] Therefore, any charitable deduction must be based on the cost basis in the work.

Further, a transfer of a copyright without the underlying tangible asset (e.g., an original artwork) constitutes a gift of other than the donor's entire interest in property and, therefore, is not deductible.[222] However, an income tax deduction for gift of a copyright where the tangible asset had little intrinsic value (i.e., a book with a large circulation) has been allowed.[223]

2. Royalty Interests

A royalty is defined in part as "amounts received for the privilege of using patents, copyrights, secret processes and formulas, goodwill, trademarks, trade brands, franchises, and other like property."[224]

The transfer of a royalty interest to a charitable remainder trust without the underlying property would, most likely, be considered an *assignment of income*. In such case, the trustor would remain liable for paying the tax on such income.[225]

If the royalty interest is transferred along with the property, the property might qualify as a capital asset (subject to related use rules). The royalty interest will, however, be considered ordinary income property for which a deduction is limited to the lesser of fair market value and its adjusted cost basis.

Finally, IRC §512(b)(2) provides that one of the modifications to be taken into account in determining unrelated business taxable income is "all royalties (including overriding royalties and net profits income) whether measured by production or by gross or taxable income from the property, and all deductions directly connected with all such income." These items are excluded in determining UBTI; however, Reg. §1.512(b)-1 cautions that all the facts and circumstances of each case must be examined to determine whether a particular item of income falls within any of the modifications provided in IRC §512(b).

a. Royalties from Working Mineral Interests

A working or *operating* interest is defined as an interest in oil and gas *in place* that is burdened with the cost of development and operation of the property.

---

[221] IRC §1221(3)

[222] Reg. §1.170A-7(b)(1)

[223] Ltr. Rul. 7944030

[224] GCM 38083

[225] Lucas v. Earl (1930), 281 U.S. 11, 8 AFTR 10287

Where an individual owns subsurface minerals *in place* and grants the right to develop those minerals to an operator in exchange for a lease bonus and a percentage of all minerals found, such income is generally considered a *non-operating* interest. Income from a non-operating interest is characterized as royalty income provided the owner does not participate in exploration, completion, or operating costs.[226]

If the owner of the non-operating interest transfers a *royalty*, *overriding royalty* interest, or *net profits interest* to a charitable remainder trust, such interests are considered interests in real property and are treated, for income tax deduction purposes, as long-term capital gain property (provided such interests are held for at least one-year), unless the interest is used by the trustor in a trade or business. In the latter case, the property is characterized under IRC §1231 and is subject to the reduction rules applicable to ordinary income property.[227] Recapture of intangible drilling costs is not applicable to non-operating interests and, therefore, has no effect on the charitable deduction.[228]

b. Carved Out Production Payments

An operator may seek outside financial resources for exploration, development, and operating expenses by *carving out* a portion of the production payments to an investor.[229] Such amounts are considered as a mortgage on the property.[230] Thus, if a charitable remainder trust is given an interest in *carved out* production payments, such payments will most likely be characterized as debt-financed income.[231]

c. Overriding Royalties or Net Profits Interest Contributed by an Operator

The transfer of an overriding royalty interest or net profits interest by the owner of an *operating* interest under an oil and gas lease to charity is not entitled to charitable contribution deduction under IRC §170(a).

Reason: The contributed interest is less than the taxpayer's entire interest within the meaning of IRC §170(f)(3) and is not an undivided portion of the taxpayer's entire interest.[232]

---

[226] IRC §614

[227] Rev. Rul. 73-428, 1973-2 C.B. 303

[228] IRC §1254

[229] Reg. §1.636-3(a)

[230] IRC §636(a)

[231] IRC §514

[232] Rev. Rul. 88-37, 1988-1 C.B. 97

3.   Patents

A transfer of *all substantial rights* to a patent is considered a transfer of a capital asset. Therefore, if the patent is held by the trustor for more than one-year prior to transfer, the trustor's charitable income tax deduction will be based on fair market value.

In order for the transfer to avoid violating the partial interest rules, the trustor must transfer "all substantial rights to the patent" (or an undivided fractional interest in the same) as described in Reg. §1.1235-2(b).

Income generated by a patent should be characterized as royalty income and thereby excepted from characterization as unrelated business income.[233]

4.   Installment Obligations

The transfer of an installment obligation (such as a note secured by a deed of trust or mortgage carried by the seller of real property) to a charitable remainder trust is considered a taxable disposition resulting in acceleration of all gain to the trustor. The charitable deduction is based on fair market value.[234]

Even though the transfer of an installment obligation to a charitable remainder trust is considered a taxable disposition under IRC §453B, the creation by the trustee of a note within the trust causes no adverse tax consequences. Further, the trust will not have debt-financed income because it is serving as lender rather than borrower.

There are several concerns regarding a trustee carrying paper. The first is security. If the buyer defaults, is the trustee prepared to foreclose and can the trust and income recipients withstand the loss of income? The second concern is valuation. Will the note be discounted and will such discount effect the annual unitrust amount? Another concern is that, in the event of a foreclosure, a lender/trustee may face CERCLA liability, may have to service a prior lien or may receive UBTI from the property.

5.   Life Insurance Contracts

The sale of a cash value life insurance contract results in the seller realizing ordinary income to the extent the sales price exceeds the owner's basis in the contract.[235] Therefore, when an insurance contract is transferred to a charitable remainder trust, the trustor's deduction is based on the lesser of fair market value and adjusted cost basis under the reduction rules applicable to ordinary income property. The trustor's basis in the contract is equal to the aggregate premiums paid, less dividends paid and outstanding policy loans. For non-modified endowment contracts, partial withdrawals from cash value are considered made on a first-in-first-out (FIFO) basis. Therefore, partial withdrawals are considered made first from basis. For modified endowment contracts (and deferred annuity contracts), withdrawals are considered made on a last-in-first-out basis (LIFO).

---

[233]   GCM 38083

[234]   IRC §453B(a); Rev. Rul. 55-157, 1955-1 C.B. 293

[235]   Comm. v. Phillips (4 Cir; 1960), 275 F.2nd 33,5 AFTR 2d 855

Therefore, a reduction in basis does not occur until all gain in the contract has first been withdrawn.

Caution: The transfer of an insurance contract with outstanding policy loans may cause the trust to have "debt-financed income" under IRC §514(c)(1)(A).

If the policy is considered paid-up, the fair market value is based on the single premium amount it would cost for a comparable policy having an equal death benefit for an individual the same age as the insured.[236] If the cash surrender value of the contributed policy exceeds the policy's replacement cost, the trustor could arguably use the interpolated terminal reserve.[237]

If the policy requires additional premiums, the fair market value is the policy's interpolated terminal reserve on the date of transfer, adjusted for the proportionate value of premiums paid that cover the period of time extending beyond the date of the gift.[238]

a. Life Insurance Contract as a Trust Investment

In 1979, the Service approved the funding of a charitable remainder unitrust with life insurance. In that ruling, a husband transferred a life insurance policy on his life to a unitrust that named his wife as the sole life income recipient. The husband then made premium payments directly to the insurance company. The trust was deemed a qualified trust to which contributions were deductible (provided the recipient trust could not be changed at the option of the insured). Further, each additional premium payment was considered an additional contribution to the trust for which the husband was allowed a deduction equal to the present value of the remainder interest.[239]

In Letter Ruling 8745013, an individual proposed to transfer appreciated non-income producing real property to a charitable remainder unitrust. The trustee intended to sell the property and use the proceeds to buy life insurance on the lives of the income recipients.

Ruled: If the trustee borrows from an insurance policy and invests proceeds to create income, acquisition indebtedness under IRC §514(c)(1)(A) will exist. The transaction will not violate Reg. §§1.664-1(a)(3) and 1.664-3(a)(4) under specified conditions. A life insurance contract not considered a jeopardizing investment under IRC §4944 under specified conditions.

---

[236]   Reg. §25.2512-6(a), Example 3

[237]   Rev. Rul. 78-137, 1978-1 C.B. 280

[238]   Reg. §25.2512-6(a); Rev. Rul. 59-195, 1959-1 C.B. 18

[239]   Ltr. Rul. 7928014

b. Insurable Interest Concerns

In 1991, the IRS ruled that a gift of a newly issued life insurance policy to charity and gifts of future premium payments were not deductible for income tax and gift tax purposes.

Reason: Under local law (New York), the charity did not have an insurable interest. Therefore, the executor of the estate could maintain an action to recover the death benefit. Since the possibility of the charity's rights in the policy being divested was not so remote as to be negligible, the transfer would be considered a nonqualified gift of a partial interest.[240]

New York and many other states subsequently amended the definition of *insurable interest* to accommodate charitable gifts of life insurance (Maryland's amendment even made specific mention of charitable remainder trusts and pooled income funds). The ruling, however, cast a cloud of doubt over the use of life insurance as an investment vehicle within charitable remainder unitrusts. In the case of a two-life trust with one of the income recipients being insured (or both via separate policies), the possibility that the proceeds will be used to provide benefits to a noncharitable survivor income recipient may be distinguishable. Refer to local law.

c. Grantor Trust Concerns

In a letter ruling, a trustor proposes to create charitable remainder trust payable for the life of the trustor and his wife. Upon creating the trust, the trustor will transfer to the trust a policy of insurance on his life, together with other assets. The trustor will assign ownership of the policy to the trustee, and the trustee will designate the trust as the beneficiary of the policy. The trustor will serve as trustee.

The governing instrument also provides that the unitrust amount will be the lesser of the trust's income, as defined in section 643(b) of the Code, and 5 percent of the net fair market value of the trust's assets valued annually. The unitrust amount for any year will include any amount of the trust's income in excess of the amount required to be distributed under the general rule above to the extent the aggregate amounts paid in prior years was less than the aggregate amounts computed as 5 percent of the net fair market value of the trust's assets on the valuation dates.

The governing instrument will provide that premiums on the insurance will be charged to the trust's principal account. Any proceeds paid on the insurance upon the death of the insured, any dividends paid on the insurance during the life of the insured, any withdrawals made from the insurance during the life of the insured, and any amount paid on the surrender of the insurance during the life of the insured will be credited to the trust's principal account. No part of any such receipt shall be credited to the trust's income account notwithstanding any statute, rule, or convention to the contrary. In addition, local (state) law has no statutory provision concerning

---

[240]   Ltr. Rul. 9110016

underproductive property that would allocate to income a portion of the proceeds received from the sale or other disposition of underproductive assets.

Rulings were requested on (a) whether the existence or exercise of the trustee's power to pay annual premiums on an insurance policy on the trustor's life causes the trustor to be treated as the owner of all or any portion of the trust under section 677(a)(3), and (b) whether the existence or exercise of such power disqualifies the trust as a charitable remainder unitrust under section 664.

Section 677(a)(3) of the Code provides that the grantor is treated as the owner of any portion of a trust whose income, without the approval or consent of any adverse party, is or in the discretion of the grantor or a nonadverse party, or both, may be, applied to the payment of premiums on policies of insurance on the life of the grantor or the grantor's spouse (except policies of insurance irrevocably payable for a purpose specified in section 170(c), relating to definition of charitable contributions).

In the present situation, any amount received by the trust with respect to insurance policies on the trustor's life, whether received during the trustor's life or upon his death, is allocated to the trust's principal, and not to income. Because the trust is a net income unitrust within the meaning of section 664(d)(3) of the Code and section 1.664-3(a)(1)(i)(b) of the regulations, the unitrust amount payable to the noncharitable recipients is limited to the trust's income (as defined in section 643(b)) if such income is less than the fixed percentage of net value of the trust's assets. Because amounts received on account of insurance policies on the trustor's life will not be allocated to income under the terms of the governing instrument, these amounts will not be used in computing the amount of the trust's income and thereby will not be used in determining the income limitation on the unitrust amount payable to the noncharitable recipients. Rather, amounts received on account of insurance policies on the life of the trustor will be allocated to principal and will become part of the remainder that is payable to qualified charitable organizations.

The Service concluded that under these circumstances the insurance policy on the trustor's life is irrevocably payable for a charitable purpose within the meaning of the parenthetical of section 677(a)(3) of the Code. Because the policy is so payable, the existence or exercise of the trustee's power to pay annual premiums on the insurance policy on the trustor's life does not cause the trustor to be treated as the owner of all or any portion of the trust under section 677(a)(3) of the Code.[241]

6.   Tax Deferred Annuity Contracts

The transfer of an existing tax deferred annuity contract to a charitable remainder trust can present special tax problems for the donor. Because of changes in the annuity rules made in 1987, a distinction is made between contracts issued before and after April 22, 1987.[242]

---

[241]   Ltr. Rul. 9227017

[242]   The use of a tax deferred annuity contract as a trust investment vehicle is discussed beginning on page 207.

a. Annuity Contracts Issued before April 22, 19 7

The transfer of a tax deferred annuity contract that was issued prior to April 22, 1987 to a charitable remainder trust will cause the donor to recognize income in the year in which the trust receives proceeds from the contract. The amount of income recognized is equal to the excess of the value of the contract over its basis.

In Friedman v. Commissioner[243], the taxpayer argued that a gift of four endowment life insurance policies to charity constituted a gift of appreciated property. As such, the donor, upon contribution, would not recognize any gain in the contract. The Court, however, characterized the appreciation element as "earned but unpaid income" rather than gain. Therefore, the donor's contribution was tantamount to an anticipatory assignment of income. Because the donor could have received the income by surrendering the policies, the court concluded that the donor would recognize income in the year in which the recipient charity actually received the policy proceeds. While the case law cites a lump-sum payment, periodic payments received by charity should have no effect on this outcome.

In addition to recognition of income, the timing of the recognition presents a potential charitable deduction tax trap for the donor. Normally, when ordinary income property is transferred to charity, the donor's income tax deduction is limited to the lesser of fair market value and adjusted cost basis.[244] However, this rule does not apply when, by reason of the transfer of the contributed property, ordinary income or capital gain is recognized by the donor *in the same year in which the contribution is made.*[245] When this exception is applied, the deduction is based on the full fair market value of the contract.

In effect, if a charity (or charitable remainder trust) does not surrender a pre-April 22, 1987 annuity contract in the same year as it is received, the donor's deduction will be limited to the lesser of fair market value and adjusted cost basis. In addition, the donor will recognize income in any tax year in which the charity (or charitable remainder trust) receives contract proceeds.

b. Annuity Contracts Issued after April 22, 19 7

If an individual who holds an annuity contract that was issued after April 22, 1987 transfers it without full and adequate consideration, the individual is treated as having received an amount equal to the excess of the cash surrender value, at the time of transfer, divided by the investment in the contract at that time.[246] Income is recognized by the trustor in the same year as the transfer regardless of when the beneficiary (charity or charitable remainder trust) receives proceeds from the contract.

---

[243]   Friedman v. Commissioner, 41 T.C. 428 (1963), aff'd 346 F.2d 506 (6th Cir. 1965)

[244]   IRC §170(e); Reg. §1.170A-4(a)(1)

[245]   Reg. §1.170A-4(a)(3)

[246]   IRC §72(e)(4)(C)

Because the recognition of income is linked to the year of transfer, a trustor's charitable contribution income tax deduction is based on the full fair market value of the contract.[247]

In summary, the transfer of an existing deferred annuity contract to a charitable remainder trust may be a poor choice regardless of when the contract was issued. If the contract is appreciated, the trustor will recognize all gain in the contract while receiving a charitable income tax deduction based only on the present value of contract's fair market value or basis. Thus, the trustor may recognize phantom income that is not entirely offset by the charitable deduction.

7. Partnership Interests

Partnership interests are often poor candidates for transfer to a charitable remainder trust because the underlying enterprise may conduct activities that could adversely impact both trustor and trust.

a. Tax Treatment of Transfer of Partnership Interest

A partnership interest is deemed a capital asset when sold or exchanged and resulting in capital gain or loss to the partner. However, any unrealized receivables and substantially appreciated inventory of the partnership are considered ordinary income property under IRC §751. Therefore, for purposes of determining a trustor's charitable contribution deduction, the fair market value of the partnership interest must be reduced by the gain attributable to any section 751 property.

b. Partnership Installment Obligations

The transfer to a charitable remainder trust of a partnership interest that owns an installment obligation accelerates any gain attributable to the installment obligation to the trustor. The amount recognized is the partner's share of the fair market value of the obligation over his or her share of the partnership's basis in the obligation. Like other transfers of installment obligations, the trustor's deduction is based on the fair market value of the obligation without reduction.

c. Debt-Encumbered Property Owned by Partnership

Debt on partnership assets is treated as a liability of the owner of the property.[248] Accordingly, the transfer of a partner's interest to a charitable remainder trust is considered a relief of such indebtedness to the partner. Such transfers expose the trustor and trust to all of the issues of debt encumbered property as discussed previously.[249]

---

[247]   Reg. §1.170A-4(a)(3)

[248]   IRC §752

[249]   Ltr. Rul. 9533014

d. Unrelated Business Income Generated by Partnership

If the partnership is engaged in an unrelated trade or business, gross income and deductions from such trade or business will be included within the trust's computation of unrelated business taxable income.[250] See Ltr. Rul. 7943062 regarding acquisition indebtedness on partnership property transferred to a charitable remainder trust.[251]

e. Publicly Traded (Master Limited) Partnerships

Whether a publicly traded or master limited partnership is suitable for transfer to or investment in a charitable remainder trust depends on whether the partnership produces unrelated business taxable income under IRC §512(c). This was not always the case, however. The Omnibus Budget Reconciliation Act of 1987 amended §512(c) by adding §512(c)(2). It provided that any organization's share (whether distributed or not distributed) of the gross income of a publicly traded partnership (as defined in section 469(k)(2)) acquired after December 17, 1987 is treated as income derived from an unrelated trade or business. The section further provided that an organization's share of partnership deductions are allowed in computing unrelated business taxable income.[252] Section 512(c)(2) was short-lived, however. The Omnibus Budget Reconciliation Act of 1993 repealed it for partnership years beginning on or after December 17, 1994. While the repeal removed the automatic classification of publicly traded partnership income as UBTI, a determination must still to be made as to whether the partnership income represents UBTI on the basis of §512(c) itself.

f. Transferability

In order for the transfer to be valid, the partnership agreement must contain language that permits the transfer of a partnership interest to a charitable remainder trust.

g. Other Potential Problems

Any transactions between a partner who transfers a partnership interest to a charitable remainder trust (now a disqualified person) and the partnership itself are subject to the self-dealing rules of IRC §4941. Further, the timing of partnership distributions and valuations might conflict with the payout sequence and valuation date of the trust.

h. Distribution Followed by Transfer

The problems created by transferring a partnership to a charitable remainder trust can be mitigated or eliminated by partial or complete distribution of partnership assets to the partner. A distributee partner realizes gain only to the extent that distributed money exceeds the partner's basis in his or her interest.[253] No gain is recognized to a

---

[250]   IRC §512(c); See also Leila G. Newhall Unitrust v. Commissioner, 104 T.C. No. 10.

[251]   *See also* Ltr. Rul. 9633007

[252]   §10213(a) of the Omnibus Budget Reconciliation Act of 1987 (OBRA 1987), Pub. L. 100-203, 101 Stat. 1330-406

[253]   IRC §731(a)(1)

distributee partner, with respect to a distribution of property other than money, until he sells or otherwise disposes of such property, except as otherwise provided by IRC §736 (relating to payments of a retiring partner or a deceased partner's successor in interest) and IRC §751 (relating to unrealized receivables and inventory items).[254] Therefore, under certain circumstances, a partner might be able to receive a distribution of property from a partnership followed by the transfer of compatible property from such distribution to a charitable remainder trust without recognition of gain.

i. Limited Partnership as Trustor

In Letter Ruling 9419021, a taxpayer asked (a) if a limited partnership is a permissible grantor of a charitable remainder trust, (b) if the partnership is a permissible recipient of the unitrust payments, and (c) whether the trust is a qualified charitable remainder unitrust under section 664(d).

The trust will pay the unitrust amount to the trustor for a term not to exceed 20 years. It has also been represented the unitrust amount will be greater than 5 percent of the net fair market value of the assets to be determined annually and that an independent trustee will be appointed.

The Service ruled there is nothing in section 664 of the Code or the underlying regulations that prohibits a partnership from being a permissible donor to an otherwise qualified charitable remainder unitrust as long as all the partners are permissible donors. The trustor is a permissible donor. Section 7701(a)(1) of the Code defines the term "person" to include an individual, trust, estate, association, company, corporation, and *partnership*.

In the present situation, the proposed trust will provide that the unitrust amount is payable to the trustor, a partnership, for a term not to exceed 20 years. Because the term of the trust is for a term of years, the recipient of the unitrust amount may be any person or persons, including a partnership, so long as at least one such person is not a charitable organization. The partners are not charitable organizations. Thus, both the partnership and the partners are permissible recipients, and the trustor is a permissible recipient of the unitrust amount.

. Limited Liability Companies

A Limited Liability Company (LLC) is an entity formed under state law by filing articles of organization as an LLC. Unlike a general partnership, none of the members of an LLC are personally liable for the LLC's debts. An LLC may be classified as a partnership or corporation for federal income tax purposes, depending on whether it has more than two of the following corporate characteristics:

- centralization of management

---

[254] Reg. §1.731-1(a)(1)

- continuity of life

- free transferability of interests

- limited liability

If an LLC is taxed as a partnership, there is a pass-through of the tax character of the distributive share to the partner. There is also a pass-through of the characterization of the distribution for purposes of determining whether or not the distributive share is unrelated business income.

9.   Qualified Plan Assets

The *rollover* of an IRA or qualified retirement plan into a charitable remainder trust will not relieve the trustor of the constructive receipt of plan proceeds for income tax purposes. As an alternative, a donor might consider transferring the *after-tax* proceeds from a lump-sum distribution from an over funded plan to a charitable remainder trust. The charitable contribution deduction will reduce the net tax attributable to the withdrawal. Furthermore, for calendar years 1997 through and including 1999, the 15 percent excise tax on excess distributions has been repealed.[255]

Planning Opportunity: Naming a testamentary charitable remainder trust as beneficiary of qualified plan proceeds will eliminate income tax otherwise attributable to income in respect of a decedent (IRD).[256] Furthermore, a transfer to a testamentary charitable remainder trust will produce an estate tax charitable deduction equal to the present value of the remainder interest. Properly designed, a trust funded with qualified plan proceeds can produce an income stream, the present value of which is, comparable to the after-tax remainder of an outright plan distribution. Such transfers, however, are not exempt from the 15 percent excise tax on excess retirement accumulations under IRC §691(c)(1)(C).

In a letter ruling, a married couple created an 8 percent net income unitrust. The husband is a participant in a qualified retirement plan as described in IRC §401(a). Under the terms of the plan, if he dies before his account balance is distributed or used to purchase an annuity, his beneficiary will be entitled to the full value of the account. The donor intends to execute a beneficiary designation, with the consent of his wife, under which a portion of his account will be distributed from the plan to the unitrust. The wife will, assuming she survives her husband, receive payments from the trust for the balance of her life.

The Service ruled 1) the trust will not be subject to any tax imposed under Subtitle A unless it has UBTI; 2) distributions will be taxed under the four-tier system; and 3) the trust will qualify for the marital deduction under IRC §2056(a).[257]

---

[255]   H.R. 3448 - The Small Business Job Protection Act of 1996, Act Section 1452, amending IRC §4980A. Note, the repeal of the 15 percent excess distributions excise tax applies only to withdrawals made during life. The 15 percent excise tax applicable to excess retirement accumulation, applicable upon the death of participant, is not affected by the Act.

[256]   Ltr. Rul. 9634019

[257]   Ltr. Rul. 9253038; See also Ltr. Rul. 9237020

J. Tangible Personal Property

There are no prohibitions against transferring tangible personal property, such as artwork or other collectibles, to a charitable remainder trust. However, the trustor's income tax deduction will be delayed until the property is sold, and it will be reduced if the property transferred has been created by the trustor or is unrelated to the charitable remainderman's tax-exempt purpose. Since the trust will presumably sell the contributed property, such a use is normally considered unrelated and the deduction will be limited to the lesser of fair market value and adjusted cost basis.[258]

1. Gift of Artwork with Retained Copyright

An original work of art and its copyright are considered separate property for gift and estate tax deduction purposes.[259] However, the transfer of artwork to a charitable remainder trust with the copyright retained by the trustor constitutes a nonqualified gift of a partial interest and therefore, produces no income tax deduction.[260]

2. Rare Coins

Rev. Rul. 69-63 holds that, for purposes of the predecessor to section 170(a)(3), a collection of rare coins held not primarily as a medium of exchange but as collector's items is tangible personal property.[261] The ruling also holds that cash is not tangible personal property within the meaning of the statute.

The Service has ruled privately that South African Krugerrand gold coins are more akin to money than to coins that have value as collector's items. South African Krugerrand gold coins are one of the best known types of gold bullion coins. They have no numismatic value. Moreover, in the case at hand, the trustee was authorized to dispose of the coins. Therefore, pursuant to the rationale of Rev. Rul. 69-63, the IRS concluded that South African Krugerrand gold coins are not tangible personal property within the meaning of section 170(a)(3) of the Code.[262]

3. Livestock, Crops, and Farm Machinery

In Letter Ruling 9413020, a taxpayer proposes to transfer "slaughter cattle" and "breeding stock" to a net income unitrust. The charitable remainderman will serve as the trustee. Once the cattle are transferred to the trust, the trustee will engage the services of an independent agent to sell them. In the meantime, the trustee will make arrangements to have them cared for and fed strictly on a maintenance basis (i.e., no attempt will be made to fatten them for market). It will use a similar procedure for disposing of any farm machinery it decides to sell. Thus, it is represented that the unitrust will not engage in regularly carried on sales of the farm items as a dealer, and that the farm items to be sold

---

[258] Ltr. Rul. 9452026; See discussion of percentage limitations applicable to tangible property on page 77.
[259] IRC §§2055(e)(4); 2522(e)(3); Reg. §§20.2055-2(e)(1)(ii); 20.2522(c)-3(c)(1)(ii)
[260] Reg. §1.170A-7(b)(1)
[261] Rev. Rul. 69-63, 1969-1 C.B. 63
[262] Ltr. Rul. 9225036

are not held by the unitrust for sale to customers in the ordinary course of any unitrust business. The donor will claim no charitable income tax deduction for any contribution of cattle, crops, or farm machinery to the trust. It is also represented that the sales of donated farm items will not involve property that is debt-financed under section 514 of the Code.

The Service ruled as follows:

- The trustor will not recognize any gross income on the transfers of farm items to the unitrust.

- Costs and expenses that the donor has incurred in raising slaughter cattle and crops transferred to the unitrust and that are properly deducted under section 162 of the Code or another Code section are allowable as deductions in the year such expenses are paid or incurred, whether or not that year is the year in which such items are transferred to the unitrust.

- The trustor will not recognize any gross income on sale by the unitrust of farm items the donor has transferred to the unitrust.

- The unitrust will not have unrelated business taxable income under sections 511 through 514 of the Code on sales of farm items the trustor has transferred to it.

- Annual distributions from the unitrust to the income recipients will have income tax characteristics, in the hands of the recipient, determined under section 1.664-1(d)(1) of the regulations.

- The trustor will not recognize any self-employment income under section 1402 of the Code on the transfers of farm items to the unitrust or on sales by the unitrust of farm items the donor has transferred to the unitrust.

- No portion of any annual distribution from the unitrust to the trustor / income recipient will be included in computing his self-employment income under section 1402 of the Code.

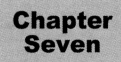

Operational Considerations

The operation and administration of a charitable remainder trust is the province of the trustee. The trustee must balance the competing interests of the income and remainder beneficiaries, acting in a prudent manner, and avoiding any act that could be considered self-dealing.

There are several general rights and duties for which a trustee is responsible:

- valuation of trust assets

- selling contributed assets

- establishing annual annuity or unitrust amounts

- receiving and disbursing revenues

- accounting under the four-tier system

- filing fiduciary tax and information returns

- maintaining the trust's tax-exempt status

- following private foundation rules

- holding and managing trust assets, and

- communicating and reporting to recipients

I. Valuation and Appraisal Requirements

The valuation of trust assets plays three distinct roles:

- determining the trustor's charitable contribution deduction for income, gift, and estate tax purposes

- assisting the trustee in establishing a sales price for contributed assets

- determining the initial annuity amount or annual unitrust amount

A. Appraisal Requirements

A qualified appraisal is required only for purposes of determining and substantiating the trustor's charitable contribution deduction. Therefore, obtaining an appraisal is the responsibility of the trustor, not the trustee. As a practical matter, because the establishment of the trust, determination of unitrust or annuity amount, and sale of contributed assets usually fall within a close span of time, a trustee will usually rely on an appraisal to assist in all three tasks.

IRS Publication 561 is designed to help trustors, trustees, and appraisers determine the value of property (other than cash) that is given to qualified organizations. It includes information required to support the charitable contribution deduction:

- fair market value, and how it is determined

- valuation of various kinds of property

- record keeping

- appraisals

B. General Overview of Appraisal Requirements

If the claimed deduction for property transferred to a charitable remainder trust is more than $5,000, ($10,000 for closely-held stock), the trustor must obtain a *qualified appraisal* made by a *qualified appraiser*. Qualified appraisals are generally not required for cash or publicly traded securities.

C. Qualified Appraisal Defined

A qualified appraisal is an appraisal document that:

- is prepared by a *qualified appraiser* not earlier than 60 days prior to the date of contribution and not later than the due date of the return (including extensions) on which the first charitable contribution is claimed;

- does not involve a prohibited appraisal fee; and

- includes specified information (discussed in detail in Pub. 561).

D. Qualified Appraiser Defined

A qualified appraiser is an individual who holds himself or herself out to the public as an appraiser (or performs appraisals on a regular basis) of the type of property being valued, is not an excluded individual, and understands the penalty for aiding and abetting an understatement of tax liability.

E. Deductibility of Appraisal Costs

Appraisal costs incurred by a trustor in determination of a charitable contribution deduction are not deductible as a charitable contribution. However, they may qualify as a miscellaneous deduction, subject to the 2 percent limit.

> **Note:** Some charitable organizations offer to pay certain implementation expenses on behalf of a trustor, including appraisal costs. The trustor should be advised that payment of such expenses is likely to be considered income to the trustor.

F. Penalties for Overstatements of Valuation

If the value of donated property claimed on the trustor's tax return exceeds the determined value by 50 percent or more, a penalty equal to 30 percent of the understated tax will be levied on the trustor.

G. Valuing Closely-Held Stock

Additional guidance in the valuation of closely-held stock is provided in Rev. Rul. 59-60[263], Rev. Rul. 77-287[264], and Rev. Rul. 83-120[265]. See discussion *infra*.

H. Valuing Restricted Securities

The IRS has ruled privately that stock that is restricted under SEC Rule 144 is not stock "for which market quotations are readily available."[266] This ruling suggests that even though the stock is traded on a public market, an appraisal may be required to substantiate value. A valuation discount may be appropriate if a lack of marketability accompanies the Rule 144 restriction.

I. Valuing Partial Interests

When a fractional interest in an indivisible asset such as real property or an interest in a closely-held corporation is transferred to a trust, the valuation must reflect the minority or majority interest, and the lack of transferability and marketability that accompanies a partial interest, even though it might be the trustor's entire interest.

II. Selling Transferred Assets

Because charitable remainder trusts are often used for the purpose of selling appreciated property, it is important to discuss the rules that preserve favorable tax treatment.

---

[263]   Rev. Rul. 59-60, 1959-1 C.B. 237

[264]   Rev. Rul. 77-287, 1977-2 C.B. 319

[265]   Rev. Rul. 83-120, 1983-2 C.B. 170

[266]   Ltr. Rul. 9247018

Gain on the sale of an appreciated asset is not considered attributable to the trustor as long as the asset is given away before sale. However, this rule is inapplicable if the trustor retains direct or indirect control over the asset or there is an express or implied prearranged obligation on the part of the trustee to sell the property. Therefore, when creating and funding a charitable remainder trust, it is imperative that the trustee have neither an express nor an implied prearranged obligation to sell the property, nor an obligation to invest the proceeds in a specified manner. Otherwise, the trustor may be taxed on the subsequent sale on one of the theories below.[267]

A. Agency Theory

An individual cannot prearrange the sale of an appreciated asset that he is planning to contribute to a charitable remainder trust and still obtain the favorable tax consequences normally associated with gifts of appreciated property. Where the sale is prearranged, any gain associated with the sale is taxable to the trustor on the theory that the trustee is merely acting as the trustor's agent in completing the sale transaction. Where creation of the trust and the sale of assets transferred to the trust are *independent transactions*, however, favorable tax consequences are preserved.

Basically, if the donative intent is formed before the decision to sell the asset, and the gift is made independently from the sale, the trustor will not be deemed to have realized a gain even if the trustee consummates a concurrent sale. As long as the decision to sell is made independently by the trustee, there are no adverse tax consequences.[268]

B. Lack of Donative Intent

Where the trustee is restricted in its ability to deal freely with the contributed assets, the IRS could also assert that the trustor lacked donative intent (i.e., there was not a release of control of the property and hence, there was no gift). However, provided the trustee is under no obligation to sell or exchange the asset transferred, or invest proceeds in a particularly restrictive manner (i.e., only in tax-exempt bonds), the cases and letter rulings dealing with the sale of an appreciated asset by the trust are generally favorable to taxpayers.[269]

C. Step Transaction Concerns

Even in situations where a sale is not prearranged, under appropriate circumstances the IRS may assert that the sales transaction is a part of a multiple step transaction and that the amount of gain on the sale should be taxed to the trustor. The courts have permitted the IRS to use this theory to collapse multiple step transactions where the intermediate steps are so interdependent the relationship created by the first transaction would be fruitless without completion of the series of steps.

---

[267]   Reg. §1.664-1(a)(3). Rev. Rul. 60-370 1960-2 C.B. 203

[268]   Martin v. Machiz 251 F. Supp. 381 (D.C. Maryland, 1966), Magnolia Development Corporation v. C.I.R. 19 T.C.M. 934, 1960-177

[269]   Rev. Rul. 78-197, 1978-1 C.B. 83

Favorable tax consequences are preserved if each step has independent significance. In other words, because the sale of an appreciated asset is anticipated or imminent is not a problem if there is an actual gift and there is an absence of an obligation to sell.[270]

In *Blake v. Commissioner*, a donor contributed highly appreciated stock to a charitable organization, which in turn sold the stock and used the proceeds to purchase the donor's yacht. The donor claimed a charitable contribution income tax deduction for the value of the stock. In the view of the IRS and tax court, however, Blake had sold the stock to the charity and donated the yacht. Further, the value and, therefore, the amount permitted as a charitable contribution deduction for the yacht was far less than the price paid for it by the charity. Even though there was no binding obligation to sell the stock or donate the yacht, the court stated that all parties had a "clear understanding" that all steps would be taken.[271]

D. Practical Application

An individual contemplating a transfer to a charitable remainder trust followed by an immediate sale most likely crosses into dangerous waters when sale negotiations between the individual and potential buyer have risen to the level of a legal obligation to proceed with the sale.

In the case of a closely-held business, the line may be drawn with the acceptance of a letter of intent, depending on its terms and conditions. In the case of real property, offer and acceptance (either verbal or written depending on local Statute of Frauds) constitutes a legal obligation. Obviously, property subject to an escrow to sell is not suitable. A broker's listing agreement is merely one party's *offer* to sell, and not an *agreement* to sell. However, the trustee should be cautious in accepting property with a listing agreement that contains a liquidated damage clause, stating that the broker is entitled to a fee if the seller refuses to accept a viable offer.

Can the trustor obtain an advance ruling? Probably not. In Rev. Rul. 60-370, the Service stated, "Since it may be necessary to go beyond the trust instrument to determine whether there is an obligation, express or implied, imposed on the trustee to sell or exchange the transferred property and invest in tax-exempt securities, no advance rulings will be issued as to whether there is such an obligation to sell or exchange the transferred property and invest the proceeds in tax-exempt securities."[272] On the other hand, the Service has ruled on lease/option cases as discussed on page 123.

Can an independent trustee negotiate a legally binding sale that is contingent upon the funding of the trust by the trustor? This question has not been addressed by the Service.

---

[270]   Palmer v. Commissioner of Internal Revenue, 62 T.C. 684, acq., aff'd (CA-8, 1975), F.2nd 1308, 36 AFTR 2d 75-5942

[271]   Blake v. Commissioner of Internal Revenue, 697 F2d 473 (2d Cir. 1982).

[272]   Rev. Rul. 60-370, 1960-2 C.B. 203

In review, the trustee must have independent ability to negotiate the transaction, change the terms, or walk away.[273]

III. Selecting a Trustee

The Code and regulations place no limitations on who the trustee of a charitable remainder trust can be. There are three general categories:

- corporate trustee

- charitable remainderman

- trustor or other individual

A. Corporate Trustee

Many banks and trust companies offer trustee services for charitable remainder trusts. However, corporate trustees vary greatly with respect to their experience regarding these specialized instruments.

A bank acting as trustee of a charitable remainder trust may invest trust assets in common trust funds maintained by the bank without jeopardizing the trust's tax-exempt status or the trustor's charitable contribution deduction.[274] Further, corporate trustees may be well suited to deal with assets that are difficult to value, or that require management (such as real property).

The are several questions that are commonly asked in evaluating a potential trustee:

- How long have they served as trustee for charitable remainder trusts?

- For how many instruments do they serve as trustee?

- What is their investment track record for charitable trusts and how is it determined?

- How are trustee fees determined?

- What are average fees for various size trusts?

- How often and in what format do they report to the trustor/income recipients?

- Does their trust accounting system track the four-tier system, or must manual computations be performed?

---

[273] See also Greene v. United States, 13 F.3d 577 (1994), aff'g [93-1 USTC 50,033] 806 F.Supp. 1165 (1992) and Ferguson v. Commissioner, 108 T.C. #14 (1997)

[274] Rev. Rul. 73-571, 1973-2 C.B. 213

- Are they structured to accommodate an independent money manager or can securities transactions be made through the trustor's choice of broker/dealer?

- What are the issues associated with managing a net income unitrust verses a standard unitrust, each funded with tax-exempt bonds?

This last question may be the most telling. In order to answer it, the trustee must understand the difference between these two types of unitrusts and the four-tier system of taxation. These issues are discussed in detail in Chapter Eight.

B. Charity as Trustee

Charitable organizations often serve as trustees of charitable trusts as a convenience and incentive to potential trustors.[275] These services are often rendered without charge to the trust or trustor.

Although expense reduction is valuable, potential trustors are well advised to evaluate the services of a charitable trustee in the same way they would scrutinize a corporate trustee with particular emphasis on the methodology by which investment decisions are made and administrative functions performed.

Who is responsible for making investment decisions? Does the organization utilize an employee, volunteer investment committee, money manager, bank, or trust company? How often is investment performance reviewed and how is it reported to the trustor?

Further, when a charitable organization serves as trustee, the Board of Directors/Trustees usually bears the fiduciary liability associated with the prudent management of trust assets. In at least one state, in the event an action is brought, the organization may be able to provide only limited indemnification of its board.[276]

C. Trustor as Trustee

Prior to 1977, it was presumed that charitable remainder trusts required the use of an independent trustee such as a bank, trust company, or charitable organization. The theory was, a trust in which a trustor retained too much control as to enjoyment, distribution, or income would be treated as a grantor trust (as described in IRC §§671 - 678). Such a trust would not qualify as a charitable remainder trust.

1.   Trustor as Trustee Permitted

Rev. Rul. 77-285 has helped clarify this issue via two examples:

In example (1), the governing instrument of an irrevocable trust provides that the trustee shall pay the specified distribution to the grantor for life and upon the grantor's death the trust will terminate and the trust assets will be distributed to an organization described in

---

[275]   Ltr. Rul 9207024 held that a trust that named a non-operating private foundation as remainderman and trustee did not constitute a prohibited act of self-dealing.

[276]   Advising California Nonprofit Corporations. California Continuing Education of the Bar 1984.

section 170(c) of the Code. The trust instrument further provides that the grantor reserves the right to remove the trustee for any reason and substitute any other person (including the grantor) as trustee. In all other respects, the trust instrument complies with the provisions of section 664 of the Code and the applicable regulations.

In example (2), the governing instrument of an irrevocable trust provides that the trustee shall pay the specified distribution to two life beneficiaries, one of whom is the grantor. The trustee may, in its sole discretion, allocate the specified distribution to or between the life beneficiaries. Upon the death of the survivor of the two life beneficiaries, the trust will terminate and the trust assets will be distributed to an organization described in section 170(c) of the Code.

The governing instrument further provides that the grantor reserves the right to remove the trustee for any reason and substitute any other person (including the grantor) as trustee. In all other respects, the trust instrument complies with the provisions of section 664 of the Code and the applicable regulations, and it includes the mandatory trust provisions prescribed in Rev. Rul. 72-395.

The specific question in both situations is whether a trust that authorizes the grantor to remove the trustee of an otherwise qualifying charitable remainder trust for any reason and substitute any person (including the grantor) as trustee qualifies as a charitable remainder trust.

Section 1.664-1(a)(4) of the regulations provides that, in order for a trust to be a charitable remainder trust, it must meet the definition of, and function exclusively as, a charitable remainder trust from the date or time of the creation of the trust. This section further provides that, solely for purposes of section 664 of the Code and the regulations thereunder, the trust will be deemed to be created at the earliest time that neither the grantor nor any other person is treated as the owner of the entire trust under subpart E, part 1, subchapter J, chapter 1, subtitle A. For purposes of the preceding sentence, neither the grantor nor the grantor's spouse shall be treated as the owner of the trust under subpart E merely because the grantor or the grantor's spouse is named as a recipient.

Sections 1.664-2(a)(3)(ii) and 1.664-3(a)(3)(ii) of the regulations provide that a trust is not a charitable remainder trust if any person has the power to alter the amount to be paid to any named person other than an organization described in section 170(c) of the Code if such power would cause any person to be treated as the owner of the trust, or any portion thereof, if sections 673 through 679 were applicable to such trust.

Section 674(a) of the Code provides the general rule that the grantor shall be treated as the owner of any portion of a trust in respect of which the beneficial enjoyment of the corpus or the income therefrom is subject to a power of disposition, exercisable by the grantor or a nonadverse party, or both, without approval or consent of any adverse party. Section 674(c) provides that section 674(a) shall not apply to a power solely exercisable by a trustee or trustees, none of whom is the grantor, to allocate the specified distribution to the income beneficiaries.

Section 1.674(d)-2(a) of the regulations provides that a power in the grantor to remove, substitute, or add trustees may prevent the trust from qualifying under sections 674(c) or 674(d) of the Code. For example, if a grantor has an unrestricted power to remove an independent trustee and substitute any person including the grantor as trustee, the trust will not qualify under section 674(c) or (d).

In Situation (1), none of the provisions of sections 673 through 679 of the Code will prevent the trust from coming into existence under section 1.664-1(a)(4) of the regulations. Further, the trust complies with all of the provisions of section 664 and the applicable regulations. Accordingly, the Service ruled, the described trust qualifies as a charitable remainder trust under section 664 of the Code and the applicable regulations.

2.   Trustor Trustee with Sprinkling Powers Not Permitted

In Situation (2), the trust fails to satisfy the requirements of sections 1.664-2(a)(3)(ii) and 1.664-3(a)(3)(ii) of the regulations because the grantor has the right to substitute the grantor as trustee. Therefore, the trustor will be treated as the owner of a portion of the trust under section 674(a) of the Code. Accordingly, the trust does not qualify as a charitable remainder trust under section 664 of the Code and the applicable regulations. The conclusion would be the same if the grantor could not serve as trustee but could name a related or subordinate party who is subservient to the wishes of the grantor as trustee.

3.   Hard-to-Value Assets

The legislative history of the Tax Reform Act of 1969 indicates that a charitable deduction will be denied when assets that do not have an objective, ascertainable market value, such as real estate or stock in a closely-held corporation, are transferred in trust, unless an independent trustee is the sole party responsible for making the annual determination of value.[277]

This rule is based on the concern that a trustor who is also the trustee can manipulate the valuation of trust assets to the detriment of the charitable remainderman. For example, because a trustee is not generally required to obtain an independent appraisal for hard-to-value trust assets for purposes of determining the annual unitrust amount, a trustor/trustee could overvalue trust assets and thereby receive a larger income distribution.

On April 18, 1997, Treasury issued proposed amendments to the regulations to solve this problem. If a charitable remainder trust holds *unmarketable* assets, and the trustee is the grantor of the charitable remainder trust, a noncharitable beneficiary, or a related or subordinate party to the grantor or the noncharitable beneficiary (within the meaning of section 672(c) and the applicable regulations), the trustee must use a current qualified appraisal, as defined in section 1.170A-13(c)(3), from a qualified appraiser, as

---

[277]   P.L. 91-172, H. Rep. No. 413 (Part 1), 91st Cong., 1st Sess. 50, 1969-3 C.B. 239.; Ltr. Rul. 8648048

defined in section 1.170A-13(c)(5), to value those assets.[278] A trustee who is not one of the parties mentioned above is considered independent and is not required to obtain a qualified appraisal to value the unmarketable assets. The amendments are proposed to be effective for trusts created on or after the date on which the final regulations are published in the Federal Register. If the governing instrument of an existing trust created before the effective date of this amendment already requires an independent trustee to value the trust's unmarketable assets, the governing instrument may be amended or reformed to conform with this provision.

It is interesting to note that the term "hard-to-value assets," as used in the legislative history, has been modified to the term "unmarketable assets." Under the proposed regulations, unmarketable assets are defined as assets that are not cash, cash equivalents, or marketable securities (within the meaning of section 731(c) and the applicable regulations). By this definition, stock that is restricted under SEC Rule 144 would not require independent valuation under these rules.[279]

4. Selling Appreciated Contributed Property

A third concern involving the trustor as trustee involves the attribution of capital gain to the trustor upon the sale of contributed appreciated property. Based on the preceding discussion concerning asset sales, the IRS would certainly have an easier time *connecting the dots* of a sale transaction if the trustee and trustor are one in the same.

5. The Special Independent Trustee

It is possible that the problems created by sprinkling powers, hard-to-value assets, and selling appreciated assets can be resolved through the use of an *independent* trustee.[280]

An *independent* trustee is one who is not the trustor and not related or subordinate to the trustor.

Related or subordinate parties include: (a) the trustor's spouse, if living with the trustor; (b) the trustor's parents, siblings, or children; (c) an employee of the trustor; (d) a corporation or employee of a corporation over which the trustor has voting control; (e) or a subordinate employee of a corporation in which the trustor is an executive. These persons are assumed to be subservient to the trustor "unless shown not to be subservient by a preponderance of the evidence."[281]

Is a professional advisor with a long-standing relationship to the trustor a subordinate party? The Service has not ruled on this question.

---

[278] Reg-209823-96

[279] It is interesting to note, however, that stock which is restricted under Rule 144 may still require an independent appraisal for purposes of determining a donor's income tax charitable contribution deduction. See discussion on page 100.

[280] IRC §674(c)

[281] Reg. §1.672(c)-1

a. Special Independent Trustee Defined

A special independent trustee is a trustee who is granted exclusive specialized fiduciary powers. Within the context of application to a charitable remainder trust, the special independent trustee is given sole discretion regarding:

- valuation of hard-to-value assets,

- the disposition of contributed assets, and

- sprinkling income among income recipients.[282]

Although the trustor often retains the right to appoint the special independent trustee, the trustor cannot exercise any of the powers of the special independent trustee.

b. Application of Special Independent Trustee

The use of carefully drafted special independent trustee provisions within a charitable remainder trust that also enables the trustor to serve as primary trustee should insulate the trustor from grantor trust problems provided state law permits the use of such rights. Therefore, state law regarding the availability of the special independent trustee provision should be thoroughly researched.

In a letter ruling, the Service concluded that a trustor / trustee's reserved right to dismiss a trustee, including any required independent trustee, will not disqualify the trust.[283] Further, a trustor's retained right to dismiss a trustee will not cause the trustor to be treated as the owner of the trust under IRC §674(a).[284]

6. Should a Trustor Be Trustee?

Transfers to charitable remainder trusts often involve assets of substantial value. The trustor's perceived loss of control of contributed assets is often a major impediment to this process. Although the solution of control can be addressed through the use of trustor/trustee provisions, an unknowledgeable trustee can cause an otherwise well conceived plan to self-destruct.

It is recommended that a trustor serve as trustee only when he or she retains an independent administrator or tax professional with specialized expertise in the unique operational requirements of charitable remainder trusts and an investment advisor with a clear understanding of the trust's investment objectives and limitations. This combination should solve the trustor's concerns while ensuring that operational, compliance, and investment matters are performed accurately and on a timely basis.

---

[282] See Rev. Rul. 77-73

[283] Ltr. Rul. 9339018

[284] Ltr. Rul. 9252023

D. Blind Trust as Trustor and Trustee

An individual who had been elected to public office transferred certain financial assets, including stock in a closely-held corporation, to a blind trust. The official intends to support projects undertaken by the corporation in his jurisdiction. In order to avoid any conflict of interest, the official proposes to instruct the trustee of the blind trust to create a charitable remainder unitrust and fund it with the closely-held stock. The unitrust agreement contains an additional provision that requires the trustee to immediately pay to charity any gains realized upon the sale of the stock that may occur during the grantor's term in office or immediately pay over any appreciation that may accrue to the stock still held at the end of the grantor's term of office.

The Service ruled the grantor will be considered as owner of the charitable remainder unitrust under section 673(a). Therefore, the grantor's direction to the trustee of the blind trust to create a charitable remainder trust will be treated for federal income tax purposes as if the grantor is establishing the trust himself. Further, the provisions directing the trustee to distribute realized gains or appreciation on the stock to charity during the trust term is permitted.[285]

IV. Private Foundation Excise Tax Rules

Prior to the Tax Reform Act of 1969, the only sanction available to a private foundation was the revocation of its tax-exempt status. In order to provide punishment commensurate with the violation, Congress created the private foundation excise taxes. Charitable remainder trusts are not private foundations. However, certain of the private foundation excise taxes are applicable to them.

Private foundation excise taxes attributable to *prohibited acts of self-dealing* and *private foundation expenditures* apply without exception to all charitable remainder trusts.[286] Charitable remainder trusts are not subject to private foundation excise taxes on *excess business holdings* and *jeopardizing investments* unless the trust includes a section 170(c) charitable organization as an income recipient.[287] Further, the tax imposed on the *undistributed income* of a private foundation does not apply to charitable remainder trusts.[288] However, if trust assets are held for the benefit of a charitable organization beyond the expiration of the income interest, the trust is converted to a private foundation and is subject to all private foundation excise taxes.[289]

A. IRS Model Trust Forms Include All Private Foundation Excise Tax Prohibitions

Even though the governing instrument is conditionally exempt from taxes on *excess business holdings* and *jeopardizing investments*, the regulations require it to include prohibitions against

[285] Ltr. Rul. 9202033

[286] IRC §4947(a)(2)

[287] IRC §4947(b)(3)

[288] IRC §4942

[289] IRC §4947(a)(2)

violating all private foundation excise tax rules.[290] Sample trust forms published by the IRS confirm this by including prohibitions against acts that would violate all private foundation excise tax rules.[291] Although these rules seemingly conflict, the requirement to include prohibitions against violating *all* private foundation excise tax rules was most likely intended to accommodate the ability of a model trust instrument to include a charitable income recipient.

B. Self-Dealing

Charitable remainder trusts are subject to private foundation excise taxes imposed on acts of self-dealing between the foundation manager (i.e., the trustee) and a *disqualified person.*

Acts of self-dealing generally include a sale, exchange or lease, loan or other credit (except a loan that bears no interest), furnishing goods, services or use of trust property, or payment of compensation, income or use of assets, between a private foundation (charitable remainder trust) and a disqualified person.[292]

With respect to a charitable remainder trust, a disqualified person is a:

1. substantial contributor (a person who contributes more than $5,000 or the creator of the trust);[293]
2. trustee (foundation manager);
3. person who owns more than 20 percent of:
   - voting power of a corporation,
   - profit interest in a partnership, or
   - the beneficial interest of a trust or unincorporated enterprise, where the entity is a substantial contributor to the trust;
4. spouse, ancestors, children, grandchildren, great grandchildren, and their spouses, of persons previously described; or
5. corporation, partnership, trust, estate or enterprise of which more than 35 percent of the total ownership, and the rights thereof, are owned by persons previously described.

1. Taxes Imposed on Acts of Self-Dealing

An initial tax of 5 percent of the amount involved is imposed on the disqualified person even though he may not have knowingly committed a prohibited act.[294] An additional tax of 2.5 percent is levied on the trustee who willfully participates in an act of self-dealing knowing it was an act unless he has reasonable cause.[295]

---

[290] Reg. §1.664-1(b); IRC §508(e)(1)

[291] Rev. Proc. 89-20, 1989-1 C.B. 170; 89-21, 1989-1 C.B. 77; Rev. Proc. 90-30, 1990-1 C.B. 534; and Rev. Proc. 90-31, 1990-1 C.B. 539

[292] IRC §4941(d)(1)

[293] IRC §507(d)(2)

[294] IRC §4941(a); Reg. §53.4941(a)-1(a)

[295] IRC §4941(a)(2)

If the act of self-dealing is not corrected during the taxable period or correction period, an additional tax of 200 percent of the amount involved is imposed on the disqualified person and a tax of 50 percent (to a limit of $10,000) is imposed on the trustee if the trustee refuses to agree to all or part of the correction.[296]

2.   Gifts of Partial Interests in Jeopardy

Many individuals are attracted to the benefits of a charitable remainder trust, yet do not wish to transfer the *entire* value of an indivisible asset to the trust. In these circumstances, the individual could transfer an *undivided fractional interest* in the property to the trust and retain the difference. The trustor then joins with the trustee via separate sales agreements in the disposition of the property. The transfer represents an undivided interest in every element of the trustor's ownership in the property and, thus, should constitute a qualified tax deductible gift of a partial interest.[297]

Problem: Letter Ruling 9114025 suggests that a transfer of an undivided fractional interest in property to a charitable remainder trust with an interest retained by a disqualified person may constitute a prohibited act of self-dealing.

The ruling stated, "Section 101(1)(2)(E) of the Tax Reform Act of 1969, Pub. L. No. 91-172, 83 Stat. 533 (1969), provides that section 4941 shall not apply to [the] use of property in which a private foundation and a disqualified person have a joint or common interest if the Interests [sic] of both were acquired before October 9, 1969. This provision contains a limited exception to application of 4941, and indicates that a disqualified person's use of jointly-owned property after October 9, 1969, will be self-dealing." Whether a common ownership interest constitutes a use of property is subject to debate. The example cited in Reg. §53.4941(d)-4(e)(2) illustrates the physical use of property, which may be distinguishable from mere ownership.

Ruling Solution: The taxpayers avoided the problem by establishing a partnership of the owners (husband and wife), and thereafter transferred portions of their partnership interests to the trust.

Alternative Solution: In most cases it is the objective of the individual to sell their retained portion of the property outside of the trust. Therefore, the self-dealing issue can be avoided by the individual first selling a portion of their property outside of the trust and then contributing their entire remaining interest to the trust.

3.   Special Exception for Disqualified Corporations

Recall from the discussion of closely-held stock, a transaction between a charitable remainder trust and a corporation that is a disqualified person (e.g., a redemption) is not an act of self-dealing if the offer to purchase stock is made to all shareholders and on the same terms.[298] In a separate ruling, the IRS stated that the retention by the trustee of a

---

[296]   IRC 4941(b)(2)

[297]   IRC §170(f)(3)(B)

[298]   IRC §4941(d)(2)(F); Ltr. Rul. 9015055

majority interest in a closely-held corporation is not a transaction that constitutes a prohibited act of self-dealing under section 4941. In the same ruling, the Service confirmed that, based on the facts of the ruling, taxes imposed under sections 4942, 4943, 4944, and 4945 do not apply.[299]

4. Application of Self-Dealing Rules to Employee Stock Ownership Plans

Section 4946(a)(1)(C) of the Code defines *disqualified person* to include a person who is an owner of more than 20 percent of the total combined voting power of a corporation that is a substantial contributor to a private foundation.

Section 53.4946-1(a)(5) of the regulations defines *combined voting power* to include the voting power represented by holdings of voting stock, actual or constructive, but does not include voting rights held only as a director or trustee.

An Employee Stock Ownership Plan's stock is subject to the direction of the individuals on whose behalf the shares have been allocated and to whom the beneficial interest in the shares has passed. Therefore, to the extent the ESOP trust has any voting power with respect to the corporation's stock, it is merely the voting power of a trustee. Thus, although the ESOP trust may hold legal title to any amount of stock that exceeds 20 percent of the total combined voting power of the corporation, it is not treated as the owner of the stock, for purposes of section 4946(a)(1)(C) of the Code.

Rev. Rul. 81-76 holds that an ESOP described in section 4975(e) of the Code is not treated as the owner of stock in a corporation where the stock is allocated to participating employees and, thus, is not a disqualified person.[300]

5. Trustor as Trustee Not Self-Dealing

The IRS has ruled privately that a charitable remainder unitrust for which the trustors, a husband and wife, serve as co-trustees does not in itself constitute an act of self-dealing unless the trust provides for income payments to charity.[301]

6. Trust Established in Satisfaction of Irrevocable Charitable Pledge or In Exchange for Recognition Not Self-Dealing

An individual made a legally binding pledge in 1987 to an educational institution that is a public charity exempt from federal income tax under section 501(c)(3) of the Code. Upon receipt of a portion of the pledge the educational institution was obligated to rename itself after the individual, which it did. There remains a large balance left to contribute to the institution in satisfaction of the pledge.

---

[299] Ltr. Rul. 9210005; *See also* Ltr. Rul. 9721035

[300] Rev. Rul. 81-76, 1981-1 C.B. 516, See also Ltr. Rul. 9542040

[301] Ltr. Rul. 8839071

The individual now proposes to create a charitable remainder trust described in section 4947(a)(2) of the Code, which names the institution as the recipient of its remainder interest. When the remainder interest is distributed to the institution at the termination of the charitable remainder trust, the fair market value of the assets distributed will be applied against the individual's remaining irrevocable pledge balance to the institution. The individual proposed to amend and restate his irrevocable pledge agreement with the institution to include the charitable remainder trust as a legal party to the irrevocable pledge agreement. The charitable remainder trust's governing instrument will be drafted to meet all the requirements of sections 170, 664, 2055, and 2512 of the Code and the accompanying regulations. The individual is a disqualified person with respect to the charitable remainder trust under section 4946(a)(1) of the Code.

In a 1992 private ruling, the Service held that the pledge agreement by the individual and his charitable remainder trust in consideration for the educational institution's name change to a name containing part of the individual's name does not constitute an act of self-dealing between the trust and the disqualified person. Further, the benefit to the individual, public acknowledgment, and recognition is incidental and tenuous under the regulations and previously cited revenue rulings.[302]

In substantiation of the latter holding, the Service cited Revenue Ruling 73-407 which provides that a contribution by a private foundation to a public charity made on the condition that the public charity change its name to that of a substantial contributor to the foundation and agree not to change its name again for 100 years does not constitute an act of self-dealing under section 4941(d)(1)(E) of the Code.[303]

In Ltr. Rul. 9714010, the Service has revoked Ltr. Rul. 9233053, citing section 53.4941(d)-2(f)(1) of the regulations which provides that an agreement, whereby the remainder interest in the trust will be credited toward a legally enforceable pledge, results in a use of trust assets for the benefit of the grantor and, therefore, is an act of self-dealing. The regulation is effective for payments in satisfaction of pledges made on or before April 16, 1973. In this case, the pledge occurred in 1986.

In its explanation, the Service stated that it had relied inappropriately on the more general provisions of section 53.4941(d)-2(f)(2), concerning incidental or tenuous benefits as received by a disqualified person as cited by Rev. Rul. 73-407. Moreover, the ruling's reliance on Rev. Rul. 77-160 was also misplaced because that ruling does not concern a legally enforceable pledge.

The donor's request for relief under section 7805(b) of the Code, which permits the donor to rely upon the findings of the original ruling, was granted.

---

[302] Ltr. Rul. 9233053
[303] Rev. Rul. 73-407, 1973-2 C.B. 383

7.   Securities Transactions and Loans between Charitable Remaindermen and Corporations Related to Trustees Not Self-Dealing

In a situation where a parent corporation owned subsidiary corporations involved separately in securities sales, lending, and trust services, transactions between the charitable remaindermen of trusts (for which the trust companies served as trustee) and the other related firms was not deemed a prohibited act of self-dealing. The Service stated, "these rules do not run upstream and thus the corporate parent of a foundation manager [trustee] is not a disqualified person with respect to the private foundation [charitable remainder trust] merely by reason of stock ownership in the manager."[304]

8.   Merger of Corporations Owned by Charitable Remainder Trust and Income Recipient Not Self-Dealing

A charitable remainder unitrust owned stock in two corporations. The income recipient of the unitrust was a shareholder, officer, and director of one of the corporations. The corporations proposed to merge; however, would the transaction be a prohibited act of direct or indirect self-dealing?

Section 4941(d)(2)(F) of the Code provides that any transaction between a private foundation and a corporation which is a disqualified person (as defined in section 4946(a)), pursuant to any liquidation, merger, redemption, recapitalization, or other corporate adjustment, organization, or reorganization, shall not be an act of self-dealing if all of the securities of the same class as that held by the foundation are subject to the same terms and such terms provide for receipt by the foundation of no less than fair market value.

Section 53.4941(d)-3(d)(1) of the Foundation and Similar Excise Taxes Regulations states that all of the securities are not subject to the same terms" unless, pursuant to such transaction, the corporation makes a bona fide offer on a uniform basis to the foundation and every other person who holds such securities.

The merger transaction would include a bona-fide offer made on a uniform basis with all holders of stock receiving the same number of shares of the acquiring corporation's stock. Thus, all the securities of the same class would be subject to the same terms. The Service approved the transaction.[305]

9.   Interest-Free Loan to Charitable Remainder Trust Permissible

The lending of money by a disqualified person to a private foundation is not a prohibited act of self-dealing as long as the loan is without interest or other charge and the proceeds are used exclusively for purposes described in IRC §501(c)(3). Furthermore, the imputed

---

[304]   Ltr. Rul. 9451069

[305]   Ltr. Ruls. 9734015; 9734016; 9734017; 9734018; 9734019

interest rules of IRC §7872 do not apply.[306] A loan may cause the trust to have acquisition indebtedness, however.[307]

10. Reasonable Compensation to Disqualified Person Not Self-Dealing

The payment of compensation from a private foundation to a disqualified person for personal services necessary to carrying on the tax-exempt purposes of a private foundation is a permitted exception to the self-dealing rules provided such compensation is not excessive.[308]

11. Reformation to Eliminate Net Income Option a Prohibited Act of Self Dealing

In 1992 an individual created a charitable remainder unitrust that included a net income option. The grantor later decided he wanted to reform the trust to remove the net income option, thereby converting the trust to a standard payout format. The Service held that such reformation would remove interests in the trust that were previously dedicated to charity and transfer them to a disqualified person. Therefore, the grantor and the trustee would participate in a prohibited act of self-dealing.[309] Furthermore, in an earlier related ruling, the Service held that such a reformation would cost the trust its qualification as a charitable remainder trust.[310]

C. Excess Business Holdings

As stated earlier, a charitable remainder trust may be exempt from taxes imposed on *excess business holdings*. In the event the trust is subject to these taxes, a private foundation's business holdings will be considered excessive if:

- the foundation owns more than 20 percent of the voting stock of a corporation reduced by the percentage of voting stock owned by all disqualified persons,[311] or

- the foundation and all disqualified persons own more than 35 percent of voting stock, or control the corporation.[312]

The trustee is allowed five years to dispose of excess holdings prior to imposition of a tax (with a possible five-year extension).[313]

---

[306]   IRC §4941(d)(2)(B)

[307]   See the discussion of unrelated business taxable income beginning on page 163.

[308]   IRC §4941(d)(2)(E)

[309]   Ltr. Rul. 9522021

[310]   Ltr. Rul. 9516040

[311]   IRC §4943(c)(1)

[312]   IRC §4943(c)(2)(B)

[313]   IRC §§4943(c)(6); 4943(c)(7)

D. Jeopardizing Investments

Charitable remainder trusts may also be exempt from tax on *jeopardizing investments*. If not, an excise tax is imposed on the trustee that invests in a manner that would jeopardize the trust's tax-exempt purpose (i.e., providing a remainder interest to a IRC §170(c) organization).

No category of investments is treated as a *per se* violation. However, the Service will closely scrutinize trading on margin (which will also cause debt-financed income), trading in commodity futures, investments in working interests in oil and gas wells, calls, puts, straddles, warrants, and selling short.[314]

Even though a violation of the rule might not cause an excise tax, a trustee who fails to exercise ordinary business care and prudence in balancing the competing interests of income recipient and remainderman may become subject to liability.

E. Private Foundation Expenditures

Private foundation expenditures as described in IRC §4945 are not relevant to charitable remainder trusts because such trusts are prevented from making payments to other than the named income recipients or charitable organizations. Therefore, a trustee would never make political contributions, grants to individuals, or donations to private foundations as described in this section.

An exception is payments for full and adequate consideration (e.g., trustee, administrative, investment management fees, etc.).[315]

V. Unrelated Business Taxable Income Concerns

If a charitable remainder trust has *any* unrelated business *taxable* income (UBTI) in its taxable year, the trust loses its tax exemption for that tax year entirely and is subject to taxes on all of its income during the entire year.[316] The purpose of denying tax-exempt status to a charitable remainder trust that has UBTI is to eliminate the unfair competitive advantage the trust otherwise enjoys over its nonexempt commercial rivals.[317]

A. Unrelated Business Taxable Income Defined

Unrelated business *taxable* income is defined as "the gross income derived by an exempt organization from any unrelated trade or business regularly carried on by it, less the deductions directly connected with the carrying out of such trade or business, both computed

---

[314] Reg. §53.4944-1(a)(2)

[315] Reg. §1.664-2(a)(4)

[316] IRC §511(b)

[317] Reg. §1.513-1(b)

---

with certain modifications."[318] Among the modifications permitted is a specific deduction of $1,000.00.[319]

B. Distinguishing UBI from UBTI

In computing UBTI, it is important to note the distinction between unrelated business income and unrelated business *taxable* income. Only the presence of the latter causes a charitable remainder trust to lose its tax-exemption. Therefore, a charitable remainder trust can have some unrelated business income and, as long as such income is offset by deductions or the specific deduction, still retain its tax-exempt status.

C. Unrelated Trade or Business

The term *trade or business* carries the same meaning as it does under IRC §162. Therefore, it is generally defined as income generated from the sale of goods or services. Presumably, any trade or business carried on by a charitable remainder trust is unrelated to its tax-exempt purpose. For this reason, most sole proprietorships and partnerships are usually unsuitable for transfer to a charitable remainder trust.

Specifically exempt from the definition of unrelated trade or business is any trade or business:

- in which substantially all the work is performed by volunteers;

- carried on by a public charity primarily for the convenience of its members, students, patients, officers or employees; and

- that consists of selling merchandise, substantially all of which has been received by the organization in question as gifts.[320]

The last exception is particularly relevant where the trustee of a charitable remainder trust must promote the sale of contributed assets via auction or other means.

D. Regularly Carried On Trade or Business

A distinction is made regarding the frequency and continuity of business operations.[321] Unlike the occasional fundraising event for which exceptions are made, the type of assets transferred to a charitable remainder trust that generate unrelated business income most commonly fall into the category of being "regularly carried on."

E. Examples of UBI Generating Assets

The following are examples, not an exhaustive list, of UBI generating assets:

---

[318] IRC §512(a)(2)

[319] IRC §512(b)(12)

[320] IRC §513(a)

[321] Reg. §1.513-1(c)(1)

1. Income from the Sale of Goods

- convenience store at a mobile home park

- coin operated food dispensers or laundry facilities connected with real property

- centrally metered utilities for which owner bills tenants at a profit

- inventory used in a trade or business

- collectibles where the trustor is considered a dealer

- artwork given by the artist

2. Income from Rendering of Services

The regulations draw a distinction between the rents and the provision of services for the convenience of the occupant. Income derived from the latter is considered UBI.

Cited examples of income derived from an unrelated business include

- hotels

- boarding houses

- apartment houses furnishing hotel services

- tourist camps or homes

- motor courts or motels

- space in parking lots

- warehouses

- storage garages

- maid services

The furnishing of heat and light; cleaning of public entrances, exits, stairways, and lobbies; or the collection of trash are not considered as services rendered to the occupant.[322]

3. Working Mineral Interests and Production Payments

Income derived from a working interest in a mineral property where the organization (trust) is responsible for either development or operating costs (i.e., income derived from

---

[322] Reg. §1.512-1(b)(4) Example 5

such property is other than a royalty, overriding royalty or net profits interest) is UBI.[323] Further, income derived from mineral production payments purchased with borrowed funds was deemed UBI.[324]

4. Debt-Financed Income

If a charitable remainder trust has any income from debt-financed property, it is treated as having unrelated business income.[325] Debt-financed property includes property that had *acquisition indebtedness* at anytime during the tax year or within 12-months of disposition of the property. In this context, the term "income" is not limited to recurring income but applies as well to gains from the disposition of property.[326]

The term "acquisition indebtedness" generally means the outstanding amount of principal indebtedness incurred prior, during, or after acquiring or improving the property.[327] Further, where property is acquired subject to an indebtedness, the indebtedness is considered as an indebtedness of the organization incurred in acquiring the property even though the organization does not assume or agree to pay such indebtedness.[328]

a. Five-and-Five Exception

Where a charitable remainder trust acquires mortgaged property by gift, the debt secured by the mortgage will not be treated as acquisition indebtedness during the ten years following the date of acquisition as long as:

- the mortgage was placed on the property more than five years prior to the gift, and

- the property was held by the trustor for more than five years prior to the gift.

This exception is inapplicable, however, if the trust assumes any part of the debt secured by the mortgage.[329]

Although this exception seemingly clears the way for the funding of a charitable remainder trust with debt-encumbered property, there are several other considerations. Refer to the discussion of contributions of debt-encumbered property in Chapter 6.

To summarize, when a charitable remainder trust accepts property subject to an indebtedness, the trust (subject to special exception) has acquisition indebtedness

---

[323] Rev. Rul. 69-179, 1969-1 C.B. 158; Reg. §1.512(b)-1(b)

[324] Rev. Rul. 76-354; See discussion of transfers of royalty interests on page 132.

[325] IRC §514(a)(1)

[326] Reg. §1.514(b)-1(a)

[327] IRC §512(c)(1)

[328] IRC §514(c)(2)(A)

[329] IRC §514(c)(2)(B)

unless it qualifies for the *five-and-five exception*. Otherwise, income and gain is included within the computation of unrelated business *taxable* income.

F. Amounts Excluded from Computation of UBTI

Some items and deductions related to such items are excluded from the computation of UBTI. These exclusions include:

- all dividends, interest and annuities, if not debt-financed;

- all royalties, if not debt-financed;

- all rents from real property, if not debt-financed;

- all rents from personal property leased with real property if such rents are an *incidental* amount, if not debt financed;[330]

- gains from the sale of property, other than inventory or property held primarily for sale to customers in the ordinary course of business, unless the property that is sold is debt-financed property;

- net operating losses;

- research income;

- charitable contributions; and

- deductions normally associated with debt-financed property.[331]

The third and fourth exclusions above do not apply if more than 50 percent of rents are attributable to personal property, or the determination of rents is based on the income or profits of a lessee (other than on a fixed percentage of gross sales).

1. Income from the Production of Crops or Livestock

The Service has ruled a sale of hay from property transferred to a charitable remainder trust would not be considered UBTI if sold within a reasonable period of time.[332]

2. Income from Sharecropping Leases

The United States Court of Appeals for the Seventh District was asked to rule on whether the rent an owner of farm property receives under a typical sharecropping contract is unrelated business income. Following are excepts from the ruling:

---

[330] Rents attributable to personal property generally are not an "incidental amount" if such rents exceed ten percent of the total rents from all the property leased. Reg. §1.512(b)-1(c)(2)(ii)(b)

[331] Reg. §1.512(b)-1

[332] Ltr. Rul. 7742063

> Sharecropping or share tenancy—tenant farming in which the rent is a fraction of the crop rather than a fixed amount of money—is an ancient institution and one found in many parts of the world. The terms of sharecropping contracts vary, but a common arrangement, and the one here, is for the owner of the farmland to contribute the land and the buildings, the tenant farmer to contribute the farm labor and the farm equipment, and owner and tenant to split the crop fifty-fifty.

> Excluded from the original concept of unrelated business income was passive investment income, including—in the original provision—all rents from real property." With rents undefined, this provision was an invitation to taxpayers to recharacterize business income as rental income. In 1969, Congress decided to levy the unrelated business income tax on rent from real property "if the determination of the amount of such rent depends in whole or in part on the income or profits derived by any person from the property leased (other than an amount based on a fixed percentage or percentages of receipts or sales).[333]

The position of the Service was that, anything more than a *de minimis* contribution by the owner to the cost of producing the farm's output transforms a sharecropping contract from a true lease to a partnership. The Court, in its affirmation of the district court, disagreed stating,

> We do not believe that the provision defining 'rent' for purposes of the unrelated business income tax was intended to bring about a revolution in agricultural or any other domain of leasing. It was intended to arm the Internal Revenue Service against efforts to reclassify business income as rent. That was not what the parties to this sharecropping contract were doing.[334]

3. Income from Contests Related to the Organization s Tax-Exempt Purpose

A trustor proposed to fund a charitable remainder trust with a condominium unit. In addition, the trustor wished to generate public interest in and raise additional money for the charitable remainderman. The trustor proposed that the trust, through an appropriate agent including, but not limited to the remainderman, conduct an essay contest in which contestants were required to write an essay suggesting how teenage pregnancies can be reduced in the United States. Each contestant would be charged an entry fee in the range of $50 to $100, such fee to be determined prior to the commencement of the contest. The essays would be judged by a panel selected by the remainderman. All persons assisting in the operation of the essay contest would be unpaid volunteers. The winner of this contest will be the entrant whose essay demonstrates the highest degree of skill and thoughtfulness in providing a solution to this social problem. The entry fees will be retained by the trust. The winner of the contest would receive the title to the condominium.

Based on all the facts and circumstances described above, the Service ruled that the entry fees received by trust would not constitute unrelated business taxable income within the meaning of section 512(a) of the Code.

---

[333]   IRC §512(b)(3)(B)(ii)

[334]   Harlan E. Moore Charitable Trust v. United States of America, United States Court of Appeals , Seventh District No. 93-1842.

In substantiating its ruling, the Service cited section 513(a) of the Code that provides, in part, that the term "trade or business" includes any activity which is carried on for the production of income from the sale of goods or the performance of services. Section 513(a)(1) of the Code provides, however, that the term "unrelated trade or business" does not include any trade or business in which substantially all the work in carrying on such trade or business is performed for the organization without compensation. Because all persons assisting in the operation of the contest would be unpaid volunteers, the entry fees from the essay contest were ruled not to constitute unrelated business income.[335]

G. Specific Deduction

A specific deduction of $1,000.00 is allowed in determining unrelated business taxable income. The deduction is not allowed in computing net operating losses, however.[336]

H. Exception for Controlled Organizations

If a charitable remainder trust owns more than 80 percent of the combined total voting power of all classes of stock in a corporation and at least 80 percent of all other classes of shares, the corporation will be considered a *controlled organization*.

Interest, annuities, royalties, or rents derived by the trust from a controlled organization are included as an item of gross income of the trust. However, a trust will not usually receive this type of income from a corporation anyway. The key is that dividends are excluded. Accordingly, even though a charitable remainder trust may own 100 percent of the stock in a closely-held corporation, the issuance of a dividend will not cause the trust to have UBTI.[337]

I. Tax Consequences of UBTI to Trust

If a charitable remainder trust has one penny of UBTI, the trust is treated as a complex trust and is taxed pursuant to the rules of IRC §§641-644 and §§661-664 applicable to complex trusts. A nonexempt charitable remainder trust is subject to tax at rates imposed by IRC §1(e) (rates similar to those for married persons filing separately). In any subsequent year, if the trust has no UBTI, it regains its tax-exempt status.

The actual effect of taxation on a charitable remainder trust having UBTI can range from benign to catastrophic. For example, a trust that has UBTI in an amount less than distributions to income recipients will pay no tax because distributions are deductible to the trust. Further, the taxation of a nonexempt charitable remainder trust does not affect the tax treatment of amounts distributed to recipients (e.g., the *throwback* provisions of IRC sections 665 through 667 are not applicable to those amounts).[338]

---

[335]   Ltr. Rul. 9517037

[336]   Reg. §1.512(b)-1(h)

[337]   Reg. §1.512(b)-(1)(l); IRC §368(c)

[338]   Reg. §§1.664-1(c); 1.664-1(d)(1)

A trust that has any UBTI in the same year in which it sells a highly appreciated asset (such as is frequently the case in the first year of the trust) is subject to tax on capital gains, depreciation recapture, and alternative minimum tax.

It is also important to note that, a trust will continue to have debt-financed property for twelve months following the disposition of the property from which the debt-financed income was produced. For example, the disposition of debt-financed property in January of 1996 will continue to produce debt-financed income into January of 1997. The trust could, therefore, have UBTI in 1997.

VI. Tax and Information Return Requirements

A. Individual Return Requirements

In addition to claiming the charitable contribution income tax deduction as an itemized deduction and including the preference amount attributable to the gift within the computation of alternative minimum tax (depending on state income tax rules), a trustor is required to file certain tax and information returns.

1.   Form   2 3 - Noncash Charitable Contributions

If the transferred property exceeds $500 in value, the trustor must attach a *Noncash Charitable Contributions* information return and include it with his or her income tax return for any year in which a contribution is made. If a qualified appraisal is required, an appraisal summary (Form 8283, Part B) must be completed and signed by the qualified appraiser and trustee.

Caution: Failure to attach the appraisal summary to the trustor's return will result in irrevocable loss of the charitable deduction unless the failure was due to a "good faith omission."

2.   Form 709 - Federal Gift Tax Return

This may come as a surprise, but any person creating a charitable remainder trust in any amount should file a federal gift tax return (Form 709) for the year in which the trust is created and in any year in which additional contributions are made, even if no gift tax is due.

The reason? Even though contributions to charity via a qualified charitable remainder trust qualify for the unlimited charitable gift tax charitable deduction under IRC §2522, charitable contributions are not one of the specific exceptions under IRC §6019 that relieves the trustor of the requirement of filing a return.

The exceptions include:

- gifts of a present interest of $10,000 or less to any person (includes charitable organizations) during the calendar year,[339]

- gifts for certain educational or medical expenses,[340] and

- gifts to a spouse.[341]

Because a gift to a charitable remainder trust constitutes a gift of a *future* interest to charity, the $10,000 annual exclusion is unavailable. Therefore, a transfer of any amount to a charitable remainder trust requires the filing of a return. Income distributions to a noncharitable income recipient, however, constitute a gift of present interest for which the annual exclusion qualifies.[342]

A failure to file a required return can cause two problems:

- A willful failure to file a return is a misdemeanor that can result in a fine of $25,000, one year in prison, or both, together with costs of prosecution.[343] The key here is probably the word, "willful." A failure to file a gift tax return for a charitable gift that results in no tax is probably closer to a good faith omission than a willful attempt to perpetrate a misdemeanor. Filing a return, however, will eliminate any doubt.

- The statute of limitations will remain open thereby subjecting the gift to review indefinitely.

The return must be filed by April 15th of the year following the calendar year when gifts are made. Check individual states for additional filing requirements.

3. Gift Incomplete when Trustor Reserves Right to Substitute Remainderman

In Letter Ruling 9326049, a husband and wife created a charitable remainder trust. With respect to his interest, the husband reserved the power to change the designation of the charitable beneficiaries. The wife did not reserve such a power with respect to her interest. The Service concluded the husband's gift to be incomplete for gift tax purposes. The wife's gift was deemed complete. Whether the wife is required to file Form 709, whereas the husband is not, is not clear.[344]

---

[339] IRC §2503(b)

[340] IRC §2503(e)

[341] IRC §2523

[342] See Chapter 5 - Gift and Estate Tax Considerations.

[343] IRC §7203

[344] See Rev. Rul. 77-275, 1977-2 C.B. 346; See also Ltr. Rul. 9204036

B. Returns Required by Trustee

The following returns are required to be filed by the trustee. Unless otherwise specified, they are due by April 15th of the year following the year for which the return is required.

1. Form 5227 - Split Interest Trust Information Return

Form 5227 reports trust income, deductions, accumulations, and distributions for the year. Extension to file may be requested on Form 2758.

2. Form 1041-A - US Information Return Trust Accumulation of Charitable Amounts

Form 1041-A is filed by the trustee to ensure the unitrust amount or annuity amount was properly distributed to the income recipients as provided for in the governing instrument. This form is not required if all net income is required to be distributed currently to income recipients.[345] Failure to file on a timely basis carries a $10 per day late penalty with a maximum of $5,000.00. An extension to file may be requested on Form 2758.

3. Form K-1

Form K-1, describing the tax character of income distributions (per the four-tier system), must be prepared for each income recipient according to his or her prorata share of income.

4. State Tax and Information Returns

Companion returns to Federal Forms 5227 and 1041-A are required in some states. Refer to state law.

C. Special Returns

1. Form 2 2 - Donee Information Return

If property transferred to a charitable remainder trust (exceeding $500 in value) is sold within two years of its contribution, the trustee is required to file Form 8282 which describes the type of donated property, when received, date sold, the price for which it was sold, and the identity of the trustor. This form enables the IRS to compare the value the trustor *claimed* as a charitable contribution to the *actual* value as determined by a sale.

Failure to file within 125-days after disposition carries a $50.00 penalty.

---

[345]   Rev. Proc. 83-32

2.   Form 1041 - U.S. Fiduciary Income Tax Return

A trust that has any unrelated business *taxable* income (under IRC §512) or otherwise is treated as a private foundation is taxed as a complex trust and is required to file Form 1041.

3.   Form 4720 - Excise Tax Return

A trustee or disqualified person who incurs a Chapter 42 excise tax (by violation of self-dealing, excess business holdings, jeopardizing investment, or taxable expenditure rules) must file Form 4720 by April 15th of the year following the calendar year in which the act occurred.

D. Written Acknowledgment from Charitable Remainderman

Starting in 1994, charitable contributions of $250 or more must be accompanied by a contemporaneous written acknowledgment from the recipient charity. The acknowledgment must be in the hands of the donor prior to the earlier of (a) the date on which the donor files a return for the taxable year in which the contribution was made, or (b) the due date (including extensions) for filing such return.[346]

Because the trustor of a charitable remainder trust is not required to designate a specific organization as the charitable remainderman at the time the trustor transfers property to the trust, there is often no designated donee organization available to provide a contemporaneous written statement to the trustor. In addition, even if a specific remainderman is designated, the designation is often revocable. For these reasons, charitable remainder trusts are exempt from the requirements of IRC §170(f)(8).[347]

VII. Powers of Amendment and Reformation

A. Limited Power of Amendment

The regulations provide that, "The trust may not be subject to a power to invade, alter, amend, or revoke for the beneficial use of a person other than an organization described in section 170(c)."[348] However, because of the extreme technical nature of charitable remainder trusts and the possibility of future changes in drafting requirements, the model forms published in the Revenue Procedures contain the following provision:

10. Limited Power of Amendment

The Trust is irrevocable. The Trustee, however, shall have the power, acting alone, to amend the Trust in any manner required for the sole purpose of ensuring that the Trust qualifies and continues to qualify as a charitable remainder trust within the meaning of section 664(d)(1) of the Code.

---

[346]   IRC §170(f)(8)

[347]   Prop. Reg. §1.170A-13(f)(13)

[348]   Section 1.664-3(a)(4)

Although this clause may provide a trustee with some ameliorative relief, it cannot be relied on to cure a trust that is defective from the time of its inception. To illustrate the narrow interpretation of this provision, the Tax Reform Act of 1986 required all trusts to adopt a calendar tax year and permitted trustees to amend existing trust instruments to bring them into compliance. In a subsequent letter ruling, a charitable remainderman who served as trustee for thirty charitable remainder trusts proposed to change the valuation date of all thirty trusts to the first day of the calendar year to coincide with the new calendar tax year requirement. The IRS held that in the case of any trust for which the prior valuation date does not occur prior to the first quarterly payment, such a change will violate regulation section 1.664-3(a)(1)(iv) and will disqualify the trust.[349]

Can a charitable remainder trust include a provision that makes it null and void and returns all the trust assets to the grantors if the Internal Revenue Service disallows a deduction for the value of the remainder interest? In Rev. Rul. 76-309, the Service ruled that it cannot citing the following reasons:

> Section 664(d)(1)(B) of the Code provides that no amount of a charitable remainder annuity trust other than the annuity payments described in subparagraph (A) may be paid to or for the use of any person other than an organization described in section 170(c).
>
> Section 664(d)(1)(C) of the Code provides that following the termination of the annuity payments described in subparagraph (A), the remainder interest in the charitable remainder annuity trust is to be transferred to, or for the use of, an organization described in section 170(c) or is to be retained by the trust for such a use.
> Under section 1.664-2(a)(4) of the Income Tax Regulations, no amount other than the annuity amount described in section 1.664-2(a)(1) of the regulations may be paid to or for the use of any person other than an organization described in section 170(c) of the Code.
>
> Under section 1.664-2(a)(6)(i) of the regulations, the entire corpus of the charitable remainder annuity trust is required to be transferred to or for the use of one or more organizations described in section 170(c) of the Code or retained for such use upon the termination of all noncharitable interests.
>
> In the instant case the condition in the trust instrument providing for the trust assets to be returned to the grantors if the Service disallows a deduction for the remainder interest presents the possibility that amounts other than the annuity payments will be paid to a person other than an organization described in section 170(c) of the Code and that the remainder interest will not be transferred to or for the use of a charitable organization or retained by the trust for such a use. Accordingly, the trust does not qualify as a charitable remainder annuity trust under section 664 of the Code and the value of the remainder interest contributed to the trust is not deductible as a charitable contribution for Federal income tax purposes.[350]

B. Reformation

It has always been the intent of Congress to encourage charitable gifts; however, abuses developed that resulted in the unrestricted support of noncharitable life interests at the expense of residual bequests (with correspondingly large tax deductions) to charitable foundations.

The Tax Reform Act of 1969 added section 664 to the Internal Revenue Code and with it the formal definition of charitable remainder trusts. Within the same legislation Congress added section 2055(e)(2). This section disallows estate tax deductions when a trust or estate creates a

---

[349]   Ltr. Rul. 8916008; See also Chapter 3 - "Changing Recipient Order Disqualifies Trust" on page 51.

[350]   Rev. Rul. 76-309, 1976-2 C.B. 196

"split interest" by bequeathing interests in the same property to both charitable and noncharitable beneficiaries.

Congress granted a limited exception to this rule with section 2055(e)(2)(A), which allows deductions for split remainder interests that take the form of a charitable remainder annuity trust, charitable remainder unitrust, or pooled income fund. The exception was substantiated by the fact that when any of these three instruments are used the IRS can determine the total cost of the bequest to the noncharitable legatee, and then accurately separate the charitable and noncharitable claims on the estate.

When this section led to harsh results in some cases, Congress enacted section 2055(e)(3) in 1974. The new section provided temporary relief by allowing an otherwise nondeductible bequest to be deductible if the will was amended so the bequest qualified as one of the three specified exceptions provided for in section 2055(e)(2). In 1984, after several extensions of this rule, Congress made the provision permanent by enacting section 2055(e)(3). This section details the requirements of a "qualified reformation."

1. Reformable Interests

In order to be a reformable interest, the trust must first be in a form that would have been deductible for estate tax purposes under the split-interest trust rules that existed prior to the Tax Reform Act of 1969. Second, the interest must be expressed as a fixed dollar amount or a fixed percentage of the annual value (as described in section 664(d)(3)). There are two exceptions to this second requirement:

- In the case of a will executed before January 1, 1979, this second requirement does not apply.[351]

- A judicial proceeding must commence no later than 90 days after the last date (including extensions) for:

    - filing the estate tax return if an estate tax return is required to be filed, or

---

[351]   In Wells Fargo v. U.S. (9th Cir.), the government attempted to prove that a codicil made after January 1, 1979 to a will originally executed prior to January 1, 1979 constituted a republication of the will for purposes of determining the application to the reformation exception under section 2055(e)(3)(C)(iv). The court stated, "In ordinary legal usage, the words 'execution' and 'republication' mean different things. The word 'execution' in connection with a document such as a will means signing it. Ballentine's Law Dictionary 433 (3d ed. 1969). The word 'publication' ordinarily means the act by the testatrix of telling her witnesses that the document is intended to be her will; see 79 AmJur 2d, Wills, section 256 (1975)."

The California statutes on execution of wills use the words in their ordinary legal significance. See Cal Prob. Code section 6110- 6113. California law treats later republication as equivalent to execution, but this is a legal fiction to accomplish the testatrix's intent, not a physical fact. The government argued that the republication of the will in 1982 amounts to execution in 1982. Under California law, republication of the will is 'tantamount' to making and executing the will at the time of republication, In re Challman's Estate, 274 P.2d 439, 442 (Cal. 1954), because "in substance, the will is re-executed as of that time." Simon v. Grayson, 102 P.2d 1081, 1082 (Cal. 1940). This general rule holds except where republication would "defeat [the] testator's most probable intention." In re McCauley's Estate, 71 P. 512, 513-14 (Cal. 1903).

The court held, however, the construction of the "will executed before January 1, 1979" language to refer only to execution, not to republication, is in accord with the generally liberal approach of other circuits toward 26 U.S.C. section 2055. Taken literally, the words "execution" and "publication" relate to different acts. The court held for the taxpayer.

- filing the income tax return, if an estate tax return is not required to be filed.

This latter requirement is intended to prevent a trustor from attempting to evade compliance by hoping not to be audited.[352]

2. Qualified Reformation

A qualified reformation is accomplished by amending the trust (in accordance with local law) to convert a reformable interest into a qualified interest. A qualified reformation is effective if:

- the actuarial value of the qualified (charitable) interest does not exceed 105 percent of the reformable interest;

- in the case of an inter vivos interest, the reformation is retroactive to the time of creation of the trust or, in the case of a testamentary trust, the reformation is retroactive to the date of death; and

- the trust term of the qualified interest is the same as the term of the reformable interest except if measured by a term exceeding twenty years; in such case, the term can be reduced to a term of twenty years.[353]

In addition, the deduction for the qualified must be no greater than the deduction for the reformable interest (had the reformable interest been qualified). Further, in the event the income recipient dies prior to the filing of the trustor's estate tax return, the reformable interest will be deemed to have met the conditions of a qualified reformation. The charitable deduction is calculated as of the date of the income recipient's death.[354]

The reformation of testamentary split interest charitable gifts into qualifying charitable remainder interests is the most frequently litigated issue by the IRS relating to charitable remainder trusts. Great care should, therefore, be taken to ensure the testator's intent to create a qualifying interest is accomplished.[355]

3. Reformation to Amend Right to Substitute Remainderman Permitted

Letter Ruling 9517020 sought judicial relief to correct a drafting error that omitted a trustor's right to substitute the charitable remainderman. The trustor proposed to reform the trust by filing a petition with the court seeking a judicial modification, *ab initio*, of the

---

[352] For more detailed examples, refer to Ltr. Ruls. 9407024 and 9422044.

[353] IRC §2055(e)(3)(B)

[354] IRC §2055(e)(3)(E)

[355] See the following letter rulings regarding reformations: Ltr. Ruls. 9515029; 9517043; 9519028; 9520041; 9523030; 9526031; 9529042; 9531003; 9535025; 9549016; 9550036; 9611019; 9613012; 9616032; 9623019; 9633004; 9635018; 9642010; 9642010; 9648042; 9716019; 9719013; 9725013; 9728007; 9733014; 9736023; 9740008; 9741022; 9745007; 9750061; 9802036; 9804019; 9811021; 9816002; 9821009; 9823037; 9827008; 9827010; 9829017

trust. In this case, the state's common law permits reformation of an irrevocable trust when it is established that, because of a drafting error, a trust's governing instrument fails to accurately reflect the trustor's original intent and that such error threatens a material purpose of the trust.

In its ruling, the Service cited section 1.664-3(a)(4) of the regulations that provides, in part, "The trust may not be subject to a power to invade, alter, amend, or revoke for the beneficial use of a person other than an organization described in section 170(c) of the Code. Notwithstanding the preceding sentence, the grantor may retain the power exercisable only by will to revoke or terminate the interest of any recipient other than an organization described in section 170(c)."

After reviewing the facts and relevant documents submitted, the Service concluded the proposed judicial reformation would not violate sections 1.664-3(a)(3)(ii) and 1.664-3(a)(4) of the regulations or any provisions under section 664 of the Code, and remaining regulations thereunder. Accordingly, it concluded the proposed judicial reformation of the trust would not adversely effect the trust's qualification as a charitable remainder unitrust.

4. Recipients Use Disclaimers to Facilitate Reformation

An individual died in 1993 having executed a revocable trust in 1992 that became irrevocable upon death. On the decedent's death, the trust was divided into two separate trusts for the benefit of two surviving beneficiaries. During their lifetimes, each beneficiary was entitled to receive the entire net income and, according to the trust instrument and at the discretion of the trustee, principal distributions from his or her trust. Upon the death of each beneficiary, the remainder interest of his or her trust would be distributed to a named charity.

Within nine months of the decedent's death each beneficiary executed and delivered to the personal representative and trustee a disclaimer disclaiming his or her rights to receive distributions of principal from the trust.

The disclaimers were subsequently filed on a timely basis with the probate court. A petition for reformation of the trust agreement with the probate court was filed shortly thereafter. Finally, waivers and consents to the reformation were filed by the beneficiaries, charity, and Attorney General.

In 1995, the probate court issued an order reforming the trusts to conform to the requirements of section 664 for charitable remainder unitrusts. The trusts would each carry a 7.4 percent payout rate and standard payout formats.

At issue were:

- whether the beneficiaries' disclaimers to principal were valid in light of the fact that the beneficiaries acquired a right to receive a unitrust payment which, if income was insufficient, would be paid from principal?

- whether a charitable deduction would have been allowed under section 2055(a) for the charitable interest at the time of the decedent's death but for section 2055(e)(2)?

- if the decedent's trust agreement precludes a charitable deduction?

With respect to the first issue, the Service ruled that a right to receive principal from the unitrust is a separate interest that will not disqualify an otherwise qualified disclaimer.

Regarding the second issue, the Service ruled that because the beneficiaries' disclaimers related back to the date of the decedent's death, a charitable deduction would have been allowed under section 2055(a) for the charitable remainder interests but for section 2055(e)(2).

Finally, the decedent's trust agreement did not preclude a charitable deduction because, as a result of the reformation process, provisions inconsistent with precluding a charitable deduction were revoked.[356]

5.   Recipient Uses Disclaimers to Accelerate Remainder Interests

A decedent created two charitable remainder unitrusts naming his brother as the sole income recipient of both. The decedent's trust provided, if the brother disclaimed his interests, the amounts would be distributed immediately and in full to the charitable remaindermen of the unitrusts to be held in specified sub-funds. The brother did disclaim his interests following the requirements for qualified disclaimers set forth in IRC §2518(b). Furthermore, the brother relinquished any power of direction over the use of the funds by the charitable recipients.

The Service ruled the decedent will be entitled to a charitable estate tax deduction for any property that passes to charity as a result of the brother's disclaimers.[357]

6.   Division of Trust into Separate Trusts to Accelerate Portion of Remainder Interest

In a request for private ruling, the trustee of a charitable remainder unitrust proposed to segregate certain assets of the trust into a separate (newly formed) trust, subject to the same terms as the existing trust. Such segregation is permissible under state law. The trustor will then assign his right as to the income interest in the newly created trust to the charitable remainderman. The merger of the income and remainder interests will terminate the new trust thereby accelerating the payment of the remainder interest. The Service approved the arrangement.[358]

---

[356]   Ltr. Rul. 9610005

[357]   Ltr. Rul. 9635011

[358]   Ltr. Rul. 9817010

This ruling offers an interesting solution for income recipients who wish to transfer other than their entire income interest to charity and receive an income tax charitable deduction. Rev. Rul. 86-60 holds that a transfer of other than an income recipient's entire income interest does not qualify for deduction.[359]

7.   Reformation to Eliminate Net Income Provision

In a proposed reformation, a taxpayer desired to convert a net income unitrust into a standard unitrust by eliminating the trust's net income option. The Service promptly denied the reformation citing Reg. §1.664-3(a)(4).[360] In a separate ruling, the Service also held that such a reformation would constitute a prohibited act of self-dealing.[361]

8.   Reformation to Correct Drafting Errors

What if a net income provision finds its way into a charitable remainder unitrust by way of a drafting error? On several occasions the IRS has approved a proposed judicial modification to correct a "scrivener's error" when the donor's intent to create a standard unitrust was clearly documented.[362] Such modification was also ruled not to be a prohibited act of self-dealing.

In separate request for ruling, a unitrust was funded with stock in a closely-held corporation. The trust instrument included a prohibition against excess business holdings under IRC §4943. However, because the trust did not provide for a portion of the unitrust amount to be paid to an organization described in IRC §170(c), the prohibition against excess business holdings was not required.[363]

The trust further permitted the remainder interest to be transferred to an organization described in IRC §509(a), which includes private nonoperating foundations. By making such provision, the trustor's income tax charitable contribution deduction would be based on the lesser of the fair market value and the trustor's adjusted cost basis in the contributed property. The trustor had always intended to name only public charities as remainderman. The IRS approved the reformation thereby enabling the trust to hold the stock and preserving the trustor's full fair market value deduction.[364]

Yet another taxpayer had the opposite problem. Again, through a drafting error, this particular trust restricted the selection of remaindermen to public charities. However, it was the trustor's intention to name one or more private nonoperating foundations.[365] In this case, the trustor had contributed publicly traded stock. In its ruling, the Service mentioned IRC 170(e)(5) which permits taxpayers to deduct contributions of publicly

---

[359]   See discussion on page 48.

[360]   Ltr. Rul. 9516040

[361]   Ltr. Rul. 9522021

[362]   Ltr. Ruls. 9506015; 9822041; 9804036

[363]   IRC §4947(b)(3)(B)

[364]   Ltr. Rul. 9743004

[365]   Ltr. Rul. 9818027

traded securities to private nonoperating foundations at full fair market value provided the contribution is made during a specified time window.[366] The trustor's contribution, however, did not qualify under the special exception. Accordingly, the trustor would have to file an amended tax return to reduce the deduction.

9. Division of Trust into Two Trusts Following Divorce

A and B, a married couple, established a charitable remainder unitrust in 1991. Following their divorce in 1993, A and B proposed to divide the trust into two separate charitable remainder trusts, each being identical to the original trust. Each party would serve as trustee of their own trust. The Service approved the arrangement, stating simply that the division of the trust would not cause the trust to fail to qualify as a charitable remainder trust.[367]

10. Rescission of Trust

The Service has ruled privately that the return of the assets of a charitable remainder annuity trust to the trust's grantor after the trust is declared void *ab initio* by a court will not be an act of self-dealing or a taxable expenditure, and will not subject the trust to the private foundation termination tax.

A husband and wife, age 77 and 73, were concerned with having sufficient income to cover living expenses and maintaining their principal. After they heard of the income benefits of a charitable remainder annuity trust, the wife executed a trust agreement. After she created the trust, her husband suffered a catastrophic illness and they were unable to live on the income from the trust and other sources. The wife filed suit for rescission of the trust and asserted that she did not understand the restrictions imposed on the trust as a charitable remainder annuity trust. The trustee disputed the grantor's assertions on the merits, but the court declared the trust void *ab initio*. The Service concluded that no valid trust existed for federal income tax purposes because the court declared the trust void from inception.[368] Accordingly, all transactions completed by the trust were deemed completed for income tax purposes by the grantor. Likewise, if the grantor had claimed an income tax charitable contribution deduction, an amended return would need to be filed to withdraw it.

Comment: This ruling speaks to several important issues: 1) the importance of balancing the income producing capabilities of the CRT with maintaining adequate estate liquidity; 2) providing prospective donors with complete written disclosure regarding all aspects of the trust, its operation, benefits, and risks; and 3) establishing donative intent as the primary motivation for making the gift.

---

[366]   The window closed on June 30, 1998.

[367]   Ltr. Rul. 9403030

[368]   Ltr. Rul. 9816030

VIII. Abusive Arrangements

When the second edition of this book was published in 1993, the authors cautioned that as charitable remainder trusts became more common, there would be the temptation to test the envelope of prudent application. The following are several examples of such tests that have come to the attention of the Service or that were discussed in the tax planning press at press-time for this edition.

A. IRS Denounces Accelerated Unitrust

The Service announced in Notice 94-78 that it will challenge transactions that attempt to use a section 664 charitable remainder unitrust to convert appreciated assets into cash while avoiding a substantial portion of the tax on the gain.[369]

In the transactions the Service is referring to, appreciated assets are transferred to a short-term unitrust that has a high percentage payout rate. The Notice offers an example of capital assets with a value of $1 million and a zero cost basis being contributed to a unitrust on January 1, 19x1. The measuring term of the trust is two years and the payout rate is set at *80* percent of the fair market value of the trust assets, valued annually. The contributed assets produce no income.

The unitrust amount required to be paid during 19x1 is $800,000; however, because of a failure on the part of the trustee to sell the contributed assets, no distributions are made to the income recipient (trustor) within the first tax year. At the beginning of 19x2, the assets are sold for $1,000,000 (plus or minus any gain or loss). The first-year $800,000 unitrust amount is distributed to the donor between January 1st and April 15th of 19x2. The unitrust amount for 19x2 is $160,000 (80 percent x $200,000 net fair market value of the trust assets). At the end of 19x2, the trust terminates and $40,000 is paid to the charitable remainderman.

Proponents of that type of transaction, the Service said, would contend the tax treatment is as follows: Because no assets are sold or distributed to the donor during the first year, the entire $800,000 unitrust amount is characterized as a distribution of trust corpus under section 664(b)(4). The $160,000 second-year unitrust amount is characterized as capital gain, on which the donor pays tax of $44,800 ($160,000 x .28). The donor is left with $915,200 in cash ($800,000 from the first year and $115,200 net after tax from the second year). If the donor had sold the assets directly, he or she would have paid a tax of $280,000 on the $1,000,000 capital gain and would have had net cash of $720,000.

The Service stated that it will challenge transactions of this type based on one or more legal doctrines, depending on the particular facts of each case, adding that "a mechanical and literal application of regulations that would yield a result inconsistent with the purposes of the charitable remainder trust provisions may not be respected."

On examination of purported charitable remainder trusts used in the type of transaction in question, the Service warned that it will apply an appropriate legal doctrine to recast the entire transaction, to characterize the unitrust amount as gross income rather than trust corpus, to

---

[369] Notice 94-78, 1994-2 C.B. 555

attribute gain on the sale of trust property to the donor, or to challenge the qualification of the trust under section 664. In appropriate circumstances, the Service might impose the section 4941 tax on self-dealing on the grounds that the trustee's postponement of the sale of trust assets beyond the first year may constitute a use of trust assets for the benefit of the donor, who is a disqualified person under section 4941(d)(1)(E). It will also apply any applicable penalties to the participants in this type of transaction. Finally, the Service notes that information sufficient to identify the type of transaction in question is required to be filed on Form 5227, Split-Interest Trust Information Return.

In support of Notice 94-78, Treasury issued proposed regulations that will require all charitable remainder annuity trusts and all standard payout format charitable remainder unitrusts to make full distribution of the annuity or unitrust by the end of the trust year in which it is due.[370] Concurrently, Congress enacted two measures designed to curtail the use of accelerated trusts: 1) a maximum payout rate of 50 percent, and 2) a minimum qualifying present value of remainder interest of 10 percent. These requirements are discussed in detail in Chapter 3.

B. The Taxable Charitable Remainder Trust

At least one practitioner has advanced a theory that is designed to circumvent the four-tier system of taxation. Suppose on January 1st, an individual transfers $1,000,000 in stock, having a $100,000 cost basis, to a 5 percent standard unitrust. The trustor is the sole income recipient. The trustee sells the stock and reinvests the proceeds in tax-exempt bonds, also yielding 5 percent. The income recipient receives $50,000 the first year.

Under the four-tier system, the distribution is taxable to the income recipient as long-term capital gain. Assuming there are no changes in valuation, the process will repeat itself for the next eighteen years until the entire $900,000 gain from the sale of the contributed stock has been distributed—so far, so good.

Imagine the same scenario; however, at the beginning of year two, the trustee sells $50,000 of the bonds and purchases an interest in a partnership that produces $2,500 per year of debt-financed income (or other UBI). In this case, the trust is determined to have UBTI and loses its tax-exempt status for the year.

The "Taxable CRT" plan relies on the fact that all income of a charitable remainder trust should be taxed if any of it is UBTI. Because a non-exempt trust is taxed as a complex trust, the four-tier system is no longer applicable. Accordingly, the $50,000 distribution to the income recipient should consist of $2,500 of ordinary income (attributable to the partnership) and $47,500 in tax-exempt income (attributable to the bonds). Because the trust has distributed all of its income, it pays no tax.

The reporter of the plan cautions that many practitioners may be reluctant to recommend this approach, "particularly in light of the IRS's recent willingness to view the use of a charitable

---

[370] Reg-209823-96

remainder trust for the grantor's tax benefit as self-dealing."[371] He also states that such a plan creates potential issues concerning fiduciary liability.[372]

Comment: While the IRS has not commented on this scenario, the authors believe it would most likely and properly attack it with at least the same amount of enthusiasm as displayed in Notice 94-78. Because the plan takes advantage of a purported legislative fiction, the authors believe its theoretical outcome is inconsistent with Congressional intent. We further speculate that because the plan relies on an express or implied understanding that the trustee will reinvest a substantial portion of the trust assets in tax-exempt bonds, the IRS would have good footing on which to attribute all capital gain to the trustor based on the theories set forth in Rev. Rul. 60-370.[373] As stated, potential issues of self-dealing are also present.

C. The Zeroed Out Charitable Remainder Trust

The so-called "zeroed out" or "near zero" charitable remainder trust concept is designed to nearly eliminate the taxable gift attributable to income interests passing to non-grantor income recipients.

For example, a parent transfers $1,000,000 to a net income unitrust bearing a 40 percent payout rate. The trust instrument defines income under IRC §643(b) and names the grantor as the sole primary income recipient for a term of ten years. Upon expiration of the term, the grantor's child or other non-grantor is named as the successor income recipient for an additional ten-year term. The combined terms equal twenty years.

The amount of the taxable gift to the non-grantor income recipient is determined at the time the trust is created. It is equal to the present value of the remainder interest (PVRI) for the first ten-year term minus the present value of remainder interest for the second ten-year term.

In this case, the PVRI for the first ten-year term is based on a fair market value of $1,000,000, a 40 percent payout rate, and a ten-year term. Given the extremely high payout rate, the PVRI is only $10,000. For purposes of calculating the PVRI for the second ten-year term, it is assumed the trust will have a fair market value of $10,000 at the beginning of the period. The PVRI based on $10,000, a 40 percent payout rate, and the remaining ten-year term is $100. The present value of the non-grantor's successor income interest (i.e., the taxable gift) is $9,900 ($10,000 minus $100).

Continuing with the example, suppose that during the initial ten-year term, the trust is invested for growth. It might be realistic to assume the trust could double in value during this period. At the beginning of the eleventh year, the investments are switched to maximize distributable net income for the benefit of the successor income recipient — all for a taxable gift of only $9,900!

This technique relies on the presence of a net income option that, when used in concert with an extremely high payout rate, creates tremendous disparity between the amount of income

---

[371] In reference to Notice 94-78, 1994-2 C.B. 555

[372] Howard M. Zaritsky, J.D., "The Joys of a Taxable CRT," *Estate Planning*, March/April 1996 Vol. 23 No. 3 p. 144.

[373] Rev. Rul 60-370, 1960-2 C.B. 203. See discussion of "The Pomona Ruling" on page 203.

the unitrust *should* distribute and the amount it *actually* distributes. It is important to note that the present value computations as described in section 664 of the regulations make no adjustment for the inclusion of a net income option.

The Achilles' heal of the technique occurs if, in the case of the example, the parent dies during the period of his or her income interest. If this occurs, the entire date-of-death value of the trust is brought back into the parent's estate under IRC §2036(a). Given the extraordinarily high payout rate, the value of the taxable transfer would exceed 99 percent of the fair market value of the trust's assets!

Reporters of this technique concluded that the trust should avoid the *sham transaction* rules of section 2702 that, if applicable, would value the donor's primary income interest at zero. They also recommend that in order to reduce exposure, (a) an independent trustee should be used, and (b) the unitrust payout rate should be in line with ordinary growth rates (e.g., 10 percent to 15 percent rather than 25 percent or higher). Finally, they further suggested the Service's best recourse for eliminating potential abuse would appear to be corrective legislation.[374]

Apparently, the IRS and Treasury read *The Journal of Taxation.* On April 18, 1997, Treasury issued proposed regulations that amend section 25.2702(c)(3) to provide that income interests retained by a donor will be valued at zero (for gift tax purposes) when someone other than (1) the donor, (2) the donor's spouse, or (3) both the donor and the donor's spouse is a non-charitable beneficiary of the trust.[375] The general explanation of the proposed regulations follows:

A. General Explanation

Section 2702 provides special rules to determine the amount of the gift when an individual makes a transfer in trust to or for the benefit of a family member and the individual or an applicable family member retains an interest in the trust. Under section 2702(a), the retained interest in these situations is generally valued at zero unless the interest is a qualified interest. Under section 2702(b), a qualified interest includes the right to receive fixed payments at least annually and the right to receive amounts at least annually that are a fixed percentage of the annual fair market value of the property in the trust.

Section 2702(a)(3)(A)(iii) was added by section 1702(f)(11)(A)(iv) of the Small Business Job Protection Act of 1996 (Public Law 104-188) as a technical correction to the Revenue Reconciliation Act of 1990 (Public Law 101-508). Section 2702(a)(3)(A)(iii) provides that section 2702(a) shall not apply to any transfer to the extent regulations provide that such transfer is not inconsistent with the purposes of the section. According to the legislative history, the regulatory authority could be used to create an exception from the application of section 2702 for a qualified charitable remainder trust that does not otherwise create an opportunity for transferring property to a family member free of transfer tax. H.R. Rep. No. 586, 104th Cong., 2d Sess. 155-56 (1996). Under section 25.2702-1(c)(3) of the Gift Tax Regulations, section 2702 does not apply to CRUTs or CRATs.

Some taxpayers have created CRUTs using an income exception method to take advantage of the section 2702 exclusion granted to charitable remainder trusts in the regulations. These taxpayers attempt to use this exclusion and the income exception feature of a CRUT to pass substantial assets to family members with minimal transfer tax consequences.

For example, a donor establishes a NIMCRUT to pay the lesser of trust income or a fixed percentage to the donor for a term of 15 years or his life, whichever is shorter, and then to the

---

[374] Simon Levin and Jay A. Soled, "Near Zero CRUT Expands the Estate Planning Possibilities of Charitable Trusts," *The Journal of Taxation*, Oct/Sept 1995.

[375] Reg-209823-96

OPERATIONAL CONSIDERATIONS

donor's daughter for her life. If the tables under section 7520 are used to value the donor's retained interest and the donor's gift to the daughter, the amount of the donor's gift to the daughter is relatively small compared to the amount the daughter may actually receive. To illustrate, the trustee may invest in assets that produce little or no trust income while the donor retains the unitrust interest, creating a substantial makeup amount. At the end of the donor's interest, the trustee alters the NIMCRUT's investments to generate significant amounts of trust income. The trustee then uses the income to pay to the donor's daughter the current fixed percentage amount and the makeup amount, which includes the makeup amount accumulated while the donor was the unitrust recipient.

The use of a CRUT as described in the above example permits the shifting of a beneficial interest in the trust from the donor to another family member and, thus, creates an opportunity for transferring property to a family member free of transfer tax that is contrary to section 2702(a)(3)(A)(iii). Therefore, the proposed regulations will amend section 25.2702-1(c)(3) to provide that the unitrust interests in a CRUT using an income exception method retained by the donor or any applicable family member will be valued at zero when someone other than (1) the donor, (2) the donor's spouse, or (3) both the donor and the donor's spouse (who is a citizen of the U.S.) is a noncharitable beneficiary of the trust. In these situations, the value of the donor's gift is the fair market value of all the property transferred to the CRUT. The present value of the remainder interest passing to the charitable organization will qualify for the deduction under section 2522. Accordingly, the amount used to calculate the donor's gift tax liability is the value of the property transferred to the trust less the value of the interest passing to charity.

Section 25.2702-1(c)(3) will continue to exclude from the application of section 2702 transfers to pooled income funds described in section 642(c)(5) and to CRATs and CRUTs that pay the unitrust amount under the fixed percentage method.
B. Proposed Effective Date

This amendment is proposed to be effective for transfers in trust made on or after May 19, 1997.

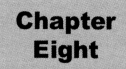

Investment Considerations

I. General Guidelines

The trustee of a charitable remainder trust has the fiduciary obligation of managing the trust for the benefit of both the income recipients and charitable remaindermen. In this connection, the trustee must balance the competing interests of each party's need for investment performance, income, and the preservation of capital.

A. Suitable Investment Assets

Previous chapters have covered a broad spectrum of issues including: design, funding, tax considerations, compliance, and administration. One can conclude that the trustee of a charitable remainder trust is well advised to invest a charitable remainder trust in assets that:

- are marketable

- are easily valued

- are diversified

- generate no debt-financed income

- generate no UBTI

- are not jeopardizing investments or would create excess business holdings, if applicable[376]

Conversely, investment assets that can, for reasons enumerated previously, cause problems for a trustee if held for investment purposes generally include:

- limited partnerships (other than those specifically designed as investment vehicles for charitable remainder trusts) and certain master limited partnerships

- real estate investment trusts

---

[376]   IRC §4944

- real property

- closely-held business interests

- installment obligations

- listed options

- margined securities

- tangible personal property

- other hard-to-value assets

B. Reasonable Return Requirement

A trust is not a charitable remainder trust if the trust includes a provision which restricts the trustee from investing the trust assets in a manner which could result in the annual realization of a reasonable amount of income or gain from the sale or disposition of trust assets.[377] The rationale for this provision is to prevent the trustor from having the ability to cause the trust to invade corpus to the detriment of the charitable remainderman.

C. Uniform Prudent Investor Act

"Over the quarter century from the late 1960's the investment practices of fiduciaries experienced significant change the Uniform Prudent Investor Act (UPIA) undertakes to update trust investment law in recognition of the alterations that have occurred in investment practice. These changes have occurred under the influence of a large and broadly accepted body of empirical and theoretical knowledge about the behavior of capital markets, often described as *modern portfolio theory.*"[378]

"Most states have legislation governing investment law. *The Uniform Prudent Investor Act* promotes uniformity of state law on the basis of a new consensus that is based on the changes and reflected in the *Restatement of Trusts 3d: Prudent Investor Rule (1992).*"[379]

There are five fundamental alterations in the former criteria for prudent investing:

- The standard of prudence is applied to any investment as part of the total portfolio, rather than to individual investments. In the trust setting the term, *portfolio* embraces all the trust's assets.[380]

- The tradeoff in all investing between risk and return is identified as the fiduciary's central consideration.[381]

---

[377] Reg. §1.664-1(a)(3)

[378] Prefatory Note: California Uniform Prudent Investor Act.

[379] *Ibid.*

[380] UPIA §2(b)

[381] *Ibid.*

- All categorical restrictions on types of investments have been abrogated; the trustee can invest in anything that plays an appropriate role in achieving the risk/return objectives of the trust and that meets the other requirements of prudent investing.[382]

- The long familiar requirement that fiduciaries diversify their investments has been integrated into the definition of prudent investing.[383]

- The much criticized former rule of trust law forbidding the trustee to delegate investment and management functions has been reversed. Delegation is now permitted subject to safeguards.[384]

Although the Act is concerned primarily with private gratuitous trusts (such as are used in traditional family wealth transfers), it also applies to charitable trusts. "In making investments of trust funds the trustee of a charitable trust is under a duty similar to that of a trustee under a private trust."[385] The effect of the Act is that it substantiates many of the investment activities that have been occurring in charitable trusts for many years.[386]

D. Restricted Investment Powers

A fairly common and unfortunate occurrence involves a charitable remainder trust which contains a provision that violates Reg. §1.664-1(a)(3). Such violations are commonly referred to as *restricted investment powers* and are illustrated by the following examples:

Example 1. Right to Veto Investments Disqualifies Trust

A trust instruments states, "The grantor reserves the right to recommend investments and to veto all investment decisions of the trustee."

In General Counsel Memorandum 36606 the Service stated, "Because the grantor has reserved the right to recommend investments and to veto all investment decisions, he could cause the trustee to invest in an unproductive asset or in assets that would produce no taxable income." Accordingly, such a power was held to violate Reg. §1.664-1(a)(3), thereby disqualifying the trust.

The Service further held, a power of administration exercisable in a *non-fiduciary* capacity to control the investment of trust funds either by directing investments or reinvestments, or by vetoing proposed investments would cause the trust to be a grantor trust.

---

[382] UPIA §2(e)

[383] UPIA §3

[384] UPIA §9

[385] Restatement of Trusts 2d: §389 (1959)

[386] At the time of this writing, California, Delaware, Georgia, Minnesota, Tennessee, and Washington have revised their prudent investor acts to emphasize the provisions of the restatement.

Example 2. Right to Name Investments Disqualifies Trust

A proposed charitable remainder trust instrument requires the trustee to invest 100 percent of the trust assets in a named mutual fund unless otherwise directed by the trustor in writing. Such language was held to be a restricted investment power.[387]

E. Permissible Restrictions

A charitable remainder trust instrument may contain provisions that restrict the trust from investing in assets which the trustor deems immoral or imprudent. For example, a trust can include a provision that permits only assets that have a readily ascertainable market value to be accepted by the trust. Further, a prohibition against holding tangible personal property, real estate, or an interest in a closely-held businesses is permissible.

The Service ruled, limitations on the types of assets the trust may accept or hold do not restrict the trustee from investing the trust assets in a manner which can result in the annual realization of a reasonable amount of income or gain from the sale or disposition of trust assets, and thus do not violate section 1.664-1(a)(3) of the regulations.[388]

Example 1. Precatory Investment Language

A provision in a charitable remainder trust that provided that the trustors *prefer* the trustee to invest trust assets exclusively in tax-exempt bonds was held not to be a restricted investment power because it was nonbinding on the trustee.[389]

Example 2. Stock Sub ect to Binding Buy-Sell Agreement

In Letter Ruling 8015036, the Service held, funding a charitable remainder trust with common stock of a closely-held corporation, subject to a binding buy-sell agreement, is not a restricted investment power.

F. Use of Investment Counselors

In Letter Ruling 8041100, a proposed charitable remainder trust instrument granted *investment counsel* the power to direct the trustee with respect to all investment decisions for the trust. Further, the trustee was relieved of any obligation or liability in connection with the review or suggestion of trust investments. These provisions were held to so restrict the trustee that he had no power over the investment of trust assets. Therefore, the trust did not fulfill the requirements of Reg. §1.664-1(a)(3).

Does this mean a trustee of a charitable remainder trust cannot employee an independent investment counselor? No. However, if an investment counselor is employed, the trustee should retain the ability, in its sole discretion, to:

- hire and fire the investment counselor with or without cause,

---

[387] Ltr. Rul. 8238085

[388] Ltr. Rul. 9138024

[389] GCM 37645; Cross reference: Ltr. Rul. 7913104

- establish and review the investment objectives of the trust with the investment counselor,

- take into consideration, but not be bound by the investment counselor's advice, and

- monitor the performance of trust investments.

A trustee cannot discharge its fiduciary obligation and liability to an investment counselor.

G. Commingling Investments of Multiple Trusts

The ability to hire institutional investment advisors with high investment minimums, reduce securities transaction costs, produce uniform performance, and streamline administration are several of the reasons a trustee might desire to commingle the investments of several charitable remainder trusts. But can they do so?

In Rev. Rul. 73-571, a bank, as trustee of a charitable remainder unitrust, invested the assets of such trust in common trust funds maintained by the bank.[390] The ruling holds that the investment by the bank of the assets of the charitable remainder unitrust in common trust funds maintained by the bank does not jeopardize the exempt status of the charitable remainder trust or the donor's charitable contribution deduction.

In Rev. Rul. 83-19, a university commingled the assets of several charitable remainder trusts with assets of the university's general endowment fund for purposes of investment.[391] The ruling holds that the joint investment of the assets will not jeopardize the exempt status of the charitable remainder trusts or the donors' charitable contribution deductions because such investment does not effect the status of the charitable remainder trusts.

In a subsequent letter ruling, X and Y, both organizations described in section 501(c)(3) of the Code, are under the common control of A. X and Y have each adopted substantially similar by-laws and have elected the same persons as directors and officers. Y has granted X authority to maintain custody of its assets and generally to conduct and manage its business affairs. X is the trustee and the remainderman of several trusts, while Y is the trustee and the remainderman of several other trusts. X and Y represent that each of the trusts qualifies as either a charitable remainder unitrust or charitable remainder annuity trust under section 664 of the Code. X and Y propose to invest jointly the assets of the charitable remainder trusts for which either is the trustee. Separate accounts and records will be maintained to identify the portion of the jointly invested assets owned by each trust and the income earned by and attributable to such portion. The Service approved the arrangement citing the previously mentioned revenue rulings.[392]

---

[390]   Rev. Rul. 73-571, 1973-2 C.B. 213
[391]   Rev. Rul. 83-19, 1983-1 C.B. 115
[392]   Ltr. Rul. 9231008

These rulings have all dealt with the commingling of assets by an institutional trustee. What if a trustor, who will also serve as trustee, desires to commingle and manage the investment assets of several trusts that he or she has created? This was the question at issue in Letter Ruling 9626007.

In 1991, a husband and wife each created six charitable remainder unitrusts. Each of the twelve trusts is similar in that the trustee will pay the unitrust amount to the creator of the trust for his or her lifetime. Upon the trustor's death, the same unitrust amount will be paid to one of the trustor's named children for his or her lifetime.

The trustees propose to invest the trusts' assets in one or more investment partnerships. The purpose of each partnership is to manage the trusts as a unit, which is made difficult with separate trusts. Each trust will hold a general partnership interest of the same class as held by all the other trusts. The trusts assert that a number of investment opportunities are not available to the trusts unless the investments are made through the vehicle of an investment partnership. The parents and children propose to manage one or more of the investment partnerships through a family owned corporation. The corporation has been providing investment and bookkeeping services on behalf of the trusts since their inception. Investment advice and consulting services are provided directly to the trusts or indirectly through the corporation by third party advisors. Tax returns for the trusts are prepared currently by an independent accounting firm. The corporation is, however, willing to prepare tax returns on behalf of the trusts for a lower fee as established by competitive bid. No family members or other disqualified persons will own an interest in any of the investment partnerships.

The trustors asked for rulings on the following issues:

- Will the joinder by one or more of the subject trusts in one or more of the proposed investment partnerships be a direct or indirect act of self-dealing under IRC §4941(d)(1)(E)?

- Will the capital contributions or distributions between the partnership be a direct or indirect act of self-dealing under IRC §4941(d)(1)(E)?

In regard to these two questions, the Service stated, "making investments through the partnership form does not constitute an act of self-dealing by virtue of the mere combination of assets or investments. An act of self-dealing is defined by section 4941 of the Code and the regulations thereunder. As long as the private foundation does not engage in any of the precluded acts described under that section, no direct or indirect act of self-dealing will occur."

Will the payment of compensation (and reimbursement of expenses) by the trusts and the proposed investment partnerships to a disqualified person for bookkeeping, accounting, and tax return preparation services (which are reasonable and necessary and at a cost not exceeding the lower of at least two bona fide proposals solicited from reputable firms for the same services) be a direct or indirect act of self-dealing within the meaning of IRC §4941(d)(1)(D) or 4941(d)(1)(E)? Will the payments be taxable expenditures within the meaning of IRC §4945(d)(5)?

In regard to these questions, the Service cited IRC §4941(d)(2)(E) which provides that the payment of compensation (and the payment or reimbursement of expenses) by a private foundation to a disqualified person for personal services which are reasonable and necessary for carrying out the exempt purposes of the private foundation shall not result in self-dealing if the compensation (or payment or reimbursement) is not excessive. The Service also mentioned Reg. §53.4941(d)-3(c)(2), which includes as permissible personal services, legal services, investment portfolio management, and general banking services.[393]

H. The Philanthropy Protection Act of 1995

The Philanthropy Protection Act of 1995 was enacted in response to a class action lawsuit. In this lawsuit an heir of an individual donor alleged that a charitable organization to which she had made a contribution in exchange for a charitable gift annuity had conspired with other charitable organizations to fix the rates they offer donors in connection with the issuance of charitable gift annuities.

Although the Act was initiated in response to litigation brought in connection with charitable gift annuities, it also specifically applies to charitable organizations that (a) serve as trustee, administrator (or have the power to remove either the trustee or administrator) for general endowment or other funds, pooled income funds, charitable remainder trusts, charitable lead trusts, and conditionally revocable assets; and (b) commingle the assets of the above mentioned funds for investment purposes.

The Act exempts charitable organizations from registration as an investment company under the Investment Company Act of 1940. The Act also excludes trustees, directors, officers, employees, or volunteers from registration as a dealer, broker, agent, or investment adviser provided such persons receive no commission or other special compensation based on the number or value of donations collected for the fund.

The Act requires charitable organizations that invest in the manner described above to provide, to each donor of the fund, written information describing the material terms of the operation of such fund. The information must be provided at the time of the donation or within 90 days after the date of enactment of the Act, whichever is later.

II. Establishing an Investment Policy

The investment policy of a charitable remainder trust is generally based on the following interrelated factors:

- unitrust or annuity trust format

- standard or net income format (unitrust only)

- payout or annuity rate

---

[393] *See also* Ltr. Rul. 9705013

- the risk tolerance of the trustee and investment horizon of the trust

- the income recipient's goals regarding taxation of income distributions

A. Effect of Annuity or Unitrust Payment Format

1. Annuity Trust Format

Charitable remainder annuity trusts are most frequently selected by those individuals who desire the assurance of a steady cash flow regardless of fluctuations in portfolio value. From an investment standpoint, the goal is to generate a total return sufficient to meet the annuity amount while preventing any diminution of principal. Since any capital growth in excess of the annuity amount will accrue solely for the benefit of the charitable remaindermen, capital preservation often takes priority, from the trustor's viewpoint, over capital appreciation.

It is interesting to suggest that although the annuity format is most often selected by conservative individuals, an annuity trust bearing a moderate to high annuity requirement subjects the trust corpus to the greatest investment risk. Why? The annuity amount remains constant regardless of changes in portfolio value. Therefore, if an annuity trust experiences a loss of corpus early in its life, it might ultimately exhaust itself prior to the charity receiving a remainder interest. With this in mind, many annuity trusts carry relatively conservative annuity amount requirements.

2. Unitrust Format

The unitrust payout format is most often selected by individuals with longer investment horizons and who desire an increasing income stream. This, however, may be easier said than done.

Notwithstanding poor investment performance, income distributions and expenses generally reduce the corpus of a charitable remainder unitrust. A third and often-overlooked component of capital reduction is inflation.

In order for annual unitrust distributions to maintain their purchasing power, the total return on investment must equal the sum of the trust's payout rate, trust administrative and transaction expenses, and annual inflation. The combination of these three elements is referred to as *erosion*.

The chart on the following page illustrates the annual erosion of a unitrust value over a fifteen-year period beginning in 1976. The chart then compares annual trust erosion to the passive investment returns generated by the bond and stock markets over the same period. The return for Treasury bills is provided to illustrate a risk-free return.

Erosion Vs Return Analysis

| | Erosion | | | | | Return | | |
| | | | | | | | | |

Year	Payout	Inflation	Expenses	Total Erosion		Bonds	Stock	T-Bills
1976	8.00%	4.80%	1.00%	13.80%		15.60%	23.80%	5.10%
1977	8.00%	6.80%	1.00%	15.80%		3.00%	-7.20%	5.10%
1978	8.00%	9.00%	1.00%	18.00%		1.20%	6.60%	7.20%
1979	8.00%	13.30%	1.00%	22.30%		2.30%	18.40%	10.40%
1980	8.00%	12.40%	1.00%	21.40%		3.00%	32.60%	11.30%
1981	8.00%	8.90%	1.00%	17.90%		7.30%	-5.30%	14.70%
1982	8.00%	3.90%	1.00%	12.90%		31.10%	21.50%	10.50%
1983	8.00%	3.80%	1.00%	12.80%		8.00%	22.60%	8.90%
1984	8.00%	3.90%	1.00%	12.90%		15.00%	6.30%	10.00%
1985	8.00%	3.80%	1.00%	12.80%		21.30%	32.20%	7.50%
1986	8.00%	1.10%	1.00%	10.10%		15.60%	18.70%	6.00%
1987	8.00%	4.40%	1.00%	13.40%		2.30%	5.30%	5.30%
1988	8.00%	4.40%	1.00%	13.40%		7.60%	16.60%	6.20%
1989	8.00%	4.70%	1.00%	13.70%		14.20%	31.70%	8.20%
1990	8.00%	6.10%	1.00%	15.10%		8.30%	-3.10%	7.80%
Annualized								
15 Yr.	8.00%	6.00%	1.00%	15.04%		10.39%	14.71%	8.28%

Assumptions

Payout rate: 8.00%

Annual transaction and administrative expenses: 1.00%

Indices

Inflation: Consumer price index

Bonds: SLH Government/Corporate bond index

Stocks: S&P 500

T-Bills: Represents a risk-free rate of return

As is illustrated, none of the stated investment indices kept pace with the investment return requirement (erosion) of an 8 percent unitrust. Granted, the investment indices represent passively invested portfolios and do not represent the returns that could have been generated by an investment advisor. However, it is interesting to note that, the performance of the S&P 500 index ranks in the top 15th percentile in the investment advisor universe. Therefore, if investment returns and expenses as assumed to be constants, the only significant room for planning involves the choice of payout rate.

The point of this exercise is, if a unitrust income recipient desires an inflation indexed return, it will become more difficult to achieve as a function of increasing payout rates. Further, as the payout rate increases, the investment style and asset allocation necessary to accomplish return goals may conflict with the trustor's risk tolerance and investment horizon (i.e., the period of time the investment policy remains unchanged).

B. Effect of Net Income Option on Investment Policy

While the use of a net income option can solve the trustee's problem regarding accepting illiquid or non-income producing assets, it may create a new one. Recall that a standard unitrust pays a fixed percentage of the trust's annual value. Therefore, like the annuity trust, a standard unitrust can invest on a *total return* basis because distributions can consist of income, capital gains, and principal if necessary. By contrast, a net income unitrust pays a fixed percentage of annual trust value or income, whichever is less. If the net income trust does not produce any income (within the meaning of the trust's definition), it distributes nothing.

The key to the investment policy of a net income unitrust is the definition of income. Most trusts define *income* as that term is defined under IRC §643(b). The section provides that income shall be "determined under the terms of the governing instrument and applicable local law." Further, "Trust provisions which depart fundamentally from concepts of local law in the determination of what constitutes income are not recognized for this [federal tax] purpose."[394]

The relevant local law in at least 38 states is either the *Uniform Principal and Income Act* or the *Revised Uniform Principal and Income Act*.[395] These acts generally describe income to include interest, dividends, rents, and royalties. Absent from the general definition of income are capital gains and principal.

Based on this definition, the trustee will seek to invest the trust portfolio in such a way as to achieve the income payout goal of the trust. For trusts bearing a 5 percent payout rate, this does not usually present a problem. However, as the payout rate increases, the trustee/investment advisor may be forced to invest a disproportionate amount of the portfolio in fixed income instruments to maximize distributable net income. In so doing, the trust might be exposed to greater interest rate risk as durations are increased or purchase premiums paid to increase yield. The trustee might also forfeit future appreciation that could be realized via investing in a portion of the portfolio in equities.

Suppose a trustor creates a 7 percent net income unitrust at the beginning of the year funding it with $100,000. Prevailing long-term bond yields are 7 percent. In an effort to maximize distributable net income, the trustee chooses to invest the entire portfolio in long bonds. During the course of the year, the trust distributes $7,000 to the income recipient. At the beginning of the next year (the annual valuation date), however, market bond rates have climbed to 9 percent causing the fair market value of trust's assets to decline to $90,000. Keeping in mind that the annual unitrust amount is based on 7 percent of the fair market value of the trust's assets on the annual valuation date, the unitrust amount in year two will decrease to $6,300 ($90,000 x 7 percent) even though the underlying trust assets continue to distribute $7,000. The $700 differential will be added to trust corpus.

It is important to note that in this example, given identical investment assumptions, a standard unitrust would have produced the same result. However, given a standard unitrust, the investment assumptions would not, most likely, have been identical. The pressure to maximize distributable net income is absent. Therefore, the trustee of the standard unitrust might have

---

[394] Reg. §1.643(b)-1

[395] *Uniform Laws Annotated, Master Edition, Vol. 7B*

elected to build a balanced portfolio comprised of fixed income instruments and equities. Given the higher average returns produced by equities and the lower risk (volatility) produced by combining asset classes, the balanced portfolio would be expected to produce a higher total return over a full market cycle.

Asset Allocation Analysis

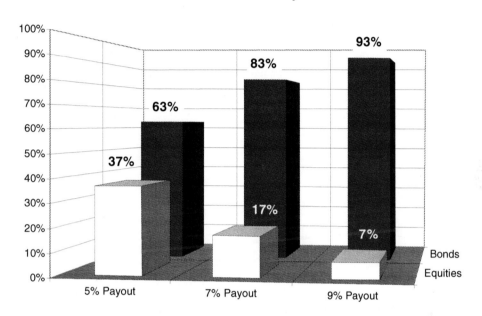

Figure 15   This chart illustrates the average asset allocation required to generate interest and dividend income sufficient to satisfy the unitrust amount of a net income unitrust over a twenty-year period (1969-1988). Illustrations use U.S. Treasury Bond yield and S&P 500 dividend statistics.

C. Modifying Income Definition to Include Capital Gain

Can the investment challenges of maximizing the distributable net income of the net income unitrust be mitigated by expanding the trust's definition of income to include gains from the sale of capital assets? Partially, and only if such definition is allowable under local law.[396]

This solution does not completely eliminate the problem, however. For purposes of determining the taxation of distributions to income recipients, capital gains are determined on a *cumulative net basis*.[397] Realized capital gains are reduced by realized capital losses in determining distributable net income. The risk this poses to the trustee/investment counselor may encourage him to retain poorly performing investments in order to avoid offsetting gains realized on the sale of appreciated investments. Also, the addition of gains to the definition of income in unitrusts containing a make-up option may require the

---

[396]   Reg. §1.643(a)-3(a)

[397]   Reg. §1.664-1(d)(1)(i)

deficiency account to be treated as a liability in determining the fair market value of the trust assets for purposes of calculating the annual unitrust amount.[398]

D. Impact of Payout or Annuity Rate

The higher the payout or annuity rate of a charitable remainder trust is, the greater the pressure will be on the trustee to generate a return in an amount sufficient to meet the distribution goal and pay the administrative expenses of the trust. A high payout rate may also conflict directly with the trustee's and income recipient's risk tolerance.

E. Risk Tolerance and Investment Horizon

Risk tolerance is defined as the ability to withstand volatility within an investment portfolio. Investment horizon is the period of time during which the investment policy of the trust remains unchanged.

Will Rogers once said, "I am not as interested in return *on* my principal as I am in return *of* my principal." The majority of charitable remainder trusts are established by and for the benefit of individuals who are retired. Many are less concerned with wealth accumulation and thinking more in terms of the conservation and distribution of their estate. Accordingly, they generally have low risk tolerances.

By contrast, a charitable remainder trust established for the benefit of younger income recipients may best serve them and charity by investing in assets that produce potentially higher long-term returns. Because this group's investment horizon is longer, they can withstand the larger bumps that might occur along the way.

F. Tax Treatment of Unitrust or Annuity Amount

The tax treatment of distributions to income recipients is determined pursuant to the rules of IRC §664 and is particularly relevant to investment selection.

A charitable remainder trust assumes the holding period and cost basis of assets transferred to it. Although the trust, in the absence of UBTI, will pay no tax on income realized through the disposition and investment of trust assets, distributions made to income recipients are considered taxable according to the *four-tier system,* described as follows:

[Reg. §1.664-1(d)(1)(i)]

(a) Ordinary Income. First, as ordinary income to the extent of the sum of the trust's ordinary income for the taxable year and any undistributed ordinary income for prior years. Any ordinary loss for the current year shall be used first to reduce undistributed ordinary income for prior years, and any excess shall be carried forward indefinitely to reduce ordinary income for future years. For purposes of this section, the amount of current and prior years' income shall be computed without regard to net operating losses provided by Code sections 172 or 642(d).

(b) Capital Gain. Second, as capital gain to the extent of the trust's undistributed capital gains. Undistributed capital gains of the trust are determined on a cumulative net basis without regard to the provisions of Code section 1212, as follows:

---

[398] See Chapter 3.

(1) Long and short-term capital gains. If, in any taxable year of the trust, the trust has both undistributed short-term capital gain and undistributed long-term capital gain, then the short-term capital gain shall be deemed distributed prior to any long-term capital gain.

(2) Long and short-term capital gains. If the trust has in any taxable year any capital losses in excess of capital gains, any excess of the short-term capital loss over the net long-term capital gain shall be a short-term capital loss in the succeeding taxable year and any excess of the net long-term capital loss over the net short-term capital gain for such year shall be a long-term capital loss in the succeeding taxable year.

(3) Capital gains in excess of capital losses. If the trust has for any taxable year capital gains in excess of capital losses, any excess of the net short-term capital gain over the short-term capital loss for such year shall be, to the extent not deemed distributed, a short-term capital gain in the succeeding taxable year and any excess of the net long-term capital gain over the net short-term capital loss for such year shall be, to the extent not deemed distributed, a long-term capital gain in the succeeding taxable year.

(c) Other income. Third, as other income (including income excluded under part III, subchapter B, chapter 1, subtitle A of the Code) to the extent of the sum of the trust's other income for the taxable year and its undistributed other income for prior years. A loss in this category for prior years and any excess shall be carried forward indefinitely to reduce income for future years.

(d) Corpus. Finally, as a distribution of corpus. For purposes of this section, the term "corpus" means the net fair market value of the trust assets less the total undistributed income (but not loss) in each of the above categories.

1. Treatment of Multiple Capital Gains Rates

The Taxpayer Relief Act of 1997 amended IRC §1(h) to provide three capital gains tax groups for noncorporate taxpayers: (1) the 28 percent group, (2) the 25 percent group, and (3) the 20 percent group (10 percent in the case of gain that would otherwise be taxed at 15 percent).[399]

- The 28 percent group consists of:

  - gains and losses on sales of long-term capital assets before May 7, 1997

  - gains and losses sales of capital assets after July 28, 1997 held 18 months or less

  - gains and losses from the sale of collectibles (held longer than one year and defined in section 408(m) without regard to paragraph (3) thereof and including gain from the sale of an interest in a partnership, S corporation, or trust attributable to unrealized appreciation of collectibles)

  - certain gains and losses from the sale of small business stock, and

  - current year short-term capital losses

- The 25 percent group consists of unrecaptured section 1250 gain (attributable to depreciation recapture)

- The 20 percent group consists of gains and losses not in the 28 percent or 25 percent group.

---

[399] Notice 97-57, 1997-45 I.R.B. 7

The question on every charitable remainder trust administrator's mind was how these new rate groups would apply to the four-tier system. Notice 98-20[400] provides guidance on the ordering a taxation of distributions under IRC §664(b)(2):

Notice 98-20

[1] This notice provides guidance on the ordering and taxation of distributions under section 664(b)(2) of the Internal Revenue Code from a charitable remainder trust (CRT) in light of the changes made to section 1(h) by the Taxpayer Relief Act of 1997 (TRA 1997). Pub. L. 105-34, section 311, 111 Stat. 788, 831. Section 1(h) provides that the Treasury may issue regulations to implement the provisions of section 1(h) for passthrough entities. The Treasury Department and the Internal Revenue Service plan to issue regulations incorporating the guidance contained in this notice.

BACKGROUND

[2] Generally, a CRT is a trust that provides for a specified distribution at least annually over a specified period to one or more noncharitable recipients (a CRT distribution), with the remainder interest in the trust held irrevocably for a charitable organization.

[3] TRA 1997 amended section 1(h) to provide for new capital gain tax rates for noncorporate taxpayers. Notice 97-59, 1997-45 I.R.B. 7, explains that a noncorporate taxpayer's long-term capital gains and losses are separated into three tax rate groups: (1) the 28 percent group, (2) the 25 percent group, and (3) the 20 percent group. The present notice uses these terms in explaining how a CRT characterizes its capital gain distribution for taxable years beginning on or after January 1, 1998. The definitions of net capital gain, net long-term capital gain or loss, and net short-term capital gain or loss were not changed by TRA 1997. Like Notice 97-59, this notice takes into account the pending retroactive legislative corrections. H.R. 2676, 105th Cong., section 605(d) (1997).

ADDITIONAL NETTING RULES

[4] CRTs will be expected to follow the netting rules in Notice 97-59 when determining net short-term and net long-term capital gains. The rules in section 1.664-1(d)(1)(i)(b)(2) and (3) of the Income Tax Regulations continue to apply in determining capital gains or losses carried forward to the succeeding taxable year.

GENERAL PRINCIPLES OF THE ORDERING RULE

[5] Section 664(b) contains the ordering rule for determining the character of a CRT distribution in the hands of the recipient. The character of a CRT's income is determined at the time the income is realized by the trust. Under section 664(b), the following ordering rule applies for determining the character of a distribution in the hands of the recipient: (1) first, as ordinary income to the extent of the trust's ordinary income for the trust's taxable year and its undistributed ordinary income for prior years, (2) second, as capital gain to the extent of the trust's capital gain for the trust's taxable year and its undistributed capital gain for prior years, (3) third, as other income to the extent of the trust's other income for the trust's taxable year and its undistributed other income for prior years, and (4) fourth, as a distribution of trust corpus.

[6] The underlying policy in the ordering rule of section 664(b) and the existing regulations thereunder is that a CRT distribution is deemed to consist first of income that is subject to the highest federal income tax rate in effect at the time of the distribution and then of income that is subject to progressively lower (or no) federal income tax rates in effect at the time of distribution. The same policy applies in the regulations under section 664 when different income tax rates apply to different groups of income within a category of the items described in section 664(b), such as short-term and long-term capital gains. Therefore, income from a group that is subject to a higher federal income tax rate is deemed distributed before other income from a group, within the same category, that is subject to a lower federal income tax rate.

[7] The following example illustrates how this principle applies to capital gain distributions after TRA 1997. Assume for the 1998 taxable year, a CRT has undistributed long-term capital gain in each of the three groups of long-term capital gain, i.e., the 28 percent group, the 25 percent group, and the 20

---

[400] Notice 98-20, 1998-13 I.R.B. 25

percent group, and also has undistributed short-term capital gain. To the extent capital gains are deemed distributed for the 1998 taxable year, the short- term capital gain is deemed distributed prior to any long-term capital gain. The long-term capital gain is deemed distributed in the following order: (1) the gain in the 28 percent group is deemed distributed prior to any other long-term capital gain; (2) the gain in the 25 percent group is deemed distributed prior to any gain in the 20 percent group; and (3) the gain in the 20 percent group is deemed distributed last of any long-term capital gain.

[8] A trustee of a CRT will be required to report each group of long-term capital gain separately on the Form 5227, "Split-Interest Trust Information Return." The trustee may use any reasonable method for determining the amount of each type of gain within a group that has been distributed when doing the required reporting or associated recordkeeping.

PRE-1997 LONG-TERM CAPITAL GAIN

[9] As of January 1, 1997, many CRTs had undistributed long- term capital gains that the CRT properly took into account before January 1, 1997 (pre-1997 long-term capital gains). These pre-1997 long-term capital gains must be assigned to one of the three groups of long-term capital gains. Section 1(h) does not specifically assign pre-1997 long-term capital gains to one group of long-term capital gain. However, section 1(h) gives the Treasury broad regulatory authority to implement the provisions of section 1(h) for passthrough entities.

[10] Pre-1997 long-term capital gains were characterized by the CRT based on the definitions of short-term and long-term capital gains applicable at the time the CRT sold a capital asset. CRTs have never been required to segregate these gains based upon the tax rate or holding period in effect at the time the gains were realized by the CRT. Thus, the undistributed pre-1997 long-term capital gains reflect gains realized when various tax rates and holding periods were in effect. Treasury will exercise its regulatory authority to treat undistributed CRT pre-1997 long-term capital gains as falling within the 20 percent group.

1997 PRE-EFFECTIVE DATE LONG-TERM CAPITAL GAINS

[11] Long-term capital gains properly taken into account from January 1, 1997, through May 6, 1997, are covered by the rules in section 1(h) regarding pre-effective date gains. Under section 1(h), for the taxable year that includes May 7, 1997, gains and losses properly taken into account by the CRT for the portion of the taxable year before May 7, 1997, must be taken into account in determining long-term capital gain in the 28 percent group. Because the taxable year for CRTs is the calendar year, long-term capital gains properly taken into account by a CRT from January 1, 1997, through May 6, 1997, are treated as long-term capital gains in the 28 percent group.

EXAMPLE ILLUSTRATING ORDERING AND CHARACTER RULES

[12] The following example illustrates how these rules will apply to the 1998 taxable year. At the end of the 1998 taxable year, CRT X has no current or undistributed ordinary income and has the following net short-term and long-term capital gains:

Net short-term capital gain	$ 5
Net long-term capital gain	$50
By tax rate group:	
28 percent group gain	- $15
($12 of gain recognized from 1/1/97 through 5/6/97; and $3 of gain recognized after 7/28/97 from an asset held for more than one year and less than 18 months)	
25 percent group gain	-$ 5
20 percent group gain	-$30
($10 of gain recognized before 1/1/97)	

X makes a CRT distribution of $25 for the 1998 taxable year. The CRT distribution is deemed to have the following characteristics in the recipient's hands:

Short-term capital gain	$ 5
28 percent group gain	$15
25 percent group gain	$ 5
20 percent group gain	$ 0

The undistributed 20 percent group gain of $30 is carried forward to 1999.

EFFECTIVE DATE

[13] The proposed regulations when published will be effective for taxable years beginning on or after January 1, 1998. CRTs and their recipients, however, may rely on the rules in this notice for the 1997 taxable year.

DRAFTING INFORMATION

[14] The principal authors of this notice are Mary Beth Collins and Jeff Erickson of the Office of Assistant Chief Counsel (Passthroughs and Special Industries). For further information regarding this notice contact Ms. Collins or Mr. Erickson on (202) 622-3070 (not a toll-free call).

2. IRS Restructuring and Reform Act of 199 Repeals 1 -Month Capital Gains Holding Period

On July 22, 1998, the President signed The Internal Revenue Service Restructuring and Reform Act of 1998 (H.R. 2676). Included in the bill is a provision that reduces the 18-month holding period for certain long-term capital gains imposed by The TRA '97 back to 12 months. The new law is effective for sales after December 31, 1997.

The new law makes sales of certain property held between 12 and 18 months eligible for less than 28 percent group treatment. However, gains and losses attributable to the sale of collectibles, certain small business stock, and section 1250 depreciation recapture are retained in the 28 percent group. At the time of this writing, the Service had not released any guidance with respect to the application of these rules to charitable remainder trusts.

3. Example of Four-Tier System

The theory of the four-tier system is most easily illustrated by example:

Suppose the Smiths transfer $1,000,000 of publicly traded stock, with a $100,000 basis, to a charitable remainder annuity trust on January 1st. The trust calls for the payment of a $50,000 (5 percent) annuity amount to be distributed at the end of each calendar year payable for the Smiths' joint lives.

The trustee sells the stock on January 2nd and buys double-tax-exempt municipal bonds. During the period of time between January 2nd and December 31st, the bonds pay $50,000 to the trust. The trustee distributes $50,000 to the Smiths on December 31st. What is the tax treatment of the income distribution to the Smiths?

Beneficiaries

The trust distribution is taxable as long-term capital gain because $900,000 of undistributed capital gain was generated when the trustee sold the stock. Because capital gain takes priority over other income (i.e., tax-exempt income), there will be no distributable tax-exempt income until all undistributed capital gain is distributed. With $850,000 of undistributed capital gain being carried over into the next year, the Smiths will not see one penny of tax-exempt income until the nineteenth year.

4. Impact of Four-Tier System on Investment Selection

In the immediate case, was the reinvestment in tax-exempt securities in the best interests of all concerned? Probably not. The reduced yield of tax-exempt securities and accompanying interest rate risk, combined with a nineteen-year delay of tax-exempt distributions, makes tax-exempt investments an inferior choice.

By contrast, if the Smiths had *contributed* tax-exempt bonds, or cash that was then used to purchase the bonds, income distributions would be tax-exempt to the Smiths from inception (provided no subsequent sales of bonds resulted in capital gain).

5. The Pomona Ruling and Its Impact on Investment in Tax-Exempt Securities

Prior to 1960, Pomona College advertised and executed arrangements whereby donors transferred appreciated property to the college with the understanding the college would sell the contributed property and invest the proceeds in tax-exempt securities. The donor avoided capital gains tax on the transfer and sale of contributed property *and* received immediate tax-exempt income from the plan.

In Rev. Rul. 60-370, better known as *The Pomona Ruling*, the Service took the position that when there is an express or implied agreement that assets be sold and reinvested in tax-exempt securities, the donor is not treated as having transferred appreciated assets; rather, he is treated as having transferred the proceeds of a taxable sale. Thus, capital gain is attributed to the donor even though the gift property is now in the hands of the college.

The 1969 Tax Reform Act (which codified charitable remainder trusts) substantially eliminated the Service's problem by creating the four-tier system of taxation. Under current law, the facts as presented in the Pomona Ruling will result in capital gain being recognized by the income recipient, more or less, on an installment basis as income distributions are received.

In the opinion of many practitioners, where there is no express or implied agreement between the trustor and trustee that sales proceeds will be invested in any particular manner (including tax-exempt securities), and the trustee invests in such securities in the normal course of carrying out its fiduciary duties, it is not likely the Service will pursue the matter.

6. Taxation of In-Kind Distributions

What happens if an individual transfers an illiquid asset such as real property or closely-held stock to a charitable remainder annuity trust or unitrust (with a standard payout format) which then fails to generate cash with which to make the required annuity or unitrust distribution? The trustee of either trust cannot borrow the money without having acquisition indebtedness. Therefore, the trustee of the annuity trust has no other choice but to make an *in-kind* distribution.

In the event a trustee makes an in-kind distribution, such amounts are treated for tax purposes as if the trustee has sold trust property (in the amount of the distribution) and distributed cash. Therefore, the income recipient will recognize any gain attributable to the distributed asset.[401]

What can the trustee of the unitrust do as an alternative? The trustee can request the trustor make additional cash contributions to the trust in an amount sufficient to make the required income distributions. The contribution will produce an additional income tax deduction to the trustor. Furthermore, the distribution back to the trustor might, depending on the status of the four-tier system, be treated as a tax-free return of principal.

Many conservative practitioners discourage the transfer of illiquid assets to charitable remainder annuity trusts. Why is the annuity trust distinguishable from a unitrust? Unlike the unitrust, it cannot accept additional contributions. Therefore, the *revolving door* strategy is unavailable.

---

[401]   Ltr. Rul. 8834039; Reg. §1.1014-4(a)(3); Rev. Rul. 68-392, 1968-2 C.B. 284

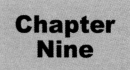

Chapter Nine

Cash Flow Planning

Charitable remainder trusts are most frequently used to convert appreciated assets into an immediate income stream. What if the trustor is at the peak of his or her income earning years and desires to use the unitrust as an income deferral vehicle for retirement planning?

The previous chapter examined the investment challenges of generating *distributable net income* within a net income unitrust. The following discussion will shift the focus from methods of maximizing distributable income to ways of deferring it.

I. Comparing the Charitable Remainder Unitrust to Traditional Retirement Plans

Charitable remainder unitrusts and qualified retirement plans share one important feature: the ability to accumulate assets free from the erosion of income taxes. That is where much of the similarity ends, however.

Compared to qualified plans, charitable remainder trusts:

- are not regulated by ERISA

- have no earned income requirements

- have no contribution limitations

- are not subject to *success* excise taxes on excess distributions or accumulations

- have no minimum or maximum retirement age

- are not integrated with social security

- have no P.S. 58 costs (for insured plans)

- are fully discriminatory in favor of key employees, and

- can be completely portable

II. Traditional Income Deferral Methods

For many years, charitable planners have considered methods by which income can be deferred within a net income unitrust. Following are examples of those methods:

A. Growth Stocks

One method of shutting off the *spigot* of DNI (distributable net income) from a net income unitrust involves investing in assets that maximize capital appreciation and minimize interest, dividends, rents, or royalties. Common growth stocks are often selected for this purpose because they produce low or no dividends, are liquid, and are easily valued. When income is desired, the trustee repositions the portfolio in assets that maximize income, such as fixed income instruments or high-dividend-paying preferred or utility stocks.

The problem with manipulating investments to control income distributions is that such decisions involve *personal timing* rather than prevailing market conditions. The necessity to invest in securities that produce capital gain to shut off income, or ordinary income to turn income on, can place investment performance at risk. Further, equities often produce some dividends, thereby creating distributable income during the accumulation phase (i.e., the spigot leaks). When this happens, the donor can contribute the income back into the trust, but only after paying taxes on the income. Finally, an investment policy of this type could give rise to questions regarding fiduciary liability and can potentially violate the reasonable return requirement of Reg. §1.664-1(a)(3).

B. ero Coupon Bonds

Another method by which income can be deferred from a net income unitrust involves the purchase of original issue discount (zero coupon) obligations. Using this approach, a trustor creates a charitable remainder unitrust that includes a net income option. The trust defines "income" as that term is defined under IRC §643(b) and under local law, and further provides that the discount element of a bond or other evidence of indebtedness purchased at a discount shall constitute income only in the year the bond is redeemed by the issuer or sold by the trust.[402]

For example, under California law, the increment in value of a bond or other obligation for the payment of money, payable at a future time in accordance with a fixed schedule of appreciation in excess of the price at which it was issued, is distributable as income. The increment in value is distributable to the beneficiary who was the income beneficiary at the time of increment from the first principal cash available or, if none is available, when realized by sale, redemption, or other disposition.[403]

If income is not produced until the bond is sold or redeemed, such sale or redemption by a trust containing a make-up option can cause a flood of DNI to the trust and, in turn, to the income recipient. This may or may not be a desired result and can be avoided by (a) the

---

[402]   Ltr. Rul. 9018015; Ltr. Rul. 8604027

[403]   California Civil Code §730.07(b)

absence of a make-up option, (b) purchasing bonds with *laddered* maturities, or (c) allocating the discount element of the bond to principal (if compatible with local law).

Using the first two methods, distributions will be triggered upon sale or redemption. In the case of the third alternative, if the discount element of the bond and capital gains are both allocated to principal, the bond will have to be sold or redeemed and the proceeds reinvested in income-producing assets before the income recipient can receive any distribution. In application, this would take considerably more time. In summary, the zero coupon bond creates little, if any, flexibility for purposes of income distribution planning from the net income unitrust.

III. Tax Deferred Annuity Contracts

Letter Ruling 9009047 presents a very creative solution to the investment challenges and income deferral possibilities of net income unitrusts. Two individuals funded a net income unitrust (with make-up option) with common stock. The trustee sold the stock and invested the proceeds in a tax deferred annuity contract issued by an insurance company.

The IRS ruled:

- The trust will qualify as a charitable remainder unitrust.

- The trust will include any annuity contract income in ordinary income for the year under IRC §72(u)(2).

- The trust will not hold the annuity for a natural person (i.e., an individual).

The published ruling does not tell the whole story of using the deferred annuity in net income unitrusts. In the trust instrument submitted with the ruling request, the trust's definition of accounting income was modified to accommodate distributions from an annuity contract. Even though the Service did not rule on this issue, such definition was found to be compatible with IRC §643(b) and local law.

In application, the results of this ruling are quite interesting:

A. Qualification of Annuity

The trust cannot hold the annuity contract for a "natural person." Therefore, income generated within the annuity contract is realized by the trust for income tax purposes when generated regardless of whether or not it is actually distributed to the trust.

A charitable remainder trust is tax-exempt; therefore, no tax is incurred as long as the trust does not become taxable for another reason (e.g., the receipt of unrelated business taxable income).

B. Generating Trust Accounting Income

Even though the trust realizes income for income tax purposes when it is generated within the annuity contract, the trust (assuming it holds no other income-producing assets) does not have accounting income until it actually receives cash from the annuity contract. Cash is produced only when the trustee makes a partial withdrawal from the contract, surrenders the contract, or receives a death benefit payment when the annuitant dies.

Distributions from an annuity contract are considered made on a last-in-first-out (LIFO) accounting basis. Therefore, to the extent that annuity withdrawals or distributions represent gain in the contract, such amounts are considered trust accounting income. The trustee must distribute net trust accounting income to the trust's income recipients to the extent of the unitrust amount due for the current tax year plus any deficiency account balance (attributable to the net income option).

C. Distribution Planning

Partial withdrawals from the annuity contract (and, therefore, distributions from the trust) are voluntary and made at the sole discretion of the trustee.

During the annuitant's life, this feature provides great flexibility in distribution planning. The planner must be mindful, however, that when an annuitant dies (absent any provisions in the contract to the contrary), the value of the contract must be distributed to its beneficiary (the trust) within five years of the date of death. If there is a surviving income recipient (such as might be the case with two-life trust for a husband and wife) and the trust has a large deficiency account balance, a large amount of income may be distributable *if the decedent was the annuitant*. The Service has not ruled on this issue as of this writing.

D. Investment Flexibility

All withdrawals from a deferred annuity contract in excess of cost basis are considered ordinary taxable income regardless of their source.

The most important and unique benefit of using a deferred annuity contract within a net income unitrust is the trustee's ability to separate the investment management of trust assets from the trust's requirement to distribute income. In application, a *variable* deferred annuity can be invested in equity, fixed income, or guaranteed sub-accounts during periods of accumulation *or* distribution. Some other deferral methods require investment within specific asset categories (i.e., stocks or zero coupon bonds) during accumulation and yet others to facilitate distributions. In the case of the deferred variable annuity, asset allocation within the contract can consider the trustee's risk tolerance, return goals, and investment horizon without concern that a particular investment choice may create undesired accounting income.

E. Application of Pre-59 1 2 Penalty Tax

IRC §72(q) provides that amounts received by a taxpayer under an annuity contract prior to the taxpayer attaining age 59 1/2 are subject to a penalty tax equal to 10 percent of the portion of such amount which is includible in gross income.

Although the Service has not ruled on this issue, the 10 percent penalty tax should not logically apply because the annuity is nonqualified (i.e., it is taxable to its owner (the trust) under IRC §72(u)).

F. Use of Make-Up Option

If the trust contains a make-up option, the trustee can make a withdrawal from the contract and distribute *the lesser of* (a) the unitrust amount for the current year plus the entire deficiency account, and (b) the amount of gain in the contract that exceeds the contract's cost basis.

Unlike other deferral methods, the trustee does not have to change investments from growth to income and then wait for income to be generated. The annuity can *store* income. This feature not only provides for immediacy of income distributions; it can also provide substantial potential distribution amounts.

> **Caution:** Private Ruling 9511007 held that the deficiency account of a net income unitrust with a make-up option must treat the amount of the deficiency account as a liability in determining the fair market value of the trust's assets for purposes of calculating the annual unitrust amount. However, the trust instrument on which the ruling was based included pre-gift gains in its definition of distributable net income. This is distinguishable from the annuity-invested unitrust in that the latter must never be able to distribute trust corpus. Accordingly, the reduction requirement of the ruling should not logically apply. The Service has not, however, addressed this question.[404] In the absence of clear guidance, the conservative trustee must fully consider the possible application of the ruling formula.

G. Valuation

The ruling stated, "The annuity contract shall be valued at its account value, i.e. the value on which interest earnings are computed, for purposes of determining the annual net fair market value of the trust assets under the terms of the trust instrument."

As a result, the annuity's full account value is used in determining the unitrust amount with no discount for possible withdrawal penalties taken into consideration.

H. Guaranteed Benefit for Charity

In a fixed annuity, principal is guaranteed by the issuing insurance company. Therefore, regardless of market conditions at the time of surrender, the charitable remainderman will receive the full market value. Further, most contracts waive all surrender penalties at the death of the annuitant.

Variable annuities handle this issue differently. Some contracts provide a death benefit that goes beyond the original investment in the contract by guaranteeing the original investment plus a stipulated compounded rate of return as a death benefit (regardless of actual account value at death). This amount is guaranteed by the contract regardless of the annuity account value on the date of the annuitant's death.

---

[404] Refer to the complete discussion beginning on page 31.

Caveat: With a "fixed" annuity, the term "guarantee" should be viewed with the understanding that a guarantee is only as good as the insurance company making it. Variable annuity sub-accounts are required by law to be held in segregated accounts in trust. In all events, careful consideration of carriers and contract provisions should always be made prior to investing.

I. Implementation Considerations

A full discussion of the administration and implementation of a deferred annuity as a trust investment is beyond the scope of this text. Although this concept creates a very compelling case for the use of a deferred annuity and although, in operation, this technique may seem simple, as with most areas of charitable trust planning, care must be taken to implement such a program correctly.

There are several issues surrounding the use of a deferred annuity as a net income unitrust investment:

- The trust instrument must be skillfully drafted to include the necessary language to permit the trustee to define and control income distributions from an annuity contract.

  Given the position in Ltr. Rul. 9009047, that a charitable remainder trust cannot act as an agent for a natural person, the definition of income should distinguish between federal "taxable" income and "distributable" trust income under state law. A specific reference to State statute(s) permitting this distinction could also be helpful if the issue is ever questioned under audit. The language contained within the trust instrument that was the subject of the original ruling excluded from the definition of trust income, " any amount with respect to an annuity or life insurance contract except for such amounts actually received by the trustee."

- The trust instrument should also include provisions that restrict the trustee from exercising any contractual rights of the contract that may be to the detriment of the remainderman. For example, the trustee could be prohibited from annuitizing the contract or selecting any death benefit option that would result in the distribution of any amount less than the original purchase amount of the contract.

- The trust instrument must require that an *independent special trustee* be given sole authority regarding the selection of maturity date, settlement options, partial surrenders of the contract, and determination of the timing and amount of payment to the trust's income recipients. Failure to do so may subject the trust to treatment as a grantor trust.

- The insurance company must be aware that no distributions below the original cost basis of the annuity should be made.

- Some practitioners have asked whether it is prudent for a charitable remainder trust to own a tax deferred annuity contract as its sole investment asset in connection with the adequate diversification requirements of the Uniform Prudent Investor Act.

This concern may have merit if the sole investment of the trust is one fixed annuity contract. If, however, a variable annuity contract (that contains multiple asset category sub-account investment options) is used, the diversification issue should come under lessened scrutiny.

These are but five of the issues that must be considered by the trustee and administrator of an annuity funded net income unitrust.

J. IRS Concerns Regarding Income Deferral

For many years, certain charitable remainder trusts have been designed and invested for the purpose of providing the trustee with flexibility regarding the timing and amount of income distributions. There has, however, been some concern by the Treasury and IRS regarding the appropriateness of such arrangements. The first evidence of such concern appeared in an internal IRS Continuing Professional Education publication article entitled, *Charitable Remainder Trusts: The Income Deferral Abuse and Other Issues.* Although the article cannot be cited as tax precedent, the authors suggested that deferring that payment of income from a charitable remainder trust may constitute a use of trust assets for the benefit of a disqualified person and, therefore, may constitute a prohibited act of self-dealing.[405]

1. Proposed Regulations and Request for Comments

On April 18, 1997, Treasury issued proposed regulations affecting charitable remainder trusts. Also included was a request for comments on net income unitrusts holding certain investments:

VII. Request for Comments on Income Exception CRUTs Holding Certain Investments

[48] The IRS and Treasury are aware that taxpayers are using income exception CRUTs to take advantage of the timing difference between the receipt of trust income (as defined in section 643(b)) and income for federal income tax purposes. For example, an income exception CRUT may hold an interest in a partnership controlled by a trustee of the trust, a grantor, a beneficiary, or a party related or subordinate to the trustee, the grantor, or a beneficiary. In such a case, an interested party controls when the trust will receive the earnings from its partnership interest and, accordingly, when the unitrust recipient will receive distributions from the trust. Although the income exception CRUT has taxable income on its distributive share of partnership items, the trust does not have trust income until it actually receives a distribution of its share of the partnership's earnings.

[49] The IRS and Treasury are studying whether investing the assets of an income exception CRUT to take advantage of the timing difference between the receipt of trust income and income for federal tax purposes causes the trust to fail to function exclusively as a charitable remainder trust. Therefore, the IRS and Treasury request comments on drafting future guidance on this issue. Revenue Procedure 97-23, to be published on April 28, 1997, in Internal Revenue Bulletin 1997-17, provides that the IRS will not issue letter rulings on whether a trust that will calculate the unitrust amount under section 664(d)(3) qualifies as a section 664 charitable remainder trust when a grantor, a trustee, a beneficiary, or a person related or subordinate to a grantor, a trustee, or a beneficiary can control the timing of the trust's receipt of trust income from a partnership or a deferred annuity contract to take advantage of the difference between trust income under section 643(b) and income for federal income tax purposes for the benefit of the unitrust recipient.

---

[405] "Charitable Remainder Trust: The Income Deferral Abuse and Other Issues *IRS Exempt Organizations Continuing Professional Education: Technical Instruction Program for FY 1997*

In November 1997, IRS and Treasury held public hearings at which public comments on this issue overwhelmingly favored permitting income deferral in charitable remainder trusts.

2.   Technical Advice Memorandum 9 25001

In January 1998, the IRS issued a Technical Advice Memorandum that addressed these issues in connection with trust created by a specific taxpayer.

In 1990, an individual created an 8 percent NIMCRUT with a portion of the stock in his closely-held corporation. The trust named the trustor and his spouse as life income recipients, and the trustor's nephew as the primary trustee. Additionally, the trust provided for a special independent trustee to deal with hard-to-value assets such as the business. In 1991, the company was sold, and with it the stock from the trust. As is common with many business sales, to aid in the transition, the seller entered into a five-year employment agreement and covenant not to compete that provided him with significant compensation over that period.

Understanding that the seller/trustor did not need any additional income during the following five years, the special independent trustee used the sale proceeds to purchase two tax deferred annuity contracts from a commercial insurance company. The intent of the trustee was to defer income distributions from the trust for the first five years, then reevaluate the income needs of the income recipients at that time. There was at least one major problem, however. The trust instrument had not anticipated the ownership of a tax deferred annuity contract for fiduciary accounting purposes; therefore, it failed to provide any guidance to the trustee with respect to whether or not income and appreciation within the annuity contract could be deferred or would be required to be distributed in the year in which it was earned. State law was also silent on the issue.

Did local law, in conjunction with the trust instrument, permit the deferral of the receipt of trust accounting income related to the annuity contracts until cash was actually received by trustee? The trustee chose to defer, making no distributions to the income recipient for several years.

In connection with a subsequent income tax audit of the unitrust, the local IRS District Office referred the following questions to the IRS National Office:

- Does the purchase of the deferred annuity policies from a commercial insurance company constitute acts of self-dealing when the named annuitants are disqualified persons?

- Would the purchase of the annuity policies jeopardize the trust's qualification as a charitable remainder unitrust under section 664 for federal income tax purposes?

- Would the annuity's withdrawal provision result in income to the trust, within the meaning of section 643(b)?

The Service advised:

- The purchase of the deferred annuity policies, based on the particular facts of this case, does not constitute an act of self-dealing under section 4941 of the Code.

- The purchase of the deferred annuity contracts does not adversely affect the trust's qualification as a charitable remainder trust under section 664 of the Code and the current regulations thereunder for federal income tax purposes.

- The trust's right to receive either the cash value or the surrender value of the contracts does not create trust accounting income under section 643(b) of the Code.

a. IRS Analysis Regarding Self-Dealing

The discussion related to the self-dealing issue was significant:

We have examined the transaction with the intention of ascertaining whether the B (the Trustee), acting in concert with A (the Trustor) on an ongoing basis, manipulated the assets of X for the personal benefit of A, by furthering his income, retirement and tax planning goals. There was a concern that the entire transaction taken as a whole; the purchase of a deferred annuity, the failure to make withdrawals from the annuity policies, and the intention to subsequently make unitrust payments to A under the "make-up" provision of the Trust; could be construed as an act of self-dealing under section 4941(d)(1)(E) of the Code by virtue of the authority provided by section 53.4941(d)-2(f)(1) of the Regulations.

In as much as A, a disqualified person, is entitled to receive the income interest from the trust, it is difficult to argue that the disqualified person receives an inappropriate benefit by deferring the income interest, particularly where such deferral is permitted under section 664 of the Code. The underlying problem is that the income beneficiary interest is in itself a use for the benefit of the disqualified person of the assets of the trust. Inherently, any investment decision regarding the trust assets that increases or decreases the amount of payout of this income interest is a use for the benefit of the disqualified person (assuming the disqualified person does not object). Section 4947(a)(2)(A) provides that section 4941 will not apply to any amounts payable under the terms of the trust to the income beneficiary. The amounts of income deferred by the investment decision in this case were payable to the income beneficiary under the terms of Trust X. Accordingly, these uses must be permitted under the income exception of section 4947(a)(2)(A) unless the disqualified person controls the investment decision and uses this control to unreasonably affect the charitable remainder beneficiary's interest.

Since charitable remainder trusts by their intrinsic nature provide for a continuous use by the disqualified person of the entire trust corpus, we conclude that the presence of an unreasonable affect on the charitable remainder interest distinguishes a permissible use of trust assets from an impermissible use.

In addition to failing to show harm to the charitable remainder interest, the facts of this case do not clearly show control by the disqualified person. X represented that an independent attorney/trustee signed the contract to purchase the deferred annuity policies. Moreover, even if we conclude that B, as trustee, purchased the deferred annuity policies, the facts are insufficient to demonstrate that A usurped control from the trustee or that he could compel or influence the trustee to purchase the deferred annuity policies in question. Instead, the trustee merely took into consideration the particular financial needs of A before reinvesting the proceeds from the sale of the trust assets.

b. Annuity Distributions as Trust Accounting Income Clarified

With respect to whether or not the trust's right to receive either the cash value or the surrender value of the contracts creating trust accounting income under IRC §643(b), a little background is in order.

In the 1990 ruling, the trust instrument expanded the definition of trust accounting income to include "distributions from a life insurance or annuity contract." This provision gave clear guidance to the trustee that only withdrawals from the annuity contract could be considered as distributable income. Because annuity withdrawals are treated for income tax purposes as being made on a last-in-first-out (LIFO) basis, any withdrawals, to the extent they exceeded the cost basis of the contract, would be accounting income, to the extent of the currently due unitrust amount and any outstanding deficiency account balance. If no cash withdrawals were made, the trust would have nothing to distribute.

In the immediate case, the trust instrument was silent and state law was ambiguous on the treatment of income withdrawals from the annuity contracts. The Service stated:

"The applicable state law, the Uniform Principal and Income Act of State, appears ambiguous on whether a trust's right to receive money is income to the trust, whether characterized as principal or income. The implication from the sections that define income and principal, however, is that a trust does not realize either until the trust actually receives possession of money or other property. See XXX Code Ann. Section XXXXX and section XXXXX (1991). Therefore, the Trust's right to receive either the cash value or the surrender value of the contracts does not create trust accounting income under section 643(b) of the Code."

3. IRS Discusses Income Deferral in 1999 CPE Text

Immediately prior to press time for this edition, the Internal Revenue Service issued its Exempt Organizations Continuing Professional Education Text for fiscal 1999 ("CPE"). Chapter P of the IRS's CPE covers recent developments in the area of private foundations, charitable remainder trusts, and chapter 42 issues.

In Chapter P, the Service addresses the issue of placing variable annuities and partnerships inside of a NIMCRUT and discusses the implications of Technical Advice Memorandum 9825001. The IRS reiterates its position as stated in the TAM, namely that the purpose of the variable annuity and the action of turning on and off fiduciary income is not an act of self-dealing. More specifically, the IRS concluded:

"Thus the negative inference of the ruling is that in some rare situations, the Service may, perhaps, be willing to find self- dealing. However, to find self-dealing of this sort, three tests must be satisfied.

The first two tests relate to the "manipulation" requirement based in Reg. 53.4941(d)-2(f)(1). (1) For the requisite "manipulation" to occur, the disqualified person and income beneficiary must control the decision of the trustee as to investment decision. Thus, such person must be serving as trustee or the facts of the case must establish that such person is acting in concert with the trustee as to these investment decisions. This is not an easy burden of proof to carry, as is demonstrated by the facts of the TAM. (2) The second element of manipulation is that the manipulation of the assets and investments is to serve the personal advantage and benefit of the income beneficiary beyond merely the receipt of the income provided by the trust instrument.

There must be specific evidence of manipulation to benefit the income beneficiary in this manner. Again, not an easy burden of proof to carry.

Finally, (3) the third test is determining whether the deferral is a permitted use, meaning the lack of a presence of an unreasonable effect on the charitable remainder interest. As a practical matter, one might speculate that it will be quite a rare situation where an income deferral NIMCRUT would disadvantage a charity to the extent that it could be said that there is an unreasonable effect on the charitable remainder interest. The unreasonable affect on the charitable remainder interest would include an evaluation of the income realized by the charitable interest as well as the appreciation in value of the charitable assets over the term of the NIMCRUT. Since the Service does not second guess the investment decisions of the trustee in this regard, the "unreasonable effect" means something more than just bad investment judgment.

In the TAM, the Service has, in theory, left open the door to apply the self-dealing prohibition for the income deferral NIMCRUT in a truly egregious situation. As a practical matter, the vast majority of income deferral NIMCRUTs adhering to ordinary fiduciary standards under state law will not run afoul of this problem. The more realistic view is that the theory aired in 1997 EO CPE Text as modified, when applied to an actual case, will rarely be applied. As such, much of the discussion in the 1997 Text suggesting an aggressive approach on IRC 4941 issues with NIMCRUTS is modified pursuant to TAM 9825001 and this article." Later in Chapter P, the Service discusses the proposed regulations on this particular issue, and indicates that final regulations should be forthcoming by the end of the year, but probably will not address the "spigot" feature. According to the Service, "[p]erhaps there may be some resolution of the IRS and Treasury study on this issue in the following year."

4. Summary

The implications of the TAM and the EO CPE text are significant. First, those who have entered into these types of arrangements and those considering them can take comfort in the fact that, even though neither a TAM or CPE text can be cited as tax precedent, the current sentiment of the Service does not discourage income deferral arrangements. The TAM also suggests that even if an existing trust instrument has not anticipated income deferral arrangements, deferral may still be permissible provided concepts of trust accounting are compatible under state law.

The authors believe that income deferral is a valuable tool in the hands of the trustee, and should be permitted based on the fact that it cannot mathematically produce a lesser charitable remainder interest than would otherwise result from an identically invested unitrust bearing a standard payout format. In essence, income deferral provides an opportunity to increase the charitable remainder as compared to the benchmark standard payout format.

The Service has confirmed in Revenue Procedure 97-23 and the proposed charitable remainder trust regulations that it is still studying and requesting comments on the issues surrounding income deferral unitrusts. Until such time as the IRS provides further guidance, planners should be mindful that the published determinations are based on very specific fact patterns that, if changed, could influence their result.

Index

Table of Authorities

CASES

INTERNAL REVENUE CODE

TREASURY REGULATIONS

REVENUE RULINGS

REVENUE PROCEDURES

GENERAL COUNSEL MEMORANDA

PRIVATE LETTER RULINGS

IRS NOTICES